New Wave Shakespeare on Screen

New Wave Shakespeare on Screen

THOMAS CARTELLI AND
KATHERINE ROWE

polity

First published in 2007 by Polity Press

Polity Press
65 Bridge Street
Cambridge CB2 1UR, UK

Polity Press
350 Main Street
Malden, MA 02148, USA

ISBN-10: 0-7456-3392-7
ISBN-13: 978-07456-3392-3
ISBN-10: 0-7456-3393-5 (pb)
ISBN-13: 978-07456-3393-0 (pb)

A catalogue record for this book is available from the British
Library.

Typeset in 9.5 on 12pt Utopia
by Servis Filmsetting Ltd, Longsight, Manchester
Printed and bound in Great Britain by MPG Books Ltd,
Bodmin, Cornwall

For further information on Polity, visit our website:
www.polity.co.uk

Contents

Plays and Films Featured in Chapters

Chapter 1
primary plays: *Romeo and Juliet, Henry V*
primary films: Baz Luhrmann's *Romeo+Juliet*, Kenneth Branagh's
    Henry V

Chapter 2
primary plays: *Richard III, The Winter's Tale, The Tempest*
primary films: Richard Loncraine's *Richard III*, Eric Rohmer's
    Conte d'hiver, Peter Greenaway's *Prospero's Books*

Chapter 3
primary play: *Hamlet*
primary films: Michael Almereyda's *Hamlet*, Laurence Olivier's *Hamlet*

Chapter 4
primary play: *Titus Andronicus*
primary film: Julie Taymor's *Titus*

Chapter 5
primary plays: *Richard III, Macbeth*
primary films: Al Pacino's *Looking for Richard*, James Gavin Bedford's
    The Street King, Billy Morrissette's *Scotland, PA*

Chapter 6
primary play: *Othello*
primary film: Geoffrey Sax's *Othello*

Chapter 7
primary play: *King Lear*
primary film: Kristian Levring's *The King is Alive*

Illustrations

Preface

The "new wave" evoked in the title of this book names two things. First, it names a surge of experiment, since the late twentieth century, in Shakespeare film adaptation. Here we lay a light claim to a famous label, "nouvelle vague": the phrase coined by French critics to embrace an aesthetically diverse group of films made by diverse artists in the late 1950s and 1960s, and which has since been loosely applied to other periodic surges of innovative art. Although not the work of a single generation of filmmakers sharing an artistic and social vision, a large subset of recent screen Shakespeares shares a propensity for visual and narrative experiments that conspicuously diverge from more classical modes of adaptation. We discuss nine such films at length in this book and touch on a number of others. Each offers vivid examples of different modes of experimentalism, which in some cases have long cinematic histories. While the label "new wave" suits this innovative turn in a historiographic sense, it fits more closely in two other ways. Like the French New Wave, these experiments in adaptation require new analytic techniques and vocabulary, and like that movement, they have helped foster a rapidly expanding body of criticism on screen Shakespeare. This expansive critical turn is the second thing we mean to invoke with the phrase "new wave." Consolidating the gains made by a generation of trailblazers, recent scholarship has mined performance studies, film and media studies, studies of globalization and popular culture, finding new resources for addressing the extraordinarily varied transformations of Shakespeare on contemporary screens.

In the pages that follow we will have more to say about our selection of films and the critical turn that our title invokes. But this book has another, more ambitious, aim than mapping recent screen experiments and the methodological rethinking they invite. We aim to integrate the new text-based and screen-based approaches in ways that will be accessible to teachers and students, as well as to scholars. Little is currently available that takes seriously what it would mean for students to move from novice to confident, expert readings of film adaptations, in the complex terms that scholars now regularly pursue. Yet students (at both the college and secondary level) provide Shakespeare films with their largest audience – and a renewable one, for whom the uses and gratifications of Shakespeare films are significantly shaped by classroom study and exhibition. The majority of course texts on Shakespeare films still begin with a version of the idea that "Shakespeare is hard while film is easy." We do not dismiss the challenges Renaissance texts pose student readers. Yet this thesis betrays long-standing and counterproductive assumptions about the relative value of word and image, primary text and adaptation. Current scholarship on Shakespeare films has traveled far from these biases in its understanding of textuality, reception, and authority; they cannot be the basis of a rigorous classroom practice. We need a resource that makes accessible to students the complexity and intellectual interest of adaptation as a cultural process, along with the different roles Shakespeare's works play and have played in that process. Respecting the separate interests of our several audiences, different sections of the book find different balances between introducing new methods and vocabulary to students, and pursuing our own film readings in conversation with other scholars.

Having sketched what we mean by "new wave" and "Shakespeare," we reserve a final word for "screen." As a critical term, "screen" marks the convergence of film and other audio-visual media, allowing scholars to generalize about increasingly diverse modes of Shakespeare exhibition. A hallmark of recent work on screen Shakespeare has been its double focus: one eye on intermedial effects (such as Branagh's use of theatrical address in the filmic long shot); the other on medium-specificity (is the internet a "lean-forward" medium, as industry analysts say, while television is a "lean-back" medium?). That double focus helps us keep track of changes in our basic categories for thinking about screen exhibition and reception. "Small screen" can now mean anything from hand-held, to laptop, to television; while TV sets, growing ever larger, may need to be thought of as medium-sized. To talk in a serious way about *screen* Shakespeare now, in other words, we have to include not just film, television, video, and DVD, domestic and global, but also web-based and cellular media, delivered via desktop, laptop, and hand-held means. And we should remind ourselves how much screen Shakespeare comes in print-based as well as audio-visual form, portable as well as fixed in an exhibition space. (Examples range from library and journal sites to the BBC's "60 Second Shakespeare," an edutainment website featuring mobile content – insult generators to impress the mates; thumbnail plots to impress the dates.) This study focuses on large to medium screens: film, television, and digital video. But we trust readers will find resources here to help them parse other emerging frames for Shakespeare.

Acknowledgments

Collaborative as this project already is, it required the support of a great many friends, students, and colleagues to bring to fruition. Many of these names appear in our notes and citations. We would like to identify here those who do not appear as well as those who have figured most prominently in our thinking and writing. Among the former are our children, who spent more time channeling Shakespeare than it might be healthy for them to admit, and our spouses, who often served as test-market audiences for our theories about film reception when they were not taking up domestic slack. Fellow Shakespeare scholars have had considerable impact on the choices made and approaches taken here, particularly Richard Burt, Peter Donaldson, Barbara Hodgdon, and Douglas Lanier. We also depended on the words, responses, advice, and example of Kenneth Rothwell, Samuel Crowl, Peter Holland, Heather James, Judith Elstein, Mark Lord, Laura Novo – and the polychronic talents of Scott Black, Claire Busse, Alice Dailey, Jane Hedley, Nora Johnson, Matt Kozusko, Laura McGrane, Steve Newman, Kristen Poole, Lauren Shohet, and Julian Yates. Richard Allen, Jennifer Horne, Jonathan Kahana, Dana Polan, and Allen Weiss were generous guides and refrained from saying "'tis new to thee" as much as they must have wished. Faculty and graduate seminars at a variety of institutions were wonderful hosts for our test drives: Penn State, University of Pittsburgh, University of Alabama, Columbia University. So were research seminars and panels of the Shakespeare Association of America (2001, 2004, 2005), the Shakespeare on Screen conference in Malaga (1999), the sixth biennial conference of the Australian and New Zealand Shakespeare Association in Auckland (2000), the International Shakespeare Conference in Stratford-upon-Avon (2004), and the 2005 conference of the American Society for Theatre Research.

We drew deeply on the patience and wisdom of our home institutions. At Muhlenberg, thanks especially to James Bloom, Francesca Coppa, James Peck, Grant Scott, and the marvelous, expeditious staff of Trexler Library. Bryn Mawr colleagues in Computing and Information Services brought unfailing patience, expertise, and a spirit of partnership to years of Katherine's technical questions. We also benefited from generous institutional support. The Hoffman Research Fellowship at Muhlenberg College enabled Tom's leave in 2004–5. A New Directions Fellowship from the Andrew W. Mellon Foundation supported Katherine's sojourn in the world of film and media studies in 2005–6; the

Department of Cinema Studies at Tisch School of the Arts graciously hosted a visitor.

Parts of chapter three and chapter five appeared in *Shakespeare, the Movie II*, edited by Richard Burt and Lynda Boose (New York & London: Routledge, 2003), pp. 37–55 and 186–99, as " 'Remember me': Technologies of Memory in Michael Almereyda's *Hamlet*" and "Shakespeare and the Street: Pacino's *Looking for Richard*, Bedford's *The Street King*, and the Common Understanding," respectively. They are reprinted in revised form here with the permission of Thomson Publishing. An early version of chapter four, by Thomas Cartelli, appeared as "Taymor's *Titus* in Time and Space: Surrogation and Interpolation" in *Renaissance Drama* 34 (2006), edited by Jeff Masten and Wendy Wall. It is reprinted here by permission of Northwestern University Press. A version of chapter seven appears in *Borrowers & Lenders: the Journal of Shakespeare and Appropriation* 1.2 (2006), and is reprinted by permission of the editors. A wonderful photograph taken by Philip Greenspun of a Marilyn Monroe display at the Colosseo Quadrato in Rome is reproduced here by permission of Mr Greenspun.

Final thanks go to all our editors at Polity Press, for keeping the faith throughout, and to our cast of anonymous readers whose reports helped make this a better book than it would have been otherwise.

INTRODUCTION

New Wave Shakespeare on and off Screen

The past 15 years have witnessed a number of new approaches to the "staging" of Shakespeare on screen, thanks in part to the development of a host of new media technologies but thanks also to the dynamic engagement with Shakespeare's plays of a group of unusually gifted filmmakers. Their numbers include Peter Greenaway, Baz Lurhmann, Julie Taymor, Kristian Levring, and Michael Almereyda, among others. Their background in fields such as painting, puppetry, costume and scenic design, music theater, experimental cinema, and television advertising differentiates these filmmakers from mainstream Hollywood directors on the one hand, and, on the other, from stage-to-screen directors who take their primary cues from theatrical conventions. The adaptations produced by these artists deliver often irreverent, broadly allusive, and richly re-imagined takes on their source material. They are avowedly self-conscious and experimental in their deployment of filmic media, and challenge their audiences to rise to the occasion of their often elliptical treatment of plot and discontinuous approach to storytelling and character. And they promiscuously take their visual and auditory cues from their vernacular surround – in this case, from contemporary advertising, television newscasts, rock video, the stylings and sounds of popular (mainly youth) culture, computer games and computer-generated special effects – as well as from more esoteric sources such as postmodern art and architecture, the visual archives of Renaissance art and design, video diaries, and the architectonics of contemporary performance art.

As with French New Wave cinema, this vernacular style is allusively rich, mixing popular and high-culture idioms in ways that provide new avenues of access to Shakespeare for scholars and popular audiences alike. Al Pacino's *Looking for Richard* (1996), for example, borrows documentary film conventions to structure his idiosyncratic engagement with *Richard III*, and throughout the film mixes casual and formal styles of address. Peter Greenaway assembles exquisite painterly tableaux in *Prospero's Books* (1991) only to have his live action *putti* urinate in unending streams into a pool where famed Shakespearean actor John Gielgud "creates" the text of Shakespeare's *The Tempest*. Best known for her theatrical adaptation of the animated film, *The Lion King* (1998), Julie Taymor reverses direction in *Titus* (1999), transforming her earlier stage production of Shakespeare's *Titus Andronicus* into a film that superimposes Mussolini's Fascist aesthetic on the foundations of ancient Rome, and dresses Shakespeare's Goths in the "borrowed robes" of contemporary "Goth" youth street-style. James Gavin Bedford's *The Street King* (2002) – which remakes *Richard III* in the idiom of East Los Angeles gang subcultures – excels at the kinds of witty visual puns typical of this group of films, notably when aspiring street king Rikki pulls out his brother Eduardo's IV tube, an aside in Roman numerals that mines the contemporary scene in terms Shakespeare scholars will respond to one way, popular audiences another.

These films are also citationally rich: participating with particular intensity in a mode of intertextuality that has become common in contemporary culture. Thus Billy Morrissette's *Scotland, PA* (2001) offers intelligent riffs on 1970s versions of screen masculinity – Michael Cimino's *The Deer Hunter* (1978), TV cop shows such as *Columbo*, *Baretta*, and *McCloud* – that unfold the vexed gender relations in *Macbeth* in generally parodic but meaningful ways. Many of these films play with the extra-textual referentiality of stars doing star-turns and "ghosting" former roles: teen-mag heart-throb Leonardo DiCaprio as Romeo; Anthony "Hannibal Lecter" Hopkins as Titus; Al (the Godfather) Pacino as Richard III; Diane Venora (one of the few contemporary female stage-Hamlets) as Gertrude; laconic comic Bill Murray as a sleazier-than-thou Polonius; "everygirl" Julia Stiles as both a stolid Desdemona and suicidal Ophelia.

Where the promise of commercial cinema is realist immersion – a viewing experience that will sink us into the filmic *mise en scène* (the cinematic frame that contains setting, costume, lighting, and the movement of actors within it), dissolving all traces of artifice and construction – the directors we discuss often press a sense of artifice or anachronism on their audiences. They call attention to the archaism of speaking Shakespearean language in a hyper-modern setting, as Luhrmann does in *William Shakespeare's Romeo + Juliet* (1996), even to the archaism of what appears to be contemporary, as Almereyda does in *Hamlet* (2000) when he has Ethan Hawke's Hamlet resume his interrupted exchanges with Gertrude and Ophelia through a payphone rather than a cellphone. And they dwell on the materials and manufacture of text and image, sometimes to a degree that undermines conventional modes of cinematic pleasure, as we find in *Prospero's Books*.

Luhrmann's film title, with its arch attribution to the playwright, highlights a generational turn in modes of adaptation shared by other Shakespeare filmmakers of this period. *Auteurism* of the kind Franco Zeffirelli launched in his groundbreaking *Romeo and Juliet* (1968) has become a received tradition. Where these directors reflect on that tradition, as Greenaway does, they tend to envision the Shakespeare text and its performances as a literary, auditory, and visual archive ripe for reinvigoration. In *Prospero's Books*, for example, where Greenaway has Gielgud recite, word by word and image by image, Shakespeare's *Tempest*, he does so with every technical device and all the cinematic "magic" at the cutting-edge filmmaker's disposal. And in Almereyda's

Hamlet, the director has his latter-day corporate prince seem to compose the Shakespearean verse he speaks at the same time as Gielgud addresses Yorick's skull on an adjacent TV screen. More often, though, the group of films we concentrate on ditches questions of authorial competition and propriety altogether. They treat Shakespeare plays and stage conventions (as earlier filmmakers such as Godard and Welles also did) as available but not privileged forms, part of a field of received cultural matter free for appropriation or recycling, according to their specific interests. This is particularly the case in films such as Gus Van Sant's *My Own Private Idaho* (1991), which pursues a discontinuous, on again, off again relationship with Shakespeare's *Henriad*, grounded in part on Orson Welles's free adaptation of this material in *Chimes at Midnight* (1966). The same combination of freedom and profound engagement with partly remembered material emerges in *The King is Alive* (2000), Kristian Levring's inspired diffraction of *King Lear* set in the brutal landscape of an abandoned mining town in the Namibian desert.

It might seem as if such richness of visual citation and appropriative freedom means leaving the playtext behind. Indeed, this fear continues to haunt other members of this generation of Shakespeare filmmakers (Kenneth Branagh, for one, takes it on explicitly). It regularly haunts teachers of Shakespeare, who lose valuable classroom time when we choose to screen films instead of just sticking to the text. Yet the opposite is often the case with these artists, who point us back to the text in compelling and fruitful ways. For example, the way Taymor translates Tamora's sons into urban Goths highlights ethnic divisions in Shakespeare's play that may otherwise remain submerged for modern audiences. "Moor" is clearly not the only ethnic category that matters in *Titus*. But neither is Taymor's rich and densely coded cinematic canvas the only object of audience attention. She takes pains to give Anthony Hopkins's Titus dramatically privileged opportunities to deliver speeches of such amplitude and grace that we hear them as if for the first time. Even films, such as *Scotland, PA*, that jettison a large part of the Shakespearean script show considerable subtlety in interpreting the text, as they seek contemporary corollaries to Renaissance motifs: for example, the Ferris wheel turning as a latter-day wheel of fortune in the opening scenes, green world motifs preserved in props, and costume grafted onto allusions to the clash of cultures in depressed, rural Pennsylvania.

The complex visual vocabularies at work in these films, their breadth of reference and formal strategies, offer obvious challenges. While undergraduates may feel more familiar with the formal idioms of film and video than with Shakespearean language, they are usually as unequipped to talk about them critically as they are to close-read a Shakespeare play. Indeed, in the case of Shakespeare, they usually assume the text requires interpretation; in the case of film, they usually assume it is transparent. General classroom introductions to film help provide a formal vocabulary for analysis. But dedicated as they are to cinema per se, these give short shrift to issues that matter crucially for Shakespeare films and especially for those of the 1990s and beyond: script-to-screen questions about the way that every Shakespeare film surrogates – reproduces and replaces – the Shakespeare play it claims as source text; the variety of adaptational modes (revival, appropriation, renovation, parody, spin-off) that are put to work in different films; formal cross-pollination between film and other media, from radio to video games; the development of filmic conventions (such as voice-over and close-ups) to substitute for dramatic soliloquies and asides.

This volume aims to address this gap in classroom resources, taking advantage of the opportunities offered by this more experimental strain of adaptation to help students and teachers move past the suspicion that film texts and print texts will always be in pedagogical competition with each other. It aims first to make sense of the different varieties of experiment at work in the films we discuss. Our selection includes pop-culture films, such as Morrissette's *Scotland, PA* and Bedford's *The Street King*; televised updatings such as the Geoffrey Sax/Andrew Davies ITV production of *Othello* (2001); art-house films, such as Eric Rohmer's *Tale of Winter* (1992), Pacino's docudramatic *Looking for Richard*, Taymor's *Titus*, Almereyda's *Hamlet*, Greenaway's *Prospero's Books*, Van Sant's *My Own Private Idaho*, and Levring's *The King is Alive*. Along the way we make reference to other contemporary screen media and to forbears of various stripes. Keeping our student audience in mind, we do so suggestively rather than comprehensively. This study is not, in other words, a history of the place of Shakespeare in European experimental cinema. Nor is it a thoroughgoing account of the debt recent Shakespeare films owe that cinema – though we think we make enough connections here to suggest that such studies deserve to be written.

In chapter 1, we expand on current narratives about the past 15 years of Shakespeare films, touching on problematics of style, canon, and reception that may be familiar to scholars but new to students. Chapter 2 identifies a number of new critical approaches to different versions of recent adaptation practices. We outline a critical vocabulary particular to screen Shakespeare that will help students grasp the way these films work, interpret them more freely, and write about them with facility and precision. Subsequent chapters put these terms into play, in open-ended readings we hope will be accessible to students and teachers, as well as scholars. The table of contents and lead pages indicate which terms we touch on in each chapter, but the discussions themselves are less explic-itly pedagogical. For films for which there is an extensive body of published criticism, we aim both to be summative (presenting a range of scholarly approaches and debates) and to take new directions of our own. In the process, we hope to meet the peculiar challenges posed by the more experimental subset of Shakespeare adaptations. These chal-lenges include, among other things, the substitution of vernacular language for Shakespearean verse; changing ideas about what constitutes a text and what constitutes the "Shakespearean;" and the plasticity and resistance of Shakespearean plots to new formats, new patterns of significance, and interpolated material.

By balancing what Richard Burt (2006) has called "Shakespeare-centric" concerns – focused on what gets done *to* the play in question – with "Shakespeare-eccentric" ones – following the pull of non-Shakespearean interests and cinematic contexts – we hope to model a variety of approaches to these complex audio-visual texts. We strive particularly to make the diverse, non-Shakespearean contexts of these films more legible to students and teachers: Almereyda's engagement with the history of memory technologies, Taymor's strong grounding in conceptual art, Pacino's devotion to the protocols of "Method" acting, Morrissette's 1970s' stylings and soundtrack, Davies and Sax's televisual borrowings, Levring's commitment to an austere European avant-garde aesthetic, and so on. This is not, then, an account of how film and television displace theatrical production or the text-based study of Shakespeare. It is, rather, an account of their ongoing negotiations with each other, which are enabled and complicated not only by the historical and technical evolution of the film medium itself and what it makes possible, but by how that medium orients itself to the one assumed constant in the negotiation process, that is, the plays of Shakespeare.

Constant though the idea of Shakespeare may be in the films we discuss, it is differently "constant" in each one of them in ways that help explain why we have chosen this set of films and not, for example, the comparatively more famous Shakespeare films of Kenneth Branagh. One reason is that Branagh's films have been far more fully explored, especially in classroom volumes. More crucially, we want to give a sustained hearing to films that draw their inspiration and subject matter from one or more Shakespeare plays but do not attempt to reproduce those plays in a clearly delineated, point-by-point manner. Such films do not try, in other words, to represent the Shakespeare play as if it could be sealed off from its contextual surround: a cultural context that not only always already assumes the existence of the play in question, but radically alters what that play does and how that play means once contact is engaged. Indeed, we entertain in the following pages films that do not even speak the same language as Shakespeare's plays, substituting contemporary British, French, or American vernacular dialogue for Shakespeare's verse, and that over-write Shakespearean plot and characters, making them part of the lived experience of the film world. Most such films signal their difference from Shakespeare in other ways as well – through updated settings, or altered titles such as *Scotland, PA*, *The Street King*, or *Men of Respect*. At the same time they sustain their ties to Shakespeare by means of allusions, citations, parody, plays-within-the-film, and, in some cases, by a casual but clearly discernible fidelity to plot. Although we may privately value one film over another, we make no formal claim for the superiority of the films we discuss at length to those that we do not. Rather, we choose those we discuss on the basis of the newness or difference they bring to what is now over a 100-year-old history of Shakespeare on screen, the resonance with which they engage the plays in question, and the opportunities they provide students and teachers for exploring the complex ways in which Western culture transmits and transforms its classic works.

At the same time, we recognize, in the next chapter in particular, tendencies that we consider more or less productive for the future of the genre itself. Thus, we trace changing notions of what it means (and has meant) to connect Shakespeare to how or where we live "now." The now of this writing is wired together by a host of rapidly emerging new media technologies that have radically altered the ways films are made and received. Yet technical sophistication is not the only ground of our interest. As noted above, the resonance of the encounter between film and play also figures mightily, as does a third, less easily defined factor of self-reflexiveness. This quality takes multiple forms: a self-consciousness about the changing conditions of cinematic and cultural reproduction; a general avoidance of mainstream editing conventions of transparency, continuity, and seamlessness; a promiscuous citationality and indulgence of anachronism and irony; a stronger interest in appropriation (using the playtexts for extra-Shakespearean purposes) than in revival or illustration; and a penchant for meditating on and deconstructing source texts, as opposed to attempting full-dress realizations. These tendencies are fueled in part by a postmodernist aesthetic shared by any number of contemporary films (even blockbusters: note, for example, the slippery allusiveness and temporal fracturings of the recent *Matrix* films). They are also fueled by a revival of the *auteurist* habit of mind comparable to that which helped orchestrate the first so-called new wave. For teachers and students, such self-reflexiveness has the advantage of foregrounding both the film-medium itself (not only the Shakespearean playtext or play-in-performance, or the referential claims of realism), and our current investments in adaptation, as matter ripe for analysis.

The films featured in this volume invite viewers back to the playtexts in fresh ways, in part because their interests go beyond the anxieties of authenticity and fidelity that worried some earlier film-adaptations of Shakespeare and that informed many scholarly and critical accounts of them. Trained in the protocols of textual- and source-study, formal analysis, genre criticism, archival research, and an old historicism that leaned heavily on the authority of "official" history and received ideas, Shakespeare scholars as a group were comparatively slow to reckon with the century-long developments of Shakespeare on film. Critical developments in the late 1970s and 1980s radically broadened the field of creditable critical discourse on Shakespeare, with signal gains being made particularly in the areas of feminist and psychoanalytic criticism, poststructuralist theory and practice, new historicism and cultural materialism, queer theory and gender studies, and stage-based performance criticism – alongside a veritable revolution in editorial theory and practice. Throughout this period, however, the study of Shakespeare on film remained a fairly marginal practice, seriously pursued by a comparatively small band of devoted trailblazers, whose numbers include, most prominently, Robert Ball, Jack Jorgens, Bernice Kliman, and Kenneth Rothwell. Drawing largely on print-based and stage-based methods of analysis, such scholars broke through considerable institutional and intellectual resistance in addressing film adaptations at all. Patiently developing accounts of Shakespeare on film from the silent period on, and registering new contributions as they made themselves felt in venues like the *Shakespeare on Film Newsletter* and, later, the *Shakespeare Bulletin*, these and other scholars effectively laid the foundation for the academic study of Shakespeare on film.

The 37 televised films produced by the BBC Shakespeare project from 1978 to 1985 greatly expanded the available canon of material for the study of Shakespeare on film, while also shifting the ground of interest from theatrical film to the flatter, but more uniformly accessible, medium of the television screen and its technical enabler, the VCR. Important academic studies of the period, notably those by James Bulman and Herbert Coursen (1988), Susan Willis (1991), and Bernice Kliman (1988), began to combine an interest in interpretation and technical analysis with a concentration on how televised Shakespeare could inform and enrich classroom teaching. Branagh's *Henry V*, and the considerable number of films that followed fast in its wake, arguably shifted the balance of power back to theatrical film, but with the crucial difference that from now on most viewers would continue to screen such films on their TVs, abetted first by the VCR, and later by the DVD player.

The sheer critical mass and variety of Shakespeare films produced throughout the 1990s, with their widely differentiated grounding in heritage conventions (*Henry V*), postmodern spectacle (*Prospero's Books*), Hollywood production practices (*Much Ado About Nothing*), popular culture (*William Shakespeare's Romeo + Juliet*), and topical updating (Richard Loncraine's *Richard III*) no doubt had much to do with the growing interest of academic scholars in the medium, and the growing respect accorded Shakespeare on screen scholarship by century's end. It also clearly contributed to some of the differences we may discern among the more influential scholars now active in the field. As the canon of Shakespeare on film has expanded well beyond the already crowded field Graham Holderness identified in "Shakespeare Rewound" (1993), so too has the canon of critical approaches Shakespeareans embrace, in the more than a dozen anthologies and nearly two dozen monographs produced in the last 15 years. These include psychoanalytic habits of critical address borrowed from film studies; the technical sophistication of new media studies; theoretically nuanced ideas about textuality and adaptation derived from performance and text studies; models of consumption, nation and transnationalism drawn from Marxist and postcolonial studies; and a wide variety of negotiations with popular culture. We draw on all these approaches here in order to put the classroom study of Shakespeare on screen on a firmer, more theoretically defensible footing, and to forge an integrated – cinematic and textual – art of close reading for film, video, and DVD.

1 Beyond Branagh and the BBC

From Verona to Verona Beach: Baz Luhrmann's *Romeo+Juliet*

In the 1977 film *Saturday Night Fever* (dir. John Badham), John Travolta's disco-dancing protagonist, Tony Manero, is trying to keep pace with the disjointed conversation of his new dance-partner, Stephanie (Karen Gorney), whose upwardly mobile goal in life is to leave Brooklyn behind and get an apartment in Manhattan where people have more class and drink tea with lemon. The conversation takes an odd turn when Stephanie mentions having recently seen Franco Zeffirelli's *Romeo and Juliet* (1968). Tony's eyes light up since this gives him the chance to contribute something intelligent like "Yeah, I read that in high school. That's Shakespeare, right?" But Tony is immediately put back in his place when Stephanie responds, "No, it's Zeffirelli, the director of the movie, you know, the movie." The conversation takes an even odder turn when the normally benighted Tony offers a fairly astute comment on the play's ending: "You know what? I never understood why Romeo took the poison so quick. I feel like he could've waited or something." Pushed out of her own zone of critical authority, Stephanie nonetheless insists, "That's the way they took poison in those days," before moving the conversation to a recent encounter she's had with Laurence Olivier, "the greatest actor in the whole world, you know, the English actor who is on TV all the time, who does those Polaroid commercials." This time it's Tony who is nonplussed and can do little more than ask whether this Olivier guy can get Stephanie a free camera.

Embedded in this exchange are a host of concerns we intend to enlarge upon in this book. These include Stephanie's cluelessness about the authorship of the play that Zeffirelli made into a celebrated film; Tony's familiarity with Shakespeare's version and intuitive grasp of its challenge to contemporary sensibilities; and Stephanie's immersion in celebrity culture and the transformation of celebrated artists like Laurence Olivier into icons of the commercial marketplace. Although the exchange is primarily designed to betray Stephanie's ignorance and naiveté (and credit the filmgoer's intelligence and sophistication), it also indicates her intuitive grasp of how the film's *auteur* effect reinforces its market effect. Films of Shakespeare's plays that are as celebrated, successful or as unique as Zeffirelli's *Romeo and Juliet* may put so prominent an identifying stamp on their product that Shakespeare's formative contributions to the subject may recede into the background of audience knowledge and attention. An audience's first point of contact, what pulls them into the theater (or draws them to the video or DVD), may continue to be the play, *Romeo and Juliet*, or the name "Shakespeare" (as it would have been for Tony had he seen the movie). But the peculiar visionary spin the individual filmmaker brings to the established subjects that fall within his or her purview may also effect a virtual transfer of ownership that privileges the filmic representation as the iconic stand-in or substitute for Shakespeare's play. The generation that grew up on Zeffirelli's film may (like Tony Manero) also have read Shakespeare's *Romeo and Juliet* in high school, may also have seen, or acted in, stage-productions of Shakespeare's play, or in *West Side Story*, which had put its own identifying stamp on *Romeo and Juliet* in the late fifties. Yet they would have had as hard a time shaking the iconic image of Olivia Hussey as Juliet or Michael York as Tybalt from their minds as an earlier generation of filmgoers would have had in erasing Marlon Brando's Stanley Kowalski from consciousness every time they heard the words *A Streetcar Named Desire.*

One of the crucial moves Zeffirelli made in bringing *Romeo and Juliet* to the screen was to break with established conventions that resisted the wholesale conversion of plays into the favored visual formats, or *mise en scène*, of film. Past masters of the genre like Olivier (whose 1944 film version of *Henry V* enraptured a younger Zeffirelli) tended to construct either expressionistic or comparatively spare indoor sets, largely modeled on those of stage plays, and to make comparatively small adjustments in how mainly stage-trained actors approached the speaking of verse (one of which was to render soliloquies as over-dubbed voice-over meditations rather than as dramatically synchronized addresses). By contrast, Zeffirelli took Shakespeare's play out into the vividly recreated sights and sounds of Renaissance Verona, and put it into vivid motion against the backdrop of a romantically compelling musical score. And rather than choose mature, stage-trained actors to play the principal parts, he chose actors whose youth and beauty could hold the eye, whose freshness and energy brought the kind of urgency and immediacy to their speech and actions that made an old play seem both new and inviting.[1]

For the current generation of moviegoers, Baz Luhrmann's *William Shakespeare's Romeo + Juliet* (1996) – far and away the most profitable and popular Shakespeare film produced in the last 30 years – has assumed the iconic status of Zeffirelli's film.[2] Where the earlier film moved the play into a period street in a realist mode, Luhrmann sets it in a hyper-realist, arguably surreal, modern cityscape. Luhrmann's *mise en scène* is equally vivid, but grittier than Zeffirelli's, and filled with visual reminders of the degree to which commercial media – including Shakespeare's plays and film itself – have saturated modern experience (Donaldson 2002b). Shakespearean phrases smudge the urban

architecture of Verona Beach, in half-legible advertising tags that reproduce the playwright's half-remembered, residual authority in popular
culture. They turn up as place-names – the funky beachside area and
pool-hall where Romeo and his friends hang out are called Sycamore
Grove and the Globe Theater, respectively – and as the name of a
message-delivery service ("Post-Haste Dispatch") that function as
ironic signifiers to the knowing viewer. The film opens and closes with
commentary on the story, delivered by the talking heads of newscasters
speaking to us directly from the frames of TV screens in cadences that
rehearse but also alter the rhythms of Shakespeare's verse. These screens
themselves dissolve into the fabric of what seems a more bracing reality
but which itself constitutes only a more densely inhabited version of
cinematic experience. The film seems to aim less at a verisimilar version
of life itself than an aesthetic of "liveness" (Auslander 1999), illustrating
how life is mediated and displayed (as fast, crowded, and compelling,
sexy and violent) in the visual language of film, TV, and advertising
(Donaldson 2002b). Even the casting choices are promiscuously citational, drawn from the covers of celebrity tabloids and the familiar faces
of second-rank actors who have more street credibility (as TV and movie
cops and criminals) than facility in speaking Shakespeare's verse.[3]

The turning-point Luhrmann's *Romeo + Juliet* marks in recent
Shakespeare on screen has even more to do with camera styles and
filmic pacing than it does with *mise en scène*. Luhrmann's camera
moves through his recreated urban landscape of Verona Beach with
vertiginous speed, borrowing the signature editing conventions and
shot selections of contemporary music videos, police dramas, and
newscasts. In visual terms, *Romeo + Juliet* takes the camera into the
aesthetic street of television, with its distinctive jump-cuts, chase
scenes, helicopter shots, and dramatic segues from talking heads to
"live" footage. And just as contemporary network TV seeks a flatness of
address, in which spoken dialogue plays about as prominent a role as
did the captions in silent film, Luhrmann chooses to flatten the
rhythms of Shakespearean verse, setting it on an anachronistic collision course with his swirling visuals and breakneck pace.

Shifting Canons: Age of Branagh?

Lurhmann's *Romeo + Juliet* not only marks a break with Zeffirelli's lushly
romantic take on the same material, but a clear-cut departure from
Kenneth Branagh's attempt to synthesize Shakespearean formalism
with the conventions of late twentieth-century Hollywood cinema, in
his celebrated 1989 version of *Henry V* and in his considerably more
plodding "full-text" *Hamlet* (released the same year as Luhrmann's
film but seemingly produced on a different planet). Each departure
defines itself in terms of specific traditions in screen Shakespeare and
mainstream commercial cinema, but leads in different directions.[4] It is
helpful to sketch the current critical narratives involving Branagh in

order to distinguish the full range of experiments taking place alongside and after his. Branagh's *Henry V* looks back to the golden age of British Shakespeare on film of the 1940s and 1950s as well as to such technicolor extravaganzas as David Lean's *Doctor Zhivago* (1965) and more recent British "heritage" films like Hugh Hudson's *Chariots of Fire* (1981). And though continuing to draw on certain theater conventions, it pointedly seeks to distance itself from the mannered, decidedly anticinematic BBC house-style of televised Shakespeare that reigned from 1978 to 1985, in an effort to initiate a Shakespeare on film revival centered on Branagh's more florid acting and direction. A number of influential Shakespeare on filmists (Mark Thornton Burnett, Deborah Cartmell, Samuel Crowl, Sarah Hatchuel, and Kenneth Rothwell) credit Branagh with having done just that in *Henry V* and in his subsequent film-versions of *Much Ado About Nothing* (1993), *Hamlet* (1996), and *Love's Labour's Lost* (1999). Crowl, for one, contends that "Branagh's 1989 film has helped to create the most concentrated release of English-language Shakespeare films in the century" (2003: 26) and claims that in fashioning such "an effective style for translating Shakespeare into the language of film," Branagh "has become as much of a film *auteur* as his great modernist predecessors Olivier and [Orson] Welles" (2003: 26–7).

Branagh's *Henry V* did jump-start a revival in Shakespeare on film production – owing in part to his demonstration of Shakespeare's marketability and successful integration of Hollywood stylings with convincing readings of Shakespearean verse, but also owing to the naturalness, conviction, and intensity of address he brought to the title role. On both accounts, Branagh was clearly modeling himself on the two precedents Crowl notes: on Olivier, whose own wartime production of *Henry V* was followed four years later by *Hamlet* (1948) and then in 1955 by his technicolor version of *Richard III*; and, to a lesser extent, on the actor-impresario, Orson Welles, who directed and starred in considerably more idiosyncratic versions of *Macbeth* (1948) and *Othello* (1952), and in his pastiche of Shakespeare's first and second parts of *Henry IV*, *Chimes at Midnight* (1966).

Branagh seems acutely conscious of his presumption at taking on Olivier in the confines of a film that was itself carefully designed to move Shakespeare on film production beyond the confines of stage-to-film conventions and comparisons. The opening moments of Olivier's *Henry V* make Olivier's interest in this project very clear. The camera literally takes flight, offering the viewer a panoramic view of London in 1599 that zooms in on the stage of a carefully recreated Globe theater as a stage-performance of Shakespeare's *Henry V* begins. Olivier here offers a richly imagined "you are there now" glimpse of the raucously social experience of playgoing in Shakespeare's England, allowing his film audience to witness from a distance actor/audience interactions and then eliding that distance by effectively having the performance play directly to the latter-day filmgoer. It is only when the "vasty fields of France" are invoked and the play requires an imaginative transfer across the Channel that the film-as-film kicks in with all the resources available to it at its moment of production. Having illustrated what the play might have looked like to a contemporary audience, Olivier goes on to demonstrate what mid-twentieth-century imagination and technology can achieve in realizing the filmic potential of Shakespeare's playtext. The flight of the camera here anticipates its later swoop through Hamlet's brain in Olivier's famously Freudian film version of *Hamlet*. With both gestures Olivier claims for cinema the power to fulfill the promise of Shakespearean theater, either by spiriting us into the epic fields of France or by taking us straight to the heart of Hamlet's mystery.

To his credit, Branagh chooses neither to repeat nor to reproduce what was, after all, Olivier's historically specific gesture at demarcating where one art-form ends and another begins. His film, after all, is not a "remake" of Olivier's film but a re-imagining of Shakespeare's play undertaken at a much later date in the development and evolution of film-art and technology. But having undertaken this film in particular, and having therefore taken on this paragon of the British theater and film establishment, Branagh also defers, sometimes anxiously, to "his" greatness (Olivier's, Shakespeare's). This becomes apparent from the start in Branagh's casting of the famous Shakespeare-actor, Derek Jacobi, in the role of Chorus (whom Branagh deploys as a kind of bridge-figure between Olivier and himself). As Chorus, Jacobi takes us behind the scenes of a film-set – showing us the apparatus of performance that film and theater have in common – before pulling back the curtain that now divides the seemingly residual traditions of theater from the emergent conventions of film. Although Branagh defers as well here to the "classic" opening movement of Olivier's film, he demonstrates his own commitment to the now dominant medium of film, positioning the filmic apparatus itself at the foreground of our attention and turning his camera's eye exclusively on the filmic *mise en scène* as soon as the curtain is parted (Donaldson 1991: 62–3). Once Jacobi opens the curtain, the camera effectively performs a time-machine function, effacing its own presentness as an apparatus, even ultimately absorbing Jacobi himself in the filmic medium. Branagh also draws on the resources of theater in powerful ways, in service to a populist vision: incorporating theatrical pacing in his long takes, directing for emotional clarity in the verse (Lanier 2002a).

In just about every additional respect, Branagh's *Henry V* achieves its goal of generating a new synthesis of Shakespearean drama and Hollywood film, and was justly celebrated at its moment of production as both a work of art and an audience-friendly cultural commodity. Branagh becomes overnight the *enfant terrible* of British cinema, the successor to the triple-threat actor-manager-director profile carved out by Olivier and Welles, and helps put Shakespeare on film back on the map as something worthy to invest in and bank on. But he also takes more than one step back. Generally celebrated for bringing a stark cinematic realism to his battlefield scenes and a camera-savvy bravado to his set pieces, Branagh has also been criticized for glorifying the triumphs of war and for flattering the burdens of royalty at the expense of its victims (Breight 1991; Hedrick 1997). *Henry V* was identified as but another bout of British imperial nostalgia in a decade marked by events like the inglorious Falklands War and by "the rage for the Raj" evinced in television mini-series such as *The Jewel in the Crown* (1984) and *The Far Pavilions* (1984), and in films like *Gandhi* (1982) and *Passage to India* (1984). While other British directors were focusing on the excesses and inequities of the Thatcher era, making socially evocative films like *Wetherby* (1985) and *The Ploughmans Lunch* (1983) and "progressive" multicultural satires like *My Beautiful Laundrette* (1985) and *Sammy and Rosie Get Laid* (1987), Branagh appeared not only to be effecting a turn to a cinematic naturalism and narrative style thriving in Hollywood, but mining a *genre*, that is, the "heritage" film, and its concomitant source, nostalgia, that made traditional British culture at this time the butt of countless Monty Python sketches and seem an altogether backward-looking affair.[5]

Although there is no gainsaying the contribution that Branagh's *Henry V* made in reviving the fortunes of Shakespeare on film production, accounts of his influence on the wide variety of Shakespeare films produced in the 1990s and beyond overstate his dominance of the "long decade" (1989–2001) Crowl has called "The Kenneth Branagh Era" and Kenneth Rothwell has termed "The Age of Branagh" (Crowl 2003; Rothwell 2004). Indeed, the story Crowl and Rothwell tell functions somewhat like a redemption narrative. Branagh takes the torch passed by his master-mentor, Olivier, and brings light from the darkness of the two preceding decades – construed as "a barren wasteland in which Shakespeare almost completely disappeared from film" (Crowl 2003: 1) – while taking careful note of what the more eccentric Welles contributed in the way of camera-work and framing, and the more exuberantly cinematic Zeffirelli contributed in the way of action, color, and sound. This is a story that leans heavily on the positive value of bringing Shakespeare on film into the popular marketplace by adopting Hollywood production values and aesthetics; it consequently situates more experimental work, which can at best hope to be screened at universities and art-houses, at the periphery of both artistic practice and critical attention. It is also a story that elides some very real differences between film-artists themselves, on the one hand, and between scholars, on the other, with respect to which version (or vision) of Shakespeare should be put on display through the medium of film and for what purpose.

Allusive Traffic

Probably few would quarrel in the abstract with the idea that it is a good thing to maximize the circulation of Shakespeare's plays in any form, particularly at a moment in history when classical musical concerts play to aging and rapidly diminishing audiences, and when classic artworks have to rely on the marketing and promotion of blockbuster exhibitions at major museums to sustain their cultural capital. But just as the marketing of catalogues, posters, and postcards, illustrated t-shirts and coffee mugs, often migrates beyond the gift-shop to the entrances of exhibition galleries themselves – not only altering the way we see and respond to art but transforming the art-object itself into merchandise – so too may the filmic reconstitution of a Shakespeare play alter and commodify our terms of engagement with it. A strain of films in the 1990s that Douglas Lanier describes as "Shakescorp *Noir*" suggests some of the troubling consequences of such commodification. For Lanier, the "age of Branagh" is better described as a period in which classics that were long understood by Hollywood as "box office poison" were systematically assimilated to the dominant visual modes, genres, and market niches of the Hollywood marketplace – particularly the teen market, with films such as *Clueless* (1995) and *10 Things I Hate About You* (1999) (2002b: 163). By making corporate competition and the rise of mass media a cause or symptom of their tragic actions, films such as Almereyda's *Hamlet* and Luhrmann's *Romeo + Juliet* suggest the costs that may be incurred when Shakespeare's works (along with those of other classic authors such as Austen, Dickens, and Woolf) are assimilated to the interests of global corporations (2002b: 162). Lanier identifies the worry reflected in these films with that articulated by social theorists such as Theodor Adorno and Fredric Jameson: that our monolithic, increasingly global culture industry circulates only what serves its institutional interests, negating "art's capacity for critique and opposition, offering its audience only the illusion of enlightenment and diversity while in fact compelling conformity to a social and aesthetic status quo" (2002b: 160–1).

These concerns are important not because Shakespeare's work is or ever has been pure of commercial interests, though sometimes it may be understood to stand for such purity. (Henry, the Hollywood-sellout in Levring's *The King is Alive*, clearly holds to this romantic vision.) They remain important because they remind us to attend to the multiple contexts in which our own practices of cultural consumption and production – including teaching Shakespeare and Shakespeare films – are shaped, and to seek out modes of expression beyond the dominant offerings of Hollywood. Thus it seems critical not to take Branagh's recontextualization of Shakespeare in terms of Hollywood practices as the only available model for the late twentieth-century development of Shakespeare on Western film, such that the one is inseparable from the other. This means not only attending to the ways in which recent films have worried about the complicity of cinema with global capital, but also turning our attention to films that rub against the grain of mainstream production practices and engage in different, often competing forms of recontextualization.[6] For example, Julie Taymor's *Titus* may follow Branagh's lead in exploiting established Hollywood strategies for arousing audience interest and attention. Yet her film also enters into sustained conversation with pop-cultural artifacts like the recent German film *Run, Lola, Run* (1998), which works within the formats of video and computer gaming; with the metamorphic iconography of Ovidian poetry; and with the conceptual frameworks of avant-garde performance art.

Branagh surely played a crucial role in bringing Shakespeare into the circuit of cineplex and art-house alike. But even Branagh's best films, like most of the Shakespeare revivals they spawned, are rooted in realist and heritage conventions that were already being superseded by a series of Shakespeare films (like *Prospero's Books* and *Titus)* that took a more radically interventionist approach to their material.[7] As we explore at greater length below, these developments can be traced in part to the work of a number of filmmakers who began experimenting with an array of expressionist, vernacular, and formalist styles in the 1950s and 1960s. Their innovations are discernible in the expressionist *auteurism* of the Shakespeare films of Welles, in the vernacular-formalism of Akira Kurosawa's "translations" of *Macbeth* and *King Lear* into the austere *Throne of Blood* (1961) and more richly cinematic *Ran* (1985), respectively, and in the similarly idiosyncratic, though very differently styled, *Macbeth* directed by Roman Polanski and *King Lear* directed by Peter Brook in 1970 (see Davies 1988). Artists such as these made their Shakespeare films during a period of great artistic ferment in the international film community, and drew inspiration from their shared commitment to the development of film as an art-form independent of, even hostile to, the commercial, mass-entertainment methods and goals of the Hollywood film industry. Their take on Shakespeare was consequently more risk-taking and formally inventive than were the Shakespeare films produced by Olivier and, subsequently, by Zeffirelli. Although they had little in common with each other apart from a shared interest in experimenting with ways to recast the Shakespearean text, each of these artists modeled ways of bringing Shakespeare on film production into closer collaboration with their own *auteuristic* objectives than with commercial film practices.

Crowl correctly notes that the period between 1971 and 1989 saw little in the way of dramatically significant work in the area of Shakespeare on film. But that period was hardly a "barren wasteland" (2003: 1), particularly if we situate the 1971 Polanski *Macbeth* at its commencement and note that during this time the BBC ambitiously produced high-prestige television films of all 37 Shakespeare plays, which were duly screened in America as Masterpiece Theatre productions, and offered as supplements to the study of Shakespeare at colleges and universities. Although it is easy to dismiss retrospectively the majority of the films generated by this project as airless, museum-quality productions, many functioned at the time (1978–85) as the only filmic realization of a given Shakespeare play ever made in the post-silent film era, and continue to do so.[8] Indeed, probably the greatest contribution made by the project was its painstaking recording of film-versions of seldom produced plays such as *Coriolanus, Timon of Athens, All's Well That Ends Well, Cymbeline, Henry VIII*, and *Measure for Measure*, which helped generate significant afterlives on the stage, in classrooms, and in scholarship and criticism.

Shakespeare also made several significant appearances in feature films in the 1980s in adventurous reworkings of *The Tempest* by the American Paul Mazursky (1982) and the British Derek Jarman (1980) as well as in *Ran*, Akira Kurosawa's extravagantly reimagined version of *King Lear*.[9] Two of the more intriguing Shakespeare films of the decade were the provocatively impertinent takes on *King Lear* and *Hamlet* (both 1987) executed by Jean Luc Godard, a pioneer of the French New Wave, and by the maverick Finnish director, Aki Kaurismaki, respectively. The studied opacity and invasive self-reflexivity of Godard's *King Lear* undoubtedly make it ripe for easy dismissal – though, as Peter Donaldson has convincingly contended, there is considerably more here than meets the eye (1990: 189–225). In a manner that the classroom scene in his 1964 film, *Bande à part* (*The Outsiders*), anticipated, Godard is less interested in updating Shakespeare than in bringing Shakespeare's status as a "classic" into collision with the variously more fluid and fractious stylings of the "modern" (see chapter 3). Godard returns to this theme with a vengeance in his *King Lear*, which begins with an unflattering portrait of Norman Mailer and his daughter as spoiled, self-important Americans, and involves throughout satirical jabs at Hollywood philistinism while recounting the "story" (so much as there can be said to be a story) of William Shakespeare, Jr, the Fifth's attempt to recover the lost plays of his famous ancestor.

Although it is difficult to find in any format, Kaurismaki's *Hamlet Goes Business*, which brings an even chillier irony and amusingly brutalist irreverence to bear on Shakespeare, also deserves more of a place in accounts of Shakespeare films of the 1980s, particularly since (like Godard's *King Lear*) it pre-dates Branagh's unerringly serious revisiting of *Henry V* by two years. Others had before taken the liberty to do completely updated filmic transformations of Shakespeare's plays – notable examples being Hughes's *Joe Macbeth* (1955), Wilcox's *Forbidden Planet* (1956), Wise and Robbins's *West Side Story* (1961), in addition to Mazursky's 1982 *Tempest*. And others had scrambled and reassembled playtexts to fit their own eccentric designs: Welles's *Chimes at Midnight* and Jarman's *Tempest*. Yet Kaurismaki is the first Western filmmaker to transpose Hamlet to a corporate setting (a move first made in Kurosawa's 1963 revenge-*noir, The Bad Sleep Well*, and thus twice-borrowed by Michael Almereyda in his own *Hamlet* film), to deploy modern media technology (such as computers and surveillance cameras) to enrich both his plot and *mise en scène*, and to have Hamlet actually contribute to (and happily take responsibility for) the killing of his father.[10] Such plot-changes may be solely construed as campy, particularly when added to a host of others (including Laertes's death by jukebox), all of which are delivered in Kaurismaki's trademark dead-pan manner. Yet when set against a backdrop that includes the examples of cinematic adventurism detailed above and those soon to be described below, one may wonder whether the transformative impulse that both Godard and Kaurismaki take to the breaking point (a point exceeded four years later in Greenaway's *Prospero's Books*), and the campiness to which it is often affiliated, may not point to a line of Shakespeare on film production which is just as continuous as – and arguably more forward looking than – the line that takes us from Olivier to Zeffirelli to Branagh.

Such distinctions, of course, may not matter much if the line in question is, for all rights and purposes, invisible, or if the period that it documents amounts to "a barren wasteland" in the popular view of things. From such a perspective, it may well seem that the only line that matters is the one that skips a few beats until it recovers its momentum in the influential work of Branagh. Godard's English instructor in *Bande à part* would no doubt recognize in Branagh's 1989 version of *Henry V* a classic instance of the "individual talent" extending the bounds of "traditional" filmic realizations of Shakespeare into the domain of the new or modern (see chapter 3). But we surely need to expand our attribution of all that follows in the next 15 years beyond the precedent of Branagh's *Henry V*. It is, for starters, impossible to credit Branagh's influence on such deeply idiosyncratic films as Gus Van Sant's *My Own Private Idaho* and Greenaway's *Prospero's Books* (both 1991) that followed closely in its wake, much less with any role in generating Zeffirelli's own blockbuster bid – the 1990 *Hamlet* starring Mel Gibson and Glenn Close, which grossed twice the amount *Henry V* earned. Whatever long-term influence Branagh might have had on films made later in the decade, such as Luhrmann's *Romeo + Juliet*, Taymor's *Titus*, and Almereyda's *Hamlet*, would seem confined to supplying confidence in their commercial viability (confidence that was roundly justified by Luhrmann's film, but clearly misplaced in the case of Taymor and Almereyda). Branagh's *Henry V* (1989) and the exuberant *Much Ado About Nothing* (1993), in which he first began to cast Hollywood stars alongside his British troupe of stage-trained actors, assuredly did help sponsor or spawn Richard Loncraine's edgy updating of *Richard III* (1995) and Trevor Nunn's estimable *Twelfth Night* (1996) (produced by Branagh's own production company) as well as Oliver Parker's *Othello* (1995), Michael Hoffman's *Midsummer Night's Dream* (1999), and even Michael Radford's recent film-version of *The Merchant of Venice* (2004). However, Branagh's effort in his even more lavishly produced 1996 *Hamlet* to serve a few too many masters – which include his opportunistic concessions to blockbuster film conventions and celebrity casting – did more than help "fashion an effective style for translating Shakespeare into the language of film." It sustained the momentum of a "revival" that combined the conventions of British "heritage film" with the homogenizing imperatives of Hollywood and the bombast and sentimentalism of Andrew Lloyd Webber musicals.[11] In so doing it helped generate the kinds of films that hark back to the famously anachronistic Max Reinhardt/William Dieterle *Midsummer Night's Dream* (1935) and evoke many of the characteristics of what Clement Greenberg shortly thereafter classified as *kitsch* in his influential 1939 essay, "Avant-garde and Kitsch," and which Richard Burt has more recently designated as "schlock" (Harbord 2002: 40; Burt 2002a).

Precedents Branagh set both in *Much Ado* and in *Hamlet* – which were arguably anticipated by Zeffirelli's 1990 *Hamlet* but even more so by his largely forgotten facilitating of Elizabeth Taylor's and Richard Burton's star-turns in his 1967 *Taming of the Shrew* – can be held directly accountable for the mismatched casting choices and overt commercialism of any number of later films. These include Parker's *Othello* (featuring Branagh in the role of Iago), Hoffman's cloyingly sentimental *Midsummer Night's Dream*, Branagh's own lackluster *Love's Labour's Lost*, and Radford's *Merchant of Venice*, in which imperatives to serve the youth market repeatedly clash with the director's efforts to do some kind of rough justice to his depiction of Shylock. Branagh's and Hoffman's films in particular show a marked nostalgia for the generic trappings of Hollywood film: ranging from 1930s Busby Berkeley filmic extravaganzas, to westerns like *The Magnificent Seven* (1960), to the heroic iconography of Charlton Heston, to the "heritage" of schlocky screwball comics from Michael Keaton and Jack Lemmon to Billy Crystal and Robin Williams. They show equal nostalgia for English theatrical traditions (note, for example, the casting of Derek Jacobi in *Henry V* and *Hamlet*) and "heritage" conventions (embodied by Emma Thompson in *Henry V* and *Much Ado* and Kate Winslet in *Hamlet*).

Of all the films produced by this group, only Loncraine's "campy" *Richard III* (Buhler 2000) can truly be construed as experimental insofar as none of the others show the least familiarity with, or interest in, the cinematic innovations pioneered as long ago as the French New Wave and elaborated on with considerable energy and panache by their American and European successors of the 1970s and 1980s – much less the varied approaches to narrative explored in new media art, commercial or otherwise. As James Loehlin observes of the rest of this group of typically "realist" films: "The realist Shakespeare film is characterized by the sort of mid-range naturalistic acting, cinematography, and editing that is used in most Hollywood films. The characters are represented as 'real people', in plausible make-up and costumes, and the film relates the narrative straightforwardly without calling attention to the medium" (2003: 173–4).[12] The effort of these films to bring a sense of cinematic naturalism to the screen (both in *mise en scène* and adherence to familiar conventions of continuity editing), at the same time as their market-driven casting choices insist on the presentism of their actors' mode of cinematic address, reveals the extent to which they have been assembled out of a mix of commercial motivations and formulaic aesthetic criteria that damps down any sense of artistic urgency.[13] The result, in our opinion, is an updated but unmistakable version of kitsch.

Kitsch, as Janet Harbord writes, is "a formulation of the derivative nature of mass culture" that "draws its powers from its pretence of serious culture, which becomes 'debased,' a 'simulacra' of the real" (Harbord 2002: 43). As Clement Greenberg observes, "Kitsch is mechanical and operates by formulas. Kitsch is vicarious experience and faked sensations. Kitsch changes according to style, but always remains the same. Kitsch is [in short] all that is spurious in the life of our times" (Greenberg 1939: 35). It is crucial to note here that, at its moment of composition, Greenberg's all-out attack on mass culture was motivated by his effort to defend "serious art practice" from what he took to be "a frivolous, stylized mass culture" that had already come close to compelling serious artists to retreat into "the formalist preoccupations of art for art's sake" (Harbord 2002: 41). In our own time, it is pointless to lament the fact that mass culture now commands the field of what is commonly taken for artistic practice, that what Greenberg anticipated has long ago eventuated in the mainstreaming of kitsch and the delegation of "serious art practice" in the production and display of film to independent directors and producers and to a dwindling number of underfunded art-houses and museums. However, it is by no means inevitable that serious artists will retreat into empty formalism rather than directly engage with the dominance of kitsch and its close associate, schlock. Nor is it too late to draw distinctions between how individual filmmakers, particularly those who take Shakespeare as their material (in either its raw or refined state), respond to that dominance in the cinematic marketplace.[14]

To draw these distinctions, we will rely on yet another term recently put back into circulation by Harbord, which has been famously associated with Susan Sontag's 1964 essay, "Notes on Camp." For Sontag, *camp* is a style "appearing only in surface phenomena; it has no depth" (Harbord 2002: 44). Rather than trying to function as "an intrinsically subversive text or act," camp is "a general mode of being 'alive to a double sense in which some things can be taken' " (Harbord 2002: 44; Sontag [1964] 1999: 57). As Sontag writes, "Camp is art that proposes itself seriously, but cannot be taken altogether seriously because it is 'too much' " (1999: 59). And, as Harbord concludes, "If Greenberg's statement on kitsch positions mass culture as a replica attempting the status of the original, Sontag rewrites it as a sensibility cut off from the original and yet illuminating the distance. It is at once innocent and performative, a 'way of seeing the world as an aesthetic phenomenon' " (Harbord 2002: 44; Sontag 1999: 54).

Although we are committed here to maintaining a wary distance from definitions and classifications that tend to close down, rather than open up, dialogue and debate, Harbord's discussion of the differences between kitsch and camp bears closely on our own effort to differentiate most of the films made, spawned, or sponsored by Branagh from those made by Bedford, Greenaway, Luhrmann, Taymor, Almereyda, and Morrissette in particular. This need not mean that Branagh's productions are all kitsch, or those of the latter all camp; rather, it means that we find a sufficient number of these generic characteristics at work within them to underwrite such distinctions. The chief difference between the kitschiness of Branagh's appropriative moves in *Much Ado* and *Hamlet* and the campiness of those of Lurhmann and Taymor in *Romeo + Juliet* and *Titus*, respectively, is that in Branagh (as in Hoffman and Radford) such moves are often occasioned by the mixed motives of comic debasement, heroic inflation, and sentimental reassurance. So eager are these directors to please that they happily diminish what can be sold cheaply while holding fast to the "pretence" that this is the best, possibly the only, way to keep the art-object circulating in the market at all, thereby condescendingly conflating the popular with the populist. Consider, for example, the swashbuckling behavior of the pumped-up Prince as he swings down on a chandelier to assail Claudius in Branagh's *Hamlet*; the bottom-line casting and characterizations of the lovers in Hoffman's *Midsummer Night's Dream* and of Dogberry and Verges in Branagh's *Much Ado*; and the patronizing representation of the bumptious Moorish retinue in Radford's *Merchant* which frees the film's Portia from having to discriminate openly in the way the play's Portia does. Consider also how Hoffman gives Kevin Kline's Bottom both a heart and a mind that are considerably softer than the ones Shakespeare endowed Bottom with in *A Midsummer Night's Dream*.

By contrast, in Luhrmann and the others a consistent self-consciousness or doubleness is discernible such that the film and the originary play are set on separate, parallel tracks, the heaviness of the one casting an occasional shadow over the lightness of the other and vice versa. The effect aimed at here is less translation than transposition, less cynicism that wants to be taken seriously than seriousness rendered with a lighter, ironic touch. While kitsch wants both to please and to succeed, camp is always already pleased with itself and comparatively indifferent to its effect on its audience. It embeds material in its filmic fabric which signals its doubleness to the knowing viewer and confidently assumes a viewer clever enough to notice.

The Counter-mainstream

The "story" we have told thus far points in two occasionally overlapping but also differentiated directions taken by recent Shakespeare films: toward kitschy, commercially driven, and conventionally formatted "realist" films on the one hand, and toward more campy, unconventional, and/or new media-savvy films on the other that may be just as commercially driven as Branagh's and Hoffman's (Lurhmann's *Romeo + Juliet*, Bedford's *The Street King*) or not (Pacino's *Looking for Richard*,

Levring's *The King is Alive*). But our storyline has deeper roots. It builds, first, on a genealogy that fastens on earlier versions of Shakespeare on film (films such as Welles's *Macbeth* and *Chimes at Midnight*, Kurosawa's *Throne of Blood* and *The Bad Sleep Well*, Polanski's *Macbeth*, and Brook's *King Lear*, among others) that have served the filmmakers of the 1990s and beyond with both established precedents and models of creative adaptation.

Our intention in proposing a post-war genealogy for the films we plan to discuss is not to replace one Shakespeare on film canon with another but to foreground the mechanics of canon formation itself, and to map the diverging faultlines of both Shakespeare on film production and scholarly accounts of it. As Rothwell and others have demonstrated, films that draw directly or indirectly on Shakespeare have been produced in virtually every corner of the world since the silent film era. Many of these remain all but invisible to anyone apart from students of the genre. But several of them – most notably *Throne of Blood* – have recontextualized Shakespeare in ways that both local and global audiences can appreciate and that both cutting-edge film scholars and tradition-bound Shakespeareans can celebrate. Certainly, practices that are characteristic of the 1990s "cross-over" films of Branagh and Hoffman – like the casting of Hollywood icons to fill prominent roles, the deployment of comic actors whose signature tics and gestures are consciously exploited in their film performances, the mixing of British Shakespeare actors with American movie stars – are broadly apparent in groundbreaking films like the 1935 Reinhardt/Dieterle *Midsummer Night's Dream* and Joseph Manciewicz's 1953 production of *Julius Caesar*. Yet so too are impulses to render Shakespeare in the fractured, fragmented, and expressionist vein of *My Own Private Idaho* and *The King is Alive* modeled on and responsive to such earlier examples as Welles's *Chimes at Midnight* and Brook's *King Lear*.

The films we have described as constituting a new wave of Shakespeare on screen also draw on the innovative approaches to cinematic art pioneered by the self-styled *auteurs* of the French New Wave of the late 1950s and 1960s (particularly the work of Jean-Luc Godard) and pursued by similarly innovative filmmakers from that time to the present. Their numbers include Federico Fellini, Michelangelo Antonioni, Louis Malle, John Cassavetes, Martin Scorsese, Stanley Kubrick, Nicholas Roeg, Peter Weir, Francis Ford Coppola, Werner Herzog, Wim Wenders, Jim Jarmusch, Peter Greenaway, David Lynch, and Lars von Trier, among others. Although one or two of these artists have since made manifest concessions to Hollywood production conventions (most notably, Scorsese), most pursued and several continue to pursue more experimental cinematic designs. These include a discontinuous approach to storytelling (Antonioni, Fellini, Cassavetes, Greenaway); the assumption of detached, ironic, and parodic points of view (Greenaway, Kubrick, Lynch, Jarmusch); disorienting cinematography (Roeg, Herzog, Wenders, von Trier); technical inventiveness (Godard, Fellini, Roeg, Greenaway); an intensely rendered embrace of the mysterious, violent, and inexplicable in modern experience (Antonioni, Kubrick, Scorsese, Weir, Herzog, Lynch, von Trier); the variable use of painfully long takes, jump-cuts, and rapid-fire montage (Antonioni, Wenders, Cassavetes, Godard, Roeg); and the mix of realist, surreal, and expressionist visual imagery (Fellini, Wenders, Von Trier, Greenaway, Lynch). These design principles run directly counter to such privileged Hollywood conventions as chronological storytelling, unified characterization, seamless montage, high-gloss production values, and cinematic naturalism, not to mention such bottom-line goals as audience satisfaction and box-office success.

The names of such artists seldom appear in treatments of Shakespeare on screen, and may, in fact, be comparatively foreign to younger students of the genre whose viewing experiences have understandably been confined to what the local multiplex makes available. When non-Shakespeare-related films enter into such discussions, they are often Hollywood products cited as illustrations of the market-driven concerns that have motivated artists such as Branagh, Zeffirelli, Loncraine, Parker, Hoffman, Luhrmann, and even Taymor and Almereyda to find ways of "crossing over" into the domain of the "popular." Conversely, developments in cultural studies have made us relatively more attentive to patterns of Shakespearean allusion in popular culture: from political punditry (Hillary Clinton as "Lady Macbeth of Little Rock") to mainstream Hollywood films such as *Renaissance Man* (1994), *L.A. Story* (1991), *Last Action Hero* (1993), and spin-offs designed to appeal to younger audiences, such as *10 Things I Hate About You* (1999), *Shakespeare in Love* (1999), and Tim Blake Nelson's *O* (2001). Such back and forth traffic between high and popular culture has made us especially alert to the "ghosting" effects of global celebrity. Those effects allow Mel Gibson's fiery star turns in *Lethal Weapon* (1987) and *Lethal Weapon II* (1989), for example, to migrate into the promotional field of the Shakespeare film in question, in this case Zeffirelli's 1990 *Hamlet*, thus generating an aggressive impression of the usually more cerebral and indecisive Danish Prince.[15]

We need to bring into this field of productive cultural traffic not only more kinds of filmic practices and precedents, but also non-filmic influences and inspirations that fly below the radar of many mainstream film audiences. And, as a number of scholars have argued, we need to remain attuned to the very real differences among the films in question in terms of *how* they explore and exploit their expansive field of citation and borrowing. Our aim in the chapters that follow is to continue to widen the contextual field for reading the films we concentrate on, by focusing closely on less familiar and more contrarian filmic idioms.

A film such as Taymor's *Titus* typifies both the challenges and ongoing interest of widening our contextual fields in this way. *Titus* draws promiscuously on a host of references to popular culture, and choreographs its many scenes of violence in ways that would be familiar to any seasoned viewer of horror and action-adventure films. But it also draws liberally on a vividly colored *mise en scène* of monumental excess and surreal spectacle lifted from Fellini's *Satyricon* (1969) and *Roma* (1972) and Peter Greenaway's *The Cook, the Thief, His Wife & Her Lover* (1989). The film's striking conceptual apparatus is, moreover, closely modeled on Taymor's earlier music theater-pieces and the performance designs of avant-garde theater and dance creators such as Robert Wilson, Martha Clarke, and Pina Bausch. Taymor's indulgence in the lurid, the unlikely, and the absurd may surely tend at times towards schlock (Burt 2002a). Yet the effects aimed at in scenes that include Titus's cooling of his human meat-pies on a window-sill may also tilt towards the campy targets (wherein the domestic coolly conflates with the horrific) that are repeatedly hit by David Lynch in *Blue Velvet* (1986) and *Mulholland Drive* (2001), and by Jim Jarmusch in his brilliantly deadpan *Dead Man* (1995).

Even Baz Luhrmann's aesthetic involves considerably more than an abject catering to his youth audience's need for constant visual and aural stimulation, drawing as it does on influences and inspirations as disparate as the costumes worn in Sydney's annual Gay and Lesbian Mardi Gras (Donaldson 2002b: 72–3 *et passim*) and the stylized violence of Stanley Kubrick's *A Clockwork Orange* (1971). The film-noirish mood and atmospheric stylings of Michael Almereyda's *Hamlet* hark back not only to popular American films of the 1950s and corporate dramas such as *Wall Street* (1987), but to the brilliantly precise visual and auditory framings of Wim Wenders's *The American Friend* (1977). The immersion of Hamlet himself in the solitary filming, playing, and replaying of video imagery in his effort to solve the mystery of his disjointed family evoke earlier films that range from Antonioni's *Blow-Up* (1966) and Coppola's *The Conversation* (1974) to Sadie Benning's Pixelvision diaries (see chapter 3). The wider our field of reference, in other words, the more unstable our calculations of any given allusive effect; but with that instability comes an increasing complexity of interpretation.

The films we have singled out for sustained attention not only enter into dialogue with specific Shakespearean playtexts, but into conversation with their own filmic contemporaries and forbears as well as with collateral developments in digital technology, computer graphics, performance art, and popular culture. These intertextual conversations are as varied as the cultural matter they draw on: typically dialogic, disintegrative, collaborative, or parodic in orientation. Yet in all of these modes these films maintain a measured distance from their source-texts – even when they launch most fully into them – that reminds us we are entertaining performances, not revivals, of classic works. In this way, as we discuss in the next chapter, they help expand our understanding of adaptation as a cultural process.

2 Adaptation as a Cultural Process

What does it mean to say that film-adaptation is a cultural process and not just a way of translating an artwork from one expressive medium into another? To use two examples from the previous chapter, we need think only of the very different forms of cultural surround that inform and invade Zeffirelli's 1968 film-adaptation of *Romeo and Juliet* and Lurhmann's 1996 *William Shakespeare's Romeo + Juliet.* Both films clearly attempt to "keep faith" with Shakespeare's tale of exuberantly youthful "star-crossed lovers" caught up in the throes of "true" love for the first time. But the casting choices, the look of the actors, and their preferred acting styles are as different from each other as Renaissance Verona is from Verona Beach. From Harold Perrineau's transvestite "voguing" as Mercutio to John Leguizamo's demonic turn as Tybalt, we recognize from the start that these films are operating in radically different cinematic terrain. They reflect not only different ideas about Shakespeare's plays and classic works more generally, but a different *cultural imaginary*: that prevailing set of fantasies, values, desires, and assumptions which effectively identifies a specific cultural moment and differentiates it from other cultural moments past or to come. This is not to say that sexual role-playing, drug-taking, and youth-gang violence are more characteristic of our time than of the 1968 of Franco Zeffirelli (or the 1961 of *West Side Story*), though they well may be. It is rather to say that prevailing ideas, fantasies, and assumptions about sex and youth-culture take *this* form as opposed to the form they took when Zeffirelli modeled the innocence, beauty, and passion of his young lovers on the youth culture of the 1960s – or when Arthur Laurents and Stephen Sondheim took their inspiration from street riots involving *chicanos* in Los Angeles, transposing their conception of embattled innocence to the clash of immigrant cultures on New York's West Side.

All adaptations necessarily operate within their specific cultural imaginaries.[1] But some also explicitly reflect on the dynamics of adaptation in this cultural key. Because so many of Shakespeare's plays have the status of classic works – indeed, have come to represent the idea of a "Classic Work" in the Western cultural imaginary – Shakespeare adaptations invite such self-reflexiveness. Of the films we just compared, Luhrmann's is the one that most explicitly takes up this invitation, as its title immediately makes clear by laying claim to and marking its distance from Shakespearean authorship. The pictograph that links the lovers' names – either a Gothic cross or a +, depending on where the title appears – evokes a host of resonances that belong not to Shakespeare's playtext but to the cultural imaginary that animates this version. The pictograph suggests playground graffiti and adolescent crushes, the transposition of a verbal art into the visual field of cinema, the film's re-appropriation of religious symbols from their kitschy half-life as commodities, and the problematic of faith and infidelity that attaches to many adaptations (Donaldson 2002b). The campy dissonance of Luhrmann's title illuminates the distance between this postmodern "copy" and its "original" while also back-handedly pressing the point that it is only the practice of copying that creates – and confers authority on – an original (Derrida 1981: 206).

In the following pages we focus on adaptation not only as a cultural process but also as a specifically film- and Shakespeare-related phenomenon. Synthesizing ideas from film theory, performance theory, and new media theory, we introduce some basic critical terms applicable to the study of Shakespeare on screen and particularly to the films discussed in this book. As we shall see, the interest these films share in the cultural dynamics of adaptation reflects changing attitudes about classic art, creativity, the relationship between past and present, and the relationship between old and new media.

Fast-forwarding the Bard

A good place to begin is a moment in Almereyda's *Hamlet* when the film rather boldly cites the pre-existence and persistence of a play called *Hamlet* by showing a brief clip on "Hamlet's" monitor. As the camera pans past Ethan Hawke, seated at a digital editing station, it quotes a famous scene (Hamlet addressing the skull of Yorick) and a famous Shakespearean actor (John Gielgud). We can guess that Hamlet must have clipped the scene himself since we often see him working with such found materials. So at this moment we might say that Almereyda is "confessing" the extent to which his film is one in a series of *Hamlet*s going back in time. Yet Almereyda's film does not pursue the question of what Shakespeare's *Hamlet means* to his video-collaging main char-acter. We never actually see Hamlet working with the clip the way we see him working with Thich Nhat Hanh's Buddhist riff on the "To be" speech that he also plays back on his monitor. Because of this, the film leaves open the question of how we are to understand that gesture backward. Is Almereyda's film a belated *hommage* to or after-image of the original play and later films? Or is it an image of Hamlet "now," understood to replace those earlier versions? Or do all these versions together constitute some larger, composite work that Western culture names *Hamlet*?

We gravitate towards the last notion: that in this brief moment the film presents itself not as a copy of an original but as a reframing of earlier framings, an addition to a larger body of work that by implication

2.1 *Hamlet* as a text series

includes many *Hamlets*. Jerome McGann and Joseph Grigely have described this kind of additive versioning of classic works in terms that underpin much recent scholarship on Shakespeare performances on and off screen, and much of our thinking in this book. A *work* – we will call it "Shakespeare's *Hamlet*" – is properly understood as a *series* of *texts* (Grigely 1995: 99; McGann 1983: 52). That series may include print editions, textbooks, children's versions, and graphic novels as well as non-print "texts" such as stage performances, opera, ballet, screen versions, multi-media installations, hypertext, and so on. Each of the texts in this series re-presents or re-iterates prior texts in the series, each varying from those that come before and after it (Grigely 1995, 99–100). The series that constitutes a work, in this way, should not be thought of as summable in any simple sense, as if one could add up all the different versions of *Hamlet* to get a sum total of potential variations that would equal "Hamlet" (1995: 99).[2] Nor should we think of the earliest texts in a series as originals. In the case of Shakespeare's works, the earliest play-texts usually exist in multiple versions: early print editions (quartos and the Folio of 1623); lost manuscripts from which the print editions were set; prompter's copies; performances in different venues. Moreover, Shakespeare's plays reiterate even earlier works, making each playtext a "tissue of quotations" from many genres and *intertexts* (Barthes 1977: 146). The tragedy of *Hamlet* belongs to the family of English nationalist dramas that retell Germanic histories and also to the popular genre of revenge plays. So, too, Almereyda's film belongs to the families of Shakespeare adaptation, film noir, and corporate or "Wall Street" drama, and it quotes indie video works along with Gielgud and Luhrmann's film. In this way, Almereyda's *Hamlet* presents itself as one of a series of texts that plays variations on a *work* that is not reducible to a single authorized version.

The Gielgud citation is a bold gesture because it invites a reaction that updatings are usually supposed to hide. Even if we have never heard the words before, what we are watching is material that may seem rather exhausted because of its very status as classic work. Yet the fact that Hamlet comes to the most familiar material of the play – his "To be" speech – by reusing someone else's (screened) riff on Shakespeare's playtext is precisely the point. The reason that Hawke sounds so fresh when he delivers those famous lines is that the audience hears them being rehearsed in this layered way – accommodating the fact that we have already heard the speech repeated in whole or fragments many times.[3] In this way, the film allows us to hear the speech as at once entirely scripted *and* performed in the moment, received *and* just now invented. And we may recognize Hamlet as acting by way of repeated citation or "restored behaviors" that are part of a long history of the reuse of Shakespeare plays in Western culture (Schechner 1985: 36–7). Performance scholars think of such actions as "restored" in several senses (Roach 1996: 3). They are played back (and given back) to us; they are represented *as* playable, repeatable givens; they are stored up for future replaying and thus conserved for the culture; they are constituted serially, through repetition and variation.

Extending the idea of a work as a text series, Grigely suggests that every copy, edition, display, publication, exhibit, recording, or performance of an artwork is fundamentally an *adaptation*, in that it reframes prior versions of that work in new environments, periods, and material, and for new purposes. Adaptation in this sense is the very mechanism by which culture transmits its classic works: unmaking and remaking them, renegotiating their meaning in specific reception contexts (Grigely 1995: 32). Even a new print edition of *Hamlet* remakes the play in a way that changes its meaning, in perceptible and imperceptible ways. Each modern edition composes different elements of the three Renaissance playtexts into a new, unified or multi-text version. It adds an apparatus of *paratexts* suited to specific readers: footnotes, introduction, historical materials, and illustrations.[4] It materializes the work (using page-layout, scene breaks, jacket notes, cover illustrations, synopses, etc.) in ways that suit contemporary notions about the shape and readability of a book. And it circulates the work to a specific market of readers: high school, college, theater, Shakespeare buffs, etc. Film-adaptations expand on the verbal and visual media of print to include other perceptual tracks (spoken dialogue as well as written words, music, foley sounds, and moving images), other paratexts, and other production and post-production choices (casting and performance, cinematography, editing, budget and marketing constraints) (Stam 2005a: 17). In such ways, works are "ontologized," Grigely explains, "contextualized semantically" or made meaningful, through a host of local choices shaped "by the temporal history that surrounds their composition" (1995: 103). Thus, a "text" in any medium can be understood as a *performance* of a work, a relatively transient but powerful actualization that gives the work a local habitation and a name. As a series of texts, that work makes certain constellations of meanings and material available to be renegotiated in performance and reception by local users – readers, performers, artists, filmmakers, auditors, teachers, students.

Thinking about Shakespeare adaptations in these terms puts some pressure not just on the question of what a particular work makes available to those adapting it, but of how these resources are negotiated in the light of earlier negotiations. In terms of actual performance by an actor, this requires something that cites his secondariness (such as the Gielgud quotation) and/or something that exceeds a mere playing of the role. Audience familiarity with Shakespearean story and language may be as much an issue in theatrical re-stagings of Shakespeare as it is in screen reproductions. So it is useful to think about the challenges cinematic and theatrical audition share. Consider, for example, how difficult it is for someone conversant with Shakespeare to get caught up in yet another "new" stage-production of *Hamlet* or *Macbeth*. For such a playgoer, there is essentially no *drama* in the offing since she not only knows virtually everything about the play in question and how it will turn out, but also anticipates most of the lines the actors will speak and even how they will probably say them. Beyond the pleasure of hearing beautiful language recited, the only reason for watching may be the hope that someone will say or do something *differently* : will *perform* the roles (that is, call overt attention to their doubleness or belatedness) rather than merely *play* them (that is, fit into them as one fits into a well-worn seat or suit).

It may seem as if only those deeply familiar with the plays could feel the pressure of belatedness, in this way. But that pressure has as much to do with the way the plays circulate throughout the culture and with a given production's attentiveness to the uncanny effects of that circulation. The conditions of mainstream theatrical production often preclude the kind of performativity we have in mind here, as does the residually theatrical conditioning of conventionally realist Shakespeare films (ranging from Branagh's *Much Ado About Nothing* to Michael Radford's *William Shakespeare's The Merchant of Venice* (2004)). Even updated stage-productions are regularly performed in an isolated space – a theater – that separates their audiences from immersion in an everydayness that would contextualize the plays far more densely and that reflects their own fragmentary but persistent life in popular culture. But set an actor who calls himself Hamlet in a profoundly multi-mediated and updated cinematic setting – the streets of New York City, a Blockbuster outlet – and a whole world that always already contains and rearticulates Shakespeare appears before our eyes.

Citational Environments

All adaptations make their habitations not only in specific geographic milieux and media but also in *citational environments*: generic and cultural fields that incorporate specific stances towards source materials and rules for handling them. We borrow the phrase from W.B. Worthen, who, in applying Grigely's ideas to Luhrmann's film, observes that the film resituates Shakespeare's playtext "in a specific citational environment – the verbal, visual, gestural, and behavioral dynamics of youth culture, of MTV" (Worthen 1998: 1104). Thus, for example, we find the distinctive presentational rules of MTV videos scripting our introduction to Romeo, as he sits alone with his melancholy musings at the ruined theater. Here the audiotracks (Romeo's voice-over, intertwining with a feature-song music track) bridge short, fast visual montages "self-consciously parading" the "perfected techniques of cinematography, *mise en scène*, and editing" (Manovich 2001: 262). These conventions are very different from the citational rules applied in Al Pacino's *Looking for Richard*. That film dips into brief sections of playtext, sampling it in a way that might at first seem more discontinuous. But the narrative structures of theater rehearsal and documentary ensure those fragments will be revisited and repeated – providing a sense of a "whole" experience, if not of the playtext, then of the actor's immersion and engagement with it. At the same time, documentary rules for handling received material call for some degree of irreverence, experimentation, and exposed artifice. These rules reinforce Pacino's self-presentation as someone rescuing Shakespeare – by way of the vernacular idioms of film and the investigative modes of Method acting – from the stiff old pretenses of British theater (see chapter 5).

Several of the films we concentrate on resituate Shakespeare's plays in citational environments in which the history of citation itself – the cultural use of iconic works – is a long-standing concern. We find this reflexiveness at work in Kristian Levring's *The King is Alive*, as a group of castaways struggle their way through rehearsals of *King Lear*. This film relocates "good old Lear" in cinematic frameworks (the survival film, the experimental film) and in locations (the African desert, an abandoned mining settlement) that evoke a vexed history of Anglo-European narratives imposed on colonial cultures. The film tips its hand early on, in an absurdly donnish debate among the castaways about the correct source of a dance track (is it *Saturday Night Fever*?) and the "right" way to dance. The multiple errors and dislocations in this scene raise fundamental questions about what it means to perform received words and gestures (including those of a Shakespeare play) here and now. The film invites us to reflect on the systems of rules that govern such expression and how different heres and nows may change the way we remember and forget received matter (see chapter 7).

Attention to the rules and practices of different citational environments helps us identify the complex effects of different artistic formats converging and recombining. Taymor's *Titus* makes an especially clear example of such convergence. The film is organized in set pieces that do not precisely correspond to scene divisions in modern editions. Some of these are *interpolations* (new material inserted into the story) in the form of Taymor's "Penny Arcade Nightmares;" some are cinematic reorganizations of dramatic entrances, exits, and arcs of action (see chapter 4). These set pieces disrupt and sometimes arrest the narrative flow of the film, in spatial montages that resemble the moving tableaux of conceptual theater, where Taymor has her artistic roots. This organizing principle becomes more evident in the DVD edition of the film, where it is reflected in chapter divisions with titles such as "Prosthetic Branches" and "A Visit From Revenge." The citational rules here seem to be drawn both from the theater and from a Shakespeare we read; not as we might read a long prose narrative but in the discontinuous way that we might consult an archive of multimedia images, like a book of Renaissance emblems. Structured around labeled entries or "chapters" and with an indexed commentary, the DVD "textualizes" the film, giving it a longer horizon of reception than the traditionally evanescent moment of its theatrical release (Burt and Boose 2003: 4). *Titus* is engaging in part because of the ways it negotiates these and other citational environments. Through the passage of performance, Grigely argues, a classic work is continually "unmade (as an object) and remade (as a text and as memory)" (1995: 33).

By calling our attention to the way artworks exist in memory – individual memories and cultural memory – Grigely reminds us that they matter because they serve to anchor social networks of meaning. In this way, performance scholars have argued, texts "perform" social functions in the ritual sense of the word. A classroom edition of *Romeo and Juliet*, for example, serves multiple functions of social transmission and access, conferring a certain cultural status and inheritance on those who study it, along with its other possible effects and uses (aesthetic pleasure, boredom, occasions for seduction, etc.). Every new version of a work inherits the ritual functions of its predecessors to maintain specific networks of meaning, a process Joseph Roach calls *surrogation* (1996: 3). Thus, for example, with each production of *Hamlet*, the paternal command to "remember me" that haunts Hamlet anchors a series of changing ideas about the relationships between fathers and sons. As *Hamlet* circulates through the culture, that command acquires new meanings that in turn open up newer representational possibilities and functions for a father/son relationship. Almereyda offers a contemporary filial spin on *Hamlet* by casting and directing Sam Shepard to convey a kind of tough-but-intimate love (grabbing his son's face, embracing him) that is profoundly different from the distant, hierarchical figures of paternity we find in Branagh and Zeffirelli. Moreover, each of these versions of paternity reflects differing ideas about relationships with the dead, about revenge, and about the nature of the afterlife.

Surrogation can work at the level of plot function as well as characterization. Thus, when Jane Howell first made Young Lucius a figure who crossed fictional boundaries between past and present, in her BBC *Titus Andronicus* (1985), she coined a convention that would be picked up by Derek Jarman in *Edward II* (1991) and then fully developed by Taymor. By creating a contemporary space of witnessing, Howell added a new *character function* not just to *Titus Andronicus* but to screen Shakespeare and other adaptations besides.[5] We see this character function informing the moments of filial witnessing in Radford's recent *Merchant of Venice*, for example. The film invites us to share Tubal's horror at Shylock's sadistic obsession with Antonio's flesh, and positions us, in its final interpolation, alone with an isolated, silent Jessica (another child who has crossed world-defining boundaries) looking out over the water that now separates her from her community of birth. The device may work differently in different films: to generate a feeling of anxious complicity with violence and ethnic prejudice (making us ask what actions we can take now, in the light of our complicity); or to produce the false pathos of distance from violent prejudice (letting us think how sad it is that it once had to be that way). The endings of both Taymor's and Radford's films can be read in both ways.[6]

Similarly, *Othello* films remind us that when ambition, love, and racism intersect we call the one who takes advantage of this intersection and tells us all about it "Iago." To perform Iago is also to tell us what Iago's work means, *now* – and by reprising the role to revise and reinvent it, along with the "invisible network of allegiances, interests, and resistances," attaching to ideas about ambition, love, and race, that animate this character (Roach 1996: 39). Iago serves a particular character function that is part of the constellation of behaviors represented and restored by *Othello* in Western culture. Thinking about dramatic roles in this way means seeing them as fictional constructs that work in certain scripted ways in relation to each other: as operations, not separable entities.[7]

Where the social functions invested in a work are particularly critical or prominent, the process of surrogation by successive texts may be especially fraught, for while surrogates inevitably fall short of and exceed the memory of their predecessors they never fully escape it (Roach 1996: 3). The "double sense" to which Shakespeare films in the camp mode seem to be alive is thus an uncanny sense of both embodying and displacing their primary intertexts (Sontag [1964] 1999: 57; Roach 1996: 2). Applying Roach's and Grigely's ideas to *Romeo + Juliet*, Worthen suggests that this process of transformation through surrogation is precisely the interest of Luhrmann's film: "Citing the text – the verbal text of a play, the cultural text of Shakespeare – Luhrmann's film undertakes a shrewd reflection of the relation between classic texts and their performances, presenting this version of Shakespeare's work not as a performance of the text and not as a translation of the work but as an iteration of the work, an iteration that necessarily invokes and displaces a textual 'origin' " (Worthen 1998: 1104). In different contexts and for different plays, one or the other imperative (to embody or to displace) may seem more urgent. Indeed, as we explain in chapter 6, the inability to break away from and displace character functions that have played a formative role in modern racial stereotypes often undermines recent performances of *Othello*.

The ambivalent dynamics of surrogation are particularly pressing in Shakespeare films, which inherit anxieties about fidelity, legitimacy, and displaced origins from two gene pools: the Romantic ideal of Shakespearean authorship, on the one hand, and deeply rooted prejudices against film and film-adaptations, on the other. Much has been written about the Romantic notion of Shakespeare as a singular genius, the secular worship of the Bard, and the passion for authenticity invested in both theater and film performances.[8] In citational environments where these are the dominant values, any performance of a Shakespeare play may be an opportunity for nostalgia for a lost – definitive – original, an attempt to close the distance between that lost original and the present performance. Yet, as Robert Stam has observed, a nostalgia for originals – and the corresponding sense that any "updating" is a falling off – is especially a phenomenon of film-adaptation. Theatrical adaptations regularly re-conceptualize, reinterpret, and innovate; if they fail to do so they may not be seen as successful (2005a: 15). The same tends to be true of literary adaptations of Shakespeare, as attested by Jane Smiley's Pulitzer Prize for *A Thousand Acres* (2001), her free adaptation of *King Lear*. Both theatrical and print adaptations are more often measured on their success or failure in their own right, not – as in the case of film – on the fundamental legitimacy of adaptation as a practice.

Why should this be so? By way of an answer, Stam surveys a number of prejudices traditionally attached to film-adaptation. It is worth taking a moment to review these prejudices not only because screen Shakespeares inherit them, as all screen adaptations do, but also because they relate so closely to long-standing notions about Shakespeare's cultural legacy. Stam explains that the common sense that there are deep oppositions between film and the verbal arts is grounded on several assumptions that are themselves deeply rooted in Western culture. When the aural and verbal aspects of film are ignored, film is easily assimilated into a long Western tradition of suspicion against images, appearances, and the phenomenal world – an "iconophobia" that goes back to Plato (Stam 2005a: 5). The converse of that suspicion is a cultural "logophilia" that privileges the verbal, valorizing the book and literature in general as the highest art-forms (2005a: 6). These twinned values reinforce the sense that the arts of the word and image are locked in an eternal struggle for dominance in which gains for one mean losses for the other (2005a: 4). Iconophobia and logophilia are also linked to a persistent "anti-corporeality" in discussions of film-adaptation: a distaste for the body and bodily experience that recycles basic principles of Puritan anti-theatricality. Film is often described as appealing primarily to bodily sensations, as emotionally and morally "contagious," and as feeding lower (and lower-class) appetites rather than the higher processes of reason (2005a: 6) – just as the Renaissance public theater was. In such moralizing contexts, to eschew and destroy the seductions of the image is tantamount to affirming one's true faith (2005a: 5). These and other assumptions underpin the notion of film-adaptation as a second-order art that parasitically sucks the life from the text, as it converts it to an "image" (2005a: 3–5).

In the context of screen Shakespeares, these long-standing prejudices reinforce related ideas about Shakespearean authorship. Indeed,

Shakespeare and Shakespeare's works have come to stand iconically for many of these ideas. Latent anti-theatricality remains strong in the scholarly preference for seeing Shakespeare as a poet, an artist of words rather than of the lesser realm of the stage (supposedly lesser because its arts are commercial, bodily, and transient). Secular worship of the text and book persists in attempts to produce ideal, composite editions of the plays attributed to a single artistic genius – rather than to the many hands (and minds and voices) that contributed to the creation of a play, from stage to printing house. Finally, to read, teach, own, and love Shakespeare's works remains a reliable way for both individuals and institutions to affirm their faith in literature and Western culture more generally. The fact that a single pictographic alteration in the title of Luhrmann's film can simultaneously evoke the possibility of both faith and infidelity suggests how forcefully these dynamics converge on film-adaptations of Shakespeare's plays.

McGann's notion of a work as a text series and Grigely's concept of textual reiteration as a kind of performance build directly on poststructuralist theory that challenges these hierarchical assumptions about the relation between different art-forms.[9] Without holding us to unworkable standards of fidelity, both models of textuality help us talk about what changes – what is added and taken away – as technologies and media change, and artworks undergo the continual process of cultural recycling, recast with new settings, props, characters, and themes. These notions of textuality are particularly suited to a group of films that tend to see Shakespeare's plays as robust compendia of traces of the past, available to be recycled according to present needs and desires, rather than as objects of veneration and nostalgia (see chapter 3). Similarly, the idea of surrogation helps us think about the ways in which the social functions of earlier Shakespeare texts – plays and also previous films – are at once fulfilled and altered by these avatars. Thus, as we have seen, a film such as Luhrmann's *Romeo + Juliet* takes on the mantle of Zeffirelli's *Romeo and Juliet*: becoming *the* bridge between Shakespeare and a new generation, fulfilling a Western cultural imperative that each generation have such a bridge. Yet it also fundamentally shifts our understanding of how such bridges work and what they bridge to. The past Zeffirelli's film conveys seems immediate, knowable, and, crucially, unchanging; indeed, for all its lush immediacy, this is still a Verona in doublet and hose. By contrast, Luhrmann's film insists that any "past" we encounter is a feature and function of the present: variously reconstructed, repurposed, or ruined like the blasted Sycamore Grove theater, but never fixed or completed in any real sense.

Revivers and Recyclers

The degree to which a film is invested in the oppositions and hierarchies listed above – text vs image, sensation vs thought, original vs copy, author vs parasite – determines whether its stance towards its source-texts is one of revival or recycling. Film *revivals* are Shakespeare-centric in a way that reflects the values of unique, original authorship; they set out to convey *Shakespeare's* version of tragic love, national unity, overweening ambition, and so on, and to bring it closer to an audience and moment they define as especially ready or in need of it. The impulse to revive requires finessing or actively hiding the interplay of intertexts – particularly the plurality of Renaissance source-texts – in the interest of "myths of legitimacy and origin" invested in qualities the performance establishes as definitively "Shakespearean" (Roach 1996: 3). Richard Loncraine's *Richard III* (1995) opens with fragments of Shakespeare's *Henry VI*, typed on a teletype machine, and later adds a swinging, 1930s-style jazz rendition of Christopher Marlowe's popular Elizabethan poem, "The Passionate Shepherd" ("Come live with me and be my love . . ."). Such *interpolations* are more the rule than the exception; like Renaissance stage performances, most theater performances and most films depend on multiple scripts (Masten 1997). Yet the fact that the Marlowe borrowing supplies lyrics on the music track while the echoes from *Henry VI* appear as print, before the credits, helps maintain dialogic boundaries. Radford's *Merchant of Venice* observes a similar decorum in its dialogue-free opening, a ten-minute trip through Renaissance Venice that segregates its anti-Semitic business in an interpolated preface to the playtext. Although that business is "Schindler-ized" to reverse the flow of prejudice, the attempt to purge the playtext of such complexities cannot stem their old momentum as soon as the film proper (and Shakespearean dialogue) begins.

At their most nostalgic, revivals are invested in purified origins of many types: in restoring some past reality, conveying a "complete" text or agreed-on meaning, using the classic devices of cinematic immersion to make the past seem present, the strange familiar. Film revivals tend towards aesthetically comfortable modes of illustration, often rendering the past in well-upholstered costume dramas (Albanese 2001: 213–14). Such upholstering typically reflects the anxiety that by rendering the literary *as* image the film debases it. Thus the lighting, *mise en scène*, and camera angles in Radford's *Merchant of Venice* allude to the characteristic play of light, architecture, and perspectives in Italian humanist painting – enlisting these models not only to establish a (loosely) historical authenticity for the film's "look," but also to borrow their high cultural authority as objects for *looking at*. Revivals often perform what Stam describes as "aesthetic mainstreaming" on their source-texts "in the name of mass-audience legibility:" "a kind of purge . . . of moral ambiguity, narrative interruption, and reflexive meditation," that "smooths over sources of potential audience discomfort" (2005a: 43). The heroine cannot be truly bigoted, her rescuer cannot be genuinely greedy, his best friend cannot be actually queer; any reflexiveness about the Englishness of a play about Venetian moneylending and venture capital disappears into the house-styles of suburban, multiplex storytelling.[10]

The distinction here does not have to do with freshness of interpretation but with an *aesthetic decorum* that conforms to one or more of the hierarchical assumptions about artistic value and narrative coherence described above. Indeed, if we think of "fidelity" in this neutral way, as a principle of decorum, we immediately see how a single film may proceed along different paths at the same time, conforming to some of those hierarchies while departing from others. Thus revivals may reinterpret, find new pay-offs and ascribe new meanings to the works they perform; they may also be motivated by an interest in replaying Shakespeare's plays in new citational environments, taking advantage of new powers of communication and new audiences, as in Olivier's film revivals and the BBC television productions. Such impulses can launch a Shakespeare film on more experimental footing, as we find in Loncraine's *Richard III*, a film based on an earlier stage-production and scripted by its star, Ian McKellen. The resituation of Richard's opening soliloquy as a victory speech, with its cinematic zooms (to Richard's mouth) and cuts, follows even more explicitly cinematic effects in the credit sequence, with its teletype machine, tank, and gunshots. In these scenes, the film conjures a counter-factual version of 1930s England in which an authoritarian right wing, led by Richard of Gloucester and his brothers, has gained control of the government. Thus the film brings the authoritarian impulses of the British upper crust – both in their 1930s and latter-day manifestations – to the surface in a belated effort to attack the conservative revolution launched by Margaret Thatcher in the 1980s and carried on by her successor, John Major. In this respect, the film may well be said to work within the cultural imaginary of the late twentieth-century British left wing, insofar as it "channels" their impression that the present is witnessing a resurgence of an imperfectly suppressed past. On the other hand, the film's status as a form of costume drama and its management of dialogic boundaries reveal equally strong attachments to the decorum of a single author and a comfortably distant past.

With its interest in modern communications and their potential for abuse, Loncraine's *Richard III* finds modern correlatives for Richard of Gloucester's deceptive persuasions on a mass scale. Such cinematic *substitutions* serve as filmic equivalents for properties, behaviors, and actions that are no longer diegetically viable – that is, are no longer consistent with the "world system" of updated film. In a similar way Almereyda's *Hamlet* substitutes Denmark Corporation for the kingdom of Denmark and the Hotel Elsinore for Elsinore Castle, while Taymor's coliseum resembles the surround-space of a video game. Substitutions like these carry considerable potential for altering our understanding of the Renaissance playtext and for requiring us to "read" the film in question on its own terms. The more fully imagined and motivated such substitutions, the less Shakespeare-centric a film tends to be. Thus Donaldson describes Loncraine's film not as a revival but as cinematic reframing of Richard's story, an allegory in its own right of "the role of cinema and other modern media in the institution and maintenance of death-dealing social regimes" (2002a: 244). While lacking the full sense of doubleness and distance from the playtext that marks the more experimental films we discuss below, Loncraine's film shares with them a willingness to manipulate the playtext and interpolate materials that reflect concerns external to its main intertext.

Filmmakers approaching Shakespearean material in this use-based way may be thought of as *recycling* their playtexts, treating a selected play as one among many intertexts that partly meet their needs – including not only literary intertexts but other films, music, television, and additional visual artifacts and electronic media like architecture and computers. Films interested in recycling Shakespeare for extra-Shakespearean uses may play around with the rise and fall of intertextual awareness, as it changes from moment to moment and from spectator to spectator; these effects are particularly strong in *vernacular* adaptations and in films that embed performances or rehearsals. Several films – Levring's, Taymor's, and Eric Rohmer's 1992 adaptation of *The Winter's Tale* – seem especially interested in the cognitive sense of match and mismatch between a given performance, its context, and the work performed.

Courting both recognition and misprision in this way, recyclers address their source-texts in a variety of terms: as word- and idea-hoards (an approach Taymor, Pacino, Greenaway, and Almereyda share); as potential survival tools (Levring's interest); as playgrounds (the iconoclastic impulse of Morrissette and Bedford). Or they may frame them as liminal spaces of transformation, taking the film into "screen worlds" marked by Shakespearean language or stage-practice, passages like the "green" worlds of Shakespearean comedy and romance. Rohmer and Van Sant use their Shakespearean passages this way and Taymor's *Titus* turns towards a similar "Shakespearean" function in its final, controversial interpolation, as it imagines a way out of the play's cycles of violence and revenge. As with revival, the impulse to recycle is not exclusive to a particular style or aesthetic (Rohmer, for example, works through a kind of classical realism), though avant-garde and experimental cinema holds more closely to this impulse than to revival.

Differential Constants: Rohmer's *Conte d'hiver*, Greenaway's *Prospero's Books*

When filmmakers adapt Shakespeare in the present day they engage not only all that has been done over time to and with a specific play, but the influence and cultural status of all the plays, as an oeuvre. Shakespeare films surrogate both their specific source-texts and the idea of Shakespeare as a cultural constant. Taymor's ending reminds us that one of the functions of that apparent constant has been to tell us we can imagine a way out of existing structures and frames. Several of the films we consider construe this *Shakespearean imaginary* as a vehicle of radical transformation, variously mystical (Rohmer, Taymor), carnivalesque (Van Sant), and emotional (Pacino). The social and psychological work of a Shakespearean imaginary is staged especially clearly in Rohmer's *Conte d'hiver / A Tale of Winter* (1992), a film that too rarely appears on the map of the so-called Shakespeare on film genre. Rohmer's film helps explain how an artist such as Taymor may find herself surrogating not just a single play but the convention of the "Shakespearean ending" itself – as it functions in Shakespeare's comedies and romances – to Shakespeare's work as a whole (see Nelson 2001: 230; and chapter 4). It particularly helps explain why Taymor would seem – with her turn towards a restoration premised on impossible, implausible artifice – to be interpolating the ending of *The Winter's Tale* as an exit from *Titus Andronicus*.

Rohmer was one of the pioneers of the French New Wave, and shares with other New Wave directors an attention to the immediacy of everyday events and an eclectic range of interests. (In Rohmer's case, those interests range from adaptations of medieval romance, to realist drama, to documentaries and instructional films.) Yet his closely observed, sensual realism distinguishes his work from more abstract strains of film modernism. In *Conte d'hiver* (the second film in his "Seasons" quartet, 1990–8) Rohmer crafts a very free appropriation of Shakespeare's *Winter's Tale*, which displaces concerns about marital fidelity, jealousy, and betrayal into an altogether more modern and female-centered frame of reference. This new frame concerns finding a balance between surrender and autonomy and matching one's erotic needs to a child's need for a stable amorous alchemy between two parents. The mystery of "what women want" gets re-articulated here in terms of a tension between *choosing* a lover and being fated to love. Felicie (Charlotte Véry) begins by believing she needs to choose one of two imperfect (dialectically opposed) lovers, but finds that she has no choice to make, since she is only "herself" when accepting a prior commitment to an ideal but lost lover. The two secondary alternatives, Loic (Hervé Furic) and Maxence (Michael Voletti), are a mismatched pair: the one intellectual but amorously dull, the other intellectually dull but amorously impulsive. By contrast, Felicie's lost love, Charles (Frédéric van den Driessche), is quick on the uptake and uncomplicatedly demonstrative, even at a chance meeting after a separation of five years.

Although grounded in the mundane details of the workaday life of a single mother and her child, the film works as fully as Shakespeare's play within the Romance framework of accident, error, serendipity, miracle, and the need to awaken one's faith that wrongs will be made right.[11] The gradual clarification of Felicie's commitment to the absent, ideal Charles, and to the impossibility of settling for lesser loves, is catalyzed in the film by the paired power of prayer (in a church) and Shakespeare (in a theater). Several observations may be made about the way Shakespearean theater works its transformations here, as articulated in Hermione's restoration. First, the Shakespeare that does this work is a French version of "heritage Shakespeare." The fragment of a play-within-the-film we get to see, when Loic and Felicie go to the theater one night, is a stiffly blocked and declaimed version of the statue scene (*The Winter's Tale* 5.3) portrayed in generic "early Celtic/Roman" dress. Yet for all its layers of mediation and dated style, the *Winter's Tale* scene is marked on screen as powerfully empathetic because theatrically embodied. As in Shakespeare's play, our empathy emerges cinematically through a guided response to another's act of audition – the kind of magic Paulina works on Leontes. Here Felicie's responses to *The Winter's Tale* serve as a gauge of our own engagement and conviction, both with the play-within-the-film and (arguably for the first time in the film) with her. Up to this point the film may have seemed to ally its viewers with Felicie's two imperfect lovers. Like them, we are unable to parse her inner life, with its confusing alterations. And we may find her amorous "games" (whims or caprices) similarly infuriating. In these scenes at the theater, Rohmer gives us our first real access to Felicie's inner life, in an extended sequence of close shots that alternate between Hermione's magical restoration and Felicie's reactions. We watch Felicie weeping at the separate stages of reunion. We see her identifying with Hermione's emergence from stasis, recognizing a figure of her own "coming to self" through an act of faith in a love that may never be re-consummated.

This scene in the theater performs magical restoration at the level of cinematic reception as well as plot, converting what had been the story of an infuriatingly opaque and wandering young woman into a story of true faith rewarded. Rohmer leaves it to Felicie, critiquing the play with Loic as they drive home, to articulate this shift. Loic offers a predictable reading of the closing scene: the problem for the audience, he claims, is whether Hermione was alive all along or whether a statue truly came to life. Felicie corrects him, reminding him not to read the drama for "realism" or plausibility but as an allegory of the rewards of genuine faith. Rohmer connects the Shakespearean imaginary *as such* – identification, alignment of self and others triggered by watching Shakespeare – with this radical, mystical transformation. And indeed, for all the dated style of the *Winter's Tale* production, the film's Shakespearean identifications are refreshingly dynamic. What get transacted here are acts of discovery that are both moored to and float free of the dramatic configurations of *The Winter's Tale*.[12] A consummate work of surrogated artistry, *Conte d'hiver* provides a contemporary substitute for Shakespeare's play that need not be recognized as such to perform the kind of cultural work that it does.

Although *Conte d'hiver* refers directly to Shakespeare's play, and may even knowingly allude to the early stirrings of female self-assertion we glimpse in *The Winter's Tale*, Rohmer's film draws just as overtly on the cultural imaginary of late twentieth-century feminism, silently "quoting" and embodying emergent social changes and aspirations. With a fortuitousness that Rohmer would appreciate, but could not have anticipated, by the time Rohmer was bringing his film to realization, *The Winter's Tale* had become a significant play for Shakespearean feminist scholars, as a work that created a space for female voice, modeling related imperatives that men withhold their patriarchal powers and awake their faith. Yet Rohmer's film goes farther, in its way, towards such feminist transformations: incorporating in Felicie not only Hermione's but also Leontes' subject-positions, rendering all of its epiphanies from a female point of view. It is not just that, at a diegetic level (the fictional world of the film), Hermione's restoration models a way out of Felicie's insoluble romantic dilemma. The "Shakespearean" also figures a way out of oppressive social codes. At a meta-dramatic level, Felicie's subsequent reunion with Charles (and his with their daughter) surrogates the reunion of Hermione and Leontes so as to counter dated notions about female satisfaction.

To see Shakespeare adaptations as surrogating their predecessors in this way is to reconceive of classic works not as containers for stable meanings but as mechanisms by which a culture transacts meaning.[13] It is in this transactional sense that we speak of the constants surrogated by Shakespeare performances as "differential." They mark shared patterns and rates of change across different cultural variables, within larger social systems that are themselves continually subject to change. A cultural differential may even transfer energy (as the differential gear in a car does) from one dynamic system to another. Thus, in the late age of print, we see related changes in the notion of textuality taking place across the different fields of postmodern art, text studies, and digital communication. And we may speculate about the differential links between the changing notions of textual decorum among literary scholars (trading a view that values purity, fixity, and single authorship for one that emphasizes hybridity, mutability, and multiple hands) and the "cut and paste" functions of digital interfaces that daily call our attention to the collaborative enterprise of expression.

Such speculations return us to the idea of adaptation as a cultural process and specifically to its potential for "changing the entire infrastructure of the art-form" (Grigely 1995: 100). Many scholars have noted the increasing "bookness" of special edition DVDs, such as the recently released version of *My Own Private Idaho* (1991; DVD 2005), which includes a 64-page book broken up into five "acts" instead of chapters. The proliferation of such paratexts has become the norm in DVD editions, so much so that we may begin to see the special edition DVD as a distinct mode of adaptation in its own right, with annotation and discontinuous viewing as its hallmarks.[14] Such special editions make visible the ongoing process of *remediation*, by which emerging media adapt and are structured by the conventions of older media, surrogating the human needs they serve (Bolter and Grusin 2000). The process of remediation is continuous but not neatly chronological or linear, in part because the life cycles of so many media are long and overlapping. As an example of this cultural process we might observe that a now familiar memory aid, web-browser "favorites" or "bookmarks," provide a personalized, cognitive-mechanical interface that derives in part from once familiar habits of footnoting in humanist essays. The memorial habits of essay-reading and -writing in turn adapted the earlier practices of Renaissance commonplace books: a form that allowed individuals to gather eclectic information they wanted to remember or regularly consult, such as recipes, important prayers, and favorite poems (Black 2006).

To return to cinematic arts, we should emphasize that film has always borrowed from and been conditioned by other media. For its sound technologies alone, film draws on older performance forms such as stage melodrama and contemporary media such as the telegraph, telephones, radio, and MTV (Altman 1992). Thus, for example, as cinema develops its conventions for voice-over soliloquy, it adapts the rules of stage asides – direct address, single-speaker focalization, and shifted auditory "wall" – to the more focalized technologies of camera and microphone. In aside, the actor speaks directly to the audience, as if she has moved in front of the "fourth wall" of the proscenium stage; isolated in an auditory space temporarily outside of the scene, she serves as her own imaginary auditor for utterances no one else on stage can hear. Cinematic soliloquies accommodate these conventions using a combination of close focus (screening out the rest of the diegetic scene so that the speaker becomes isolated in a now featureless space) and voice-over (making the speaker herself the only on-screen auditor, as she listens to her own thoughts). A number of the films we discuss reflect on this process of remediation more generally, in "media allegories" that surrogate the meta-theatrical aspects of Shakespeare's plays to the rapid transformation of modern expressive media.[15] That interest is reflected in the tradition of *establishing* and *disestablishing sequences*, devices directors since Olivier have used to hide or foreground the relationships between the different media they draw on. Such opening sequences are frequent in recent Shakespeare films, which seem to need to establish relations between the old and new media they remediate, from stage and book to cinema, video, radio, record player, etc. Some films aim to smooth over or exploit the chasm between archaic and modern forms, as Radford's *Merchant of Venice* does in its opening scene, by immersing us in Renaissance Venice. There a long, dialogue-free establishing sequence piously reminds us that anti-Semitism is an old, bad, idea that led to book burning, whereas modern forms such as film can call our attention to this error and (by extension) preserve rather than destroy culture. Other films seek to destabilize our sense of what is old and new, using disestablishing sequences to call our attention to the costs and benefits of technological change – something we find in Luhrmann, Almereyda, and Morrissette.

The cross-pollinations between different media are ongoing and far from one way. Lev Manovich finds strong connections, for example, between the digital revolution and the aesthetics of avant-garde film:

> Avant-garde aesthetic strategies came to be embedded in the commands and interface metaphors of computer software. In short, the avant-garde became materialized in a computer. Digital cinema technology is a case in point. The avant-garde strategy of collage reemerged as the "cut-and-paste" command, the most basic operation one can perform on digital data. The idea of painting on film became embedded in paint functions of film-editing software. The avant-garde move to combine animation, printed texts, and live-action footage is repeated in the convergence of animation, title generation, paint, compositing, and editing systems into all-in-one packages. (Manovich 2001: 306–7)

Films working directly in the avant-garde modes Manovich describes may point to another constant in the Shakespearean imaginary: the notion that Shakespeare's work represents a *way into* new forms, because it provides an archive or experimental space that has a history of reinvention and remediation. Thus in Taymor's set pieces, for example, we find a divided screen structure that suggests the beginnings of an experiment with "broadband" cinema that Manovich calls the future of the avant-garde (2001: 322–6). Taymor's three-part collages echo the split screens of computer "window" interfaces, in a cut-and-paste mode that is allusively thicker than related experiments with "tiled" screens (as we might find in a show such as *24*), which simply multiply linear narratives on screen.

Peter Greenaway's work is perhaps the prime cinematic example of an interest in Shakespeare-play-as-archive, as his experiment with what Manovich calls "database" cinema in *Prospero's Books* (1991) attests (2001: 237–9). Greenaway completely jettisons the *drama* of *The Tempest* (along with the conventions of linear storytelling) while *performing* a wholesale recitation of the language of the playtext. An actor whose almost century-long career has been identified with Shakespeare (Gielgud), here assumes the role of a character (Prospero) that has long been seen as a surrogate Shakespeare, at once writing and speaking the lines of a play that he conjures into a surplus of visual life around him. *The Tempest* put on display in this way is unlike any version ever realized on stage or screen and it is tied to its moment of production in very specific ways. Using archival and artistic resources newly made available by computer technology, Greenaway orchestrates an archeological recovery that is also a discovery of surprising continuities. He links the visual excess of the present both to the oral richness of a receding past (the theatrical past embodied by Gielgud's voice and persona) and to an earlier moment of cutting-edge archivalism. That was the moment when the then new technology of the printed book was itself used to record and store between its bindings everything new and old under the sun. Nothing is fixed or static in

Greenaway's greenworld/screenworld of expanding storage. While Gielgud inscribes and recites, the film offers a catalogue display of rare books, testing out different methods for ordering, indexing, and retrieving the matter they store and the ways it may be presented. But it also offers a bibliophile's fantasy of books as living, interactive artifacts, whose contents both contain and spill out into the world around them, much in the way our computers serve as responsive links and open channels of communication. The result is a weird hybrid of documentary film, high-end pornography, performance piece, museum display, diorama, and Powerpoint lecture-demonstration.

Greenaway's hybrid mode of presentation foregrounds a pervasive and challenging quality of cinema: its sheer copiousness. It is not always easy to hear everything, just as it is not always easy to see everything in a frame or sequence. Real attention to such abundance requires us to acclimate to changing aural and visual rhythms – in a process not unlike the one we undergo when we acclimate to the unfamiliar rhythms and codes of Shakespearean language – and even to adjust our mode of interaction from linear reception to discontinuous sampling. If we let go of the discomforts of an unsatisfied desire for linear narrative, we may find it easier to adjust to this different kind of decorum: to an art that aims at a comprehensive audio-visual archive of the series of texts that we might call *The Tempest*. And that adjustment opens up intriguing ways to watch and listen. What texts get into Greenaway's catalogue? How are they matched with different modes of representation? What constitutes "bookness" and why does it matter to Greenaway that we learn this through the medium of film (a question Manovich pursues)? We may go even farther afield to wonder about the relationship between this passionate, avant-garde expression of database capacity and the contemporary passion for the archive found in late twentieth century, post-imperial British literature (Keen 2001).

Time and technology cohere in Greenaway's film in a manner that announces not just the brave new world of computer technologies or the triumph of the visual, but, like the Renaissance of the book it celebrates, a moment of reckoning: with cultural memory, with the media that help us remember, with the accretions of the past and what we make of them. Indeed, all the films we discuss function more in the way of archives than as ephemeral "iterations" of the Shakespeare play they revive or recycle. Some are more conscious than others of their doubleness, belatedness, and their status as "copies" or "serial texts." To these we attend most closely in what follows. Yet all recent Shakespeare films – enabled as they are by the encyclopedic impulse at work in the contemporary manufacture of "special edition" DVDs, fan writings, and classroom interactions – have the capacity to become always already archival.

We suggested earlier how a long-established iconophobia, focused on new regimes of the visual, has served to restrain the academic Shakespeare industry from fully embracing the expressly filmic dimensions of some of the more daring examples of cinematic Shakespeare. Such restraint will be harder to countenance and sustain as the repackaging of Shakespeare films into DVD archives moves forward, making them available for replaying, quoting, and other kinds of handling that have been second nature to us with print texts. Because it is on screens (like the one on which we are writing) that much "Shakespearizing" already takes place, we suspect that it is on the level of the screen and its multi-mediated interactions that most future Shakespearizing will occur. The screens that once represented the tyranny of the visual are increasingly understood to remediate the powers of print; if they become ubiquitous it will be because they satisfy our hunger for images and our logophilia alike. Indeed, it is in the screen world of our computers that much that constitutes the archive of both print and performance is now made recoverable and manifest: the delivery and downloading of primary and secondary sources alike; the assembly and "posting" of bibliographies, the contents of scholarly journals, countless depositories of images and illustrations; the playing of DVDs, capturing of stills, recording of film-clips, and so on. In the first sentence of his introduction to Julie Taymor's *Titus: The Illustrated Screenplay*, the scholar Jonathan Bate echoes Olivier's conviction that "If William Shakespeare were alive today, he would be writing and directing movies" (Taymor 2000: 8). We think Bate is half right and that if Shakespeare were alive today, he would likely be experimenting with filmmakers such as Taymor and Greenaway, collaboratively crafting the kind of audio-visual art that is awake to the fullest range of mediated experiences – aural, visual, verbal, synesthetic – that the culture and technology make possible.

3 *Hamlet* Rewound

Called many things in its 400-year career as Shakespeare's signature play, *Hamlet* has consistently served as the quintessential "text of modern life" (Emerson 1968: 211). It was transparently "modern," possibly even cutting-edge, at its moment of production in early modern England. Though hardly up to date, *Hamlet* remained "modern" when Emerson made his all-embracing generalization about Shakespeare writing "the text of modern life" in that it continued to speak (knowingly, presciently) to nineteenth-century actors, audiences, and readers. *Hamlet* became "modernist" when Freud and his disciple Ernest Jones appended it to the myth of Oedipus in the early twentieth century, and remained so when Laurence Olivier followed their psychoanalytic lead in crafting his dizzyingly Oedipal film in 1948. The play became conspicuously "postmodern" when Heiner Müller disintegrated and reincarnated it as *Hamletmachine* (1977), and it will no doubt receive additional attributions of (post)modernity as we move deeper into our own century – unless, of course, we or our descendants forget how to remember it, or forget why it has always seemed so memorable in the first place.

In his four-hour-long 1996 film-version of the play, Kenneth Branagh chose to forget nothing. Indeed, he had his actors recite more text from variant editions of the play than had probably ever been recited before on stage or film. Yet by channeling this presumptively faithful reading of *Hamlet* through an uneasy mix of blockbuster conventions and costume drama, Branagh could also be said to have forgotten other aspects of the play: first and foremost, its capacity to speak *past* its originary conditions of production and *to* whatever changes "modern life" assembles around it. But what does this privileged word "modern" mean in the first place? How can a print text or play seem so insistently "modern" – speaking to the way things are *now* – when it is the product of a past that seems positively ancient by current reckonings? The rapid proliferation of new media technologies makes it hard even to appreciate the novelty of a cellphone or laptop PC, much less a ghost that speaks acres of blank verse during a flying visit from purgatory. Humanists will tell us that if literature is the news that stays news, then works of *Hamlet's* genius and universality will always seem more modern than dated. Yet if "modernity" is (as these examples suggest) a shifting target, then it is a quality that may belong less to the text itself than to its uses.

"Everything that is new   is thereby automatically traditional."

3.1 "Everything that is new is thereby automatically traditional"

The way we calculate the up to dateness or belatedness of film-adaptations is complicated by the fact that film has long been under-stood as *the* modern art-form: developing with and dependent on industrialization; shaping and shaped by modernist aesthetics.[1] For some early theorists and filmmakers the claim of a film's modernity rested on its revolutionary exceptionalism – its difference from other media. For others, film was seen as a supremely synthetic medium, combining the aesthetic powers found in all other arts. Shakespearean drama is a frequent touchstone in both lines of argument, standing for a media past against which film plays the exceptional or synthetic present.[2] Thus to adapt Shakespeare to film is always implicitly to raise the question of what modernity means, what its signs and properties are, what relationships it proposes with the past. Jean Luc Godard, one of the most inventively allusive directors of the French New Wave, rehearses these questions in a classroom lesson in his 1964 film, *Bande à part* (*The Outsiders*).[3] The classroom is an institutional space in which Western culture regularly reforges its ties to the past and asserts the value of this process; and Godard's lesson – delivered by an English teacher – is an early version of classroom scenes that have become a dominant pattern of Shakespeare citations in popular culture.[4] The wayward itinerary of Shakespearean allusion in this scene emphasizes the uses and transformations of the past in the present, in terms that help situate the particular claims to modernity of *Hamlet* films.

The teacher begins the day's English class by declaring her difference of opinion with the school's supervisor, M. Louis, who insists that every-thing she does be *au courant*, that is, modern, up to date. She maintains that her students also know the place and importance of great English writers of the past such as Thomas Hardy and Shakespeare. To make her point, she will have her students translate passages from *Romeo and Juliet* that she reads aloud in French. But before beginning, the teacher prompts one student (Odile, played by Anna Karina) to recite from memory the mantra the teacher has derived from T.S. Eliot's landmark essay, "Tradition and the Individual Talent" (1919): "Everything that is new is thereby automatically traditional" (figure 3.1).

3.2
Recontextualized,
remediated,
remembered

In his essay, Eliot suggests not that everything new almost immediately becomes dated, but that the new text reorganizes the "tradition" it enters so that we understand that tradition differently. By extension, a classic or traditional text achieves modernity not in itself but through what gets made of it over time: how it is recontextualized, remediated, remembered. In just these ways, Shakespeare's *Romeo and Juliet* is given a surprising second life in the romantic escapades of the "outsiders" of Godard's film. Although they overtly ignore every aspect of the "lesson" the teacher is trying to convey, their flirtation not only casually reproduces the matter of the play, but the play inscribes its own understanding of the vagaries of young love on them: "Love goes toward love as schoolboys from their books." This happens literally in subtitled versions of the film.

As the instructor gets carried away by her recitations, two of her students, Artur and Odile, enact their own little drama. This drama is negotiated by Odile's longing looks and by the hastily scribbled notes Artur composes as ripe passages from *Romeo and Juliet* float unregarded above them. One of these notes playfully demonstrates *Hamlet's* uncanny receptiveness to modern and traditional applications alike; it reads, "tou bi or not tou bi contre votre poitrine, it iz ze question," which the English-language subtitle translates as "TOU BI OR NOT TOU BI AGAINST YOUR BREAST, IT IZZE QUESTION." In this translation, *Hamlet* is mated to the matter of *Romeo and Juliet* in a way that transforms Hamlet's metaphysical posturing into an erotic invitation, recontextualizing both plays in terms of the casual vernacular of the present (figure 3.3).

Nothing could be farther from Artur's flirtatious designs than Romeo's single-minded devotion to Juliet, and the only life that will be lost in this film will result from a bungled burglary. But Godard's simultaneously ironic and sympathetic take on Artur's ardor and Odile's infatuation indicates how, on one level at least, the new does, indeed, build on and grow into the traditional. For Godard, trying to make a "faithful" film-version of a play like *Romeo and Juliet* would be pointless in any event. It would block the creative channel through which any tradition or text needs to circulate in order to reclaim its modernity.

a pair of star-cross'd lovers   TOU BI OR NOT TOU BI AGAINST YOUR BREAST,   take their life.

3.3 "TOU BI OR NOT TOU BI AGAINST YOUR BREAST"

Making a highly allusive but avowedly "modern" film (that only refers directly to *Hamlet* and *Romeo and Juliet* in this one scene), Godard nonetheless manages to bring three works of art – Shakespeare's plays and his own film – into suggestive and productive relationship with each other. In this sense, the "new" can barely be said to be new at all if it lacks the vital connection forged with a powerful tradition, and the "old" can hardly hope to gain a purchase on modernity unless it proves capable not only of speaking to – but of serving the varied interests of – the vernacular surround of the present.

To be fair, Branagh's *Hamlet* is also "modern" in a number of ways most of us would recognize. It is up to date in its deployment of mainstream filmic techniques, production values, and casting choices, and innovative in exploiting conventions more common in Hollywood action-adventure than in prestige fare like Shakespeare film. But no one watching Branagh's *Hamlet* would construe it as "modern" in the way Godard's playfully ironic variations on *Hamlet* and *Romeo and Juliet* are modern or in the way Müller establishes the (post)modernity of *Hamlet* in *Hamletmachine*. Indeed, Müller's version of *Hamlet* is a thing of "shreds and patches," a remnant of "classic" dramaturgy that has been disassembled and reworked to express its new provenance as a late twentieth-century work of performance art, self-consciously speaking out of and to the experience of postwar Europe (Halpern 1997). While Branagh deploys all the conventions of 1990s commercial cinema, his very aim to revive a complete *Hamlet* in a nineteenth-century costume-drama setting – one that faithfully proceeds from point to point of its composite playtext's chronological map and carefully obscures the mechanics of that composition – may make it seem old-fashioned. It may seem especially so given the changes that have been wrought in cinematic production and display by new media technologies and more experimental directors alike. Branagh's *Hamlet* remembers Shakespeare's *Hamlet* in the way a museum might construct a diorama of days past. "Presentist" aesthetic and behavioral criteria are everywhere apparent, but the passion for faithful rendering remains a driving interest.[5] The analogy to dioramas is helpful because it reminds us how changes in representational media can alter audience perceptions of what is old or new, traditional or avant-garde. Early twentieth-century dioramas were visually lush, richly detailed experiments in perspective and *mise en scène*. Their innovations arguably shaped the arts of cinematic set-building and miniature, even as they came to seem static and artificial by comparison. Similarly, as Hollywood shifts its interest to the visual structures of newer media in films such as *The Matrix*, Branagh's identification with an earlier "mainstream" – the immersive richness of naturalistic cinema, Zeffirelli's breakthrough for Shakespeare adaptation – may come to seem dated.

Michael Almereyda's *Hamlet* chooses from the start to remember *Hamlet* differently by channeling it through the technical media and aesthetic criteria of a transient present. From its opening sequence, when we encounter Hamlet (Ethan Hawke) immersed in video gadgetry, the film seems aggressively dedicated to updating. This approach risks letting much that belongs to the Renaissance playtexts float free of their moorings and remain untranslated. It also allows for the possibility that its updatings will remediate the story in ways that may make it unmemorable to a knowing audience, incapable of being conjoined to the more familiar ways in which Shakespeare's *Hamlet* has been experienced or remembered. Almereyda's film foregrounds this conflict in an extended meditation on the resources film and digital video bring to the problem. In so doing, Almereyda effectively allegorizes his own practice, turning Hawke's Hamlet into a recorder and maker of images. This is a character who, unlike his namesake, does not so much *think* too much as seem to *look* too much, who does not live as exclusively in his head as he does in *mediated* relation with reality through an ensemble of image-making machines.

Students and scholars alike have found this tendency considerably more objectionable than they find Shakespeare's Hamlet's tendency to over-intellectualize (Burnett 2003: 66). Hawke's Hamlet's gadgetry (like his Pixelvision camera) and his compulsive recording often seem more a defense against the world than a legitimate form of engagement. Despite the character's effort to use these media to understand and command his circumstances, his reliance on such tools strikes some viewers as a dangerous over-investment in mediated experience. We, in turn, find this response puzzling. Given how wedded contemporary students and scholars alike are to our iPods, cellphones, video games, and laptops, it should seem obvious that these tools serve fundamental social as well as psychological uses. Suspicion of Hamlet's gadgets suggests how long our attachments to older forms of assessing experience persist after technological changes have altered our terms of engagement with the world. We approach this disparity between what we do with technology and how we think about it as an opportunity to make the technophobia of an increasingly technophilic age a pivotal issue in the sustained encounter with *Hamlet* and the technologies of memory that follows.

Memory and Technology

In an influential, late twentieth-century account of modernity, Pierre Nora attributes the impoverished condition of modern memory to the proliferation of new technologies. As Nora tells it, our modern condition of memory is technological dependency as well as loss. The communications and storage media we depend on to shore up the past also ruin it. They offer only "sifted and sorted" fragments of its actual plenitude (Nora 1989: 8). According to Nora, that plenitude consisted in a time of unmediated "true memory" and in "skills passed down by unspoken traditions, in the body's inherent self-knowledge, in unstudied reflexes [which were] social, collective [and] all-encompassing" (1989: 13). What remains to us now is "a mode of historical perception which, with the help of the media, has substituted for a memory entwined in the intimacy of a collective heritage the ephemeral film of current events" (1989: 7). In a trenchant critique of Nora's theory, John Frow outlines its underlying nostalgia: Nora's model opposes an idealized past, "a realm of authenticity and fullness of being," with present "forms of human association" that have been debased by modern technology (exemplified by film) (Frow 1997: 223–4; Turner 1987: 151). As Frow notes, this pattern repeats itself with every successive modern representational form: against an idealized vision of the forms that precede it, each new technology appears insufficiently responsive to both personal and collective needs (1997: 223–4).[6]

Recent defenses of new media contest this alleged impoverishment of experience. Yet these defenses betray a similar desire for immediacy projected into an idealized past. For example, Malcolm McCullough's idea of virtual "handicraft" argues for a skill-based understanding of electronic design. Virtual handicraft has the quality of being "thrown," McCullough tells us, "executed at a particular moment, with a particular degree of skill, and with particular idiosyncrasy to the result" (1996: 8). Little if anything of earlier modes of making is lost in this progressive vision, while much is gained that serves human memory and desire. Yet even such avowedly progressive models lack a real cost–benefit analysis: a fuller account of the needs we bring to any given technology, an exploration of the different losses and gains intrinsic to the varied media that serve those needs. Our current and past memory technologies are both mediated and phenomenally rich in ways that serve some interests but not others. Instead of a richer account of these qualities, nostalgic arguments like Nora's offer prejudicial contrasts, while "progressive" ones like McCullough's offer celebratory analogies.

Both these stances unduly periodize technology and idealize its relations to individual and cultural memory. As an alternative to Nora, Frow suggests we should conceive of memory as always already technological: a function of the cognitive and social practices of representation that mediate past experience (indeed all experience) and selectively describe it for the present. "Technology," in this root sense of art or craft, denotes a range of devices and practices:

> on the one hand storage-and-retrieval devices and sites such as books, calendars, computers, shrines, or museums; and on the other hand particular practices of recall – techniques of learning acquired in school, structured confession or reminiscence, the writing of autobiography or history, the giving of evidence in court, the telling of stories

related to an artifact or a photograph, and even such apparently immediate forms of recollection as the epiphanic flash of involuntary memory or the obsessive insistence of the symptom. (Frow 1997: 230)

Frow draws this integrated model of cognitive and social practice from early modern theories of memory – particularly the art of mental "writing." Writing serves him as the transhistorical type of all the above named forms and practices, which select, sort, and reproduce the matter of the past as a text. Frow's model is appealing in part because its embrace of mediated experience seems to free us from the unproductive desire for presence, and with that desire, from the feeling of loss. Yet a progressive account of memory-as-technology does not get rid of the problems Nora raises – specifically the problem of loss – any more than Hamlet's "tables" allow him, in his most famous moment of remembrance, to "wipe away" the memory of his mother (1.5.99).[7] By reducing loss to nostalgia, Frow stops short of a richer exploration of the different ways various representational forms constrain and serve human memory.

Missing most urgently from Frow's analysis is a broader recognition of the historically *composite* nature of the specific technologies through which individuals and cultures remember. Michel Serres reminds us that any technology develops *polychronically*, as a multilayered accumulation of technical solutions, practices, and uses arising from multiple historical contexts:

> In order to say "contemporary," one must already be thinking of a certain time and thinking of it in a certain way . . . what things are contemporary? Consider a late-model car. It is a disparate aggregate of scientific and technical solutions dating from different periods. One can date it component by component: this part was invented at the turn of the century, another, ten years ago, and Carnot's cycle is almost two hundred years old. Not to mention that the wheel dates back to neolithic times. The ensemble is only contemporary by assemblage, by its design, its finish, sometimes only by the slickness of the advertising surrounding it. (Serres and Latour 1995: 45)

As Godard's English teacher claims, what is construed as "new is thereby automatically traditional" because the new and the traditional reorganize each other: older technologies adapt in relation to emerging needs and new social and cultural developments; new technologies emerge in relation to needs and practices shaped by the older ones. Michael Almereyda's recent adaptation of *Hamlet* – the play to which we regularly return to play out the conflict between a desire for presence and the technologies that mediate and shore up our losses – invites us to see Hamlet's cameras and editing tools in exactly this way: not only as mediating his world but as *remediating* earlier arts of memory. By viewing these new memory arts through the lens of the Shakespearean text we learn not only how new media incorporate aspects of earlier ones but also how the long-standing human needs and habits of use that evolved with those earlier media persist in and shape the new. Over time, any given technology may turn out to be unresponsive to the desire for immediacy, the embrace of mediation, or perceptions of belatedness and loss. The same technical solution may serve some of these impulses at different moments, or even serve conflicting impulses at the same time. Finally, the meaning of immediacy itself and its relation to memory technologies may change significantly in different periods. This is just as true for the figure of "writing on tables" that dominates early modern memory arts as it is of writing with chalk on blackboards. It is equally true for the modern memory arts of the moving image.

Arts of Memory

> We are always simultaneously making gestures that are archaic, modern, and futuristic.
>
> Michel Serres, *Conversations on Science, Culture, and Time*

The first observation someone like Michel Serres might make about Almereyda's *Hamlet* is that the viewing experience most of us have of the film is not, strictly, cinematic. Most readers of this chapter will have watched the film on VHS or DVD, forms that begin to simulate something like a print-based experience that allows for non-linear reading and replay, and even (in the case of DVD) delivers the text in chapters. This is an important instance of the polychronic needs we bring to any representational form and is not incidentally an important element of Almereyda's *mise en scène*. As a medium, film exists largely as an experience in memory. For all the visual and auditory richness and collective social experience of the cinema, we tend to view films only once in this way (when we see them in a theater), only to return to this experience in memory: in later conversation, commentary (as in this chapter), or classroom analysis. Unredacted, uncited, unrehearsed films do not have a robust existence. For those with access to video and DVD, the loss of the social and aesthetic impact associated with cinema may be balanced by the more quotable and repeatable experience supported by DVD tracking and video replay.

To pursue the polychrony of film and video further, however, we need a fuller account of the earlier memory arts that these media inherit and remediate. For a film such as *Hamlet*, this means looking back not only to some of its film predecessors (for a sketch of the form and uses of film in Shakespearean adaptation), but also to Shakespeare's text and the memory arts it invokes. Recent work on Shakespeare and film has tended to leave the text behind in order to move beyond the limitations of the fidelity model of adaptation (how faithful is the film to the play being the only question the text seems to answer). This reasonable impulse effectively obscures the ways older practices of memory persist in and shape our uses of the newer forms. The same impulse makes it harder for us to see how Shakespeare's own plays allegorize (consciously represent and reflect on) their relation to media that were both new and old at the time of their earliest performance and publication. Almereyda adapts an allegory of earlier memory technologies already worked out in Shakespeare's *Hamlet* to what our new technologies of memory, playback, erasure, and editing make available. Indeed, the Shakespearean allegory is more clearly visible than it might otherwise be because of the way the film renovates the play. As an experiment in polychronic reading, then, this chapter revisits some of those early technologies, sketching the multimedia practices of early modern memory as illustrated in John Willis's 1621 manual, *The Art of Memory*, and as evoked more anxiously in Shakespeare's play.

Memory was understood in early modern Europe as a cognitive and social discipline that marshals past knowledge and experience for present uses.[8] In this model, recollection satisfies present needs by means of – rather than in spite of – technologies of representation that "sift," "sort," and otherwise manipulate the matter of the past. This view emphasizes the different kinds of cognitive leverage that different forms of representation and remembering environments provide. Thus early modern writers model their memory arts on the theater, writing and printing, painting and emblem books, and religious observance. John Willis relies on all of these media when he sets out to popularize the classical memory arts, publishing an English manual for those who aspire to the status of civil gentleman but who lack a Latin education. The arts Willis describes are accessible in part because they depend on familiar technologies of representation and storage. These include an anachronistic mix of classical and early modern technologies: mental tablets in which ideas may be cognitively inscribed (Hamlet's "tables"); pamphlets; books; emblems; the mental "house" or "theater" in which ideas can be placed until future need, often as moving and audible scenes (Willis 1621: 13). "Idea" is Willis's technical term for the visual metaphors in which we commit matter (events, information) to memory. Willis describes several orders of memory ideas, including scenes of human figures in motion – a smith working, a "duell fought betweene two combatants" – and important sayings inscribed on "tables" and hung on the wall of one's personal memory theater (Willis 1621: 12–15).

Willis's memory arts depend on modes of visual perception that combine theatrical spectation with reading. He is specific about the material conditions of *mise en page*, or layout, as well as architecture, in ways that may seem extraordinary to modern readers, since what he is talking about is an imaginary space. For example, he takes pains to explain the proper shape of letters, line spacing, marginal citation conventions, and capitalization involved in mental writing – as well as the materials involved. Your mental table should be plain, sturdily framed in oak, and the right size for what you write on it. Most importantly, your letters should "be all of such bignesse, as that they may plainly be read by him that standeth on this side of the Repositorie; like unto the writings which we see in Churches" (1621: 34). Thus, when remembering important sayings it is best to inscribe them on the tables of your brain using large initials, clearly visible to your mind's eye as they hang on a mental wall.

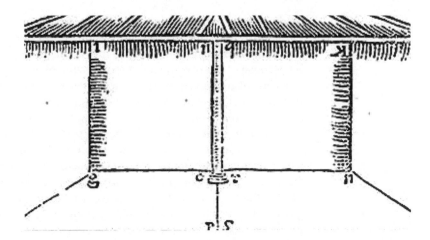

3.4 Design for a mental memory theater

Willis's remembering subject takes the position of a fixed spectator: never turning to view his other rooms (coded by color) but substituting each one into the same spatial configuration as needed. The optical constraints of this fixed position are particularly evident in the case of remembered objects. Objects that are too big to fit on the mental stage or too little to be seen need to be metaphorically reduced or enhanced. To remember a pearl, for example, you have to mentally pile a bushel of pearls on your stage (Willis 1621: 16). To remember something enormous or sublime, like a city or mountain – "whose Idea in the full bignesse, cannot be contained in a place of the Repositorie" – you have to paint it in small on the wall in your theater (1621: 17–18). Such formal techniques for manipulating remembered things help to optimize their retrieval. Retrieval typically means, for Willis, recombining the matter in memory to suit the needs of a given occasion, not playing it back sequentially. Moreover, the ability to forget impressions was as critical for successful remembering as retention (Sullivan 1999). The point to be taken here is the profound shaping force that early modern technologies of representation – architecture, theatrical performance, written texts – were understood to have on cognitive processes.

The interplay of impressions in this material psychology is especially fraught in Shakespeare's *Hamlet*. The question of whether internal disciplines actually work – and the ways in which technical supplements support or fail them – turns out to be a critical problem in the play. That problem becomes most acute when the polychronic nature of one dominant technology – writing on tables – shows most clearly, that is, when Hamlet formally accepts the Ghost's charge, "remember me:"

> Remember thee!
> Yea, from the table of my memory
> I'll wipe away all trivial fond records,
> All saws of books, all forms, all pressures past,
> That youth and observation copied there;
> And thy commandment all alone shall live

Within the book and volume of my brain,
Unmix'd with baser matter: yes, by heaven!
O most pernicious woman!

                                        (1.5. 97–105)

Much critical attention has been paid to these lines. They serve here briefly to emphasize three points. First, the "pressures past" recorded in Hamlet's memory are simultaneously bodily and immediate ("fond," "youth") and deliberate ("observation"). Second, immediacy is here an obstacle to true memory rather than – as for Nora – its privilege. Hamlet needs to forget the combined impressions of his natural and artificial memory – which he cannot quite succeed in doing, as the pun on "baser matter" makes clear. Matter implies, of course, both the rhetorical matter – "trivial fond records" – of early modern education, and the physical matter of his affections. The spontaneous break of memory in line 1.5.104 which recalls Hamlet's mother to mind suggests it may be as difficult to wipe away artful impressions (the Latin of a classical education) as natural ones. Indeed, the pun (mater/mother) suggests it may be impossible to distinguish the two.

The third point to be taken here returns us to the subject of memory technologies like writing on tables. The "table" of Hamlet's memory denotes a range of book technologies, from archaic to cutting edge: a reference to the ancient technology (and memory metaphor) of tablets; a prop that the actor carries (such as ivory writing tablets); and a new form of portable notebook with treated, erasable leaves (Chartier et al. 2004). If we resist the temptation to collapse "table," "book," "volume," and writing into a single kind of technology, we may read this passage as an exploration of the strengths and limitations of different kinds of writing-on-tables, as Hamlet gropes through a variety of storage forms seeking the one that best serves the functions of sorting and reordering the matter of the past (Chartier et al. 2004). Ancient wax tablets were reuseable but somewhat challenging to erase and they never entirely lost impressions – Hamlet's particular problem. So he reaches for the latest technology to redress the failures of an earlier one: he looks to a portable repository, invitingly separable from the matter of an embodied mind and more easily wiped. Yet judging by the force of the spontaneous recollections that follow – "O most pernicious woman!" "smiling, damned villain" – the attempt is at best a partial success.

Shakespeare and New(er) Media

The transitional, polychronic nature of early modern technologies such as Hamlet's tables provides some insight into the stances towards memory in recent film-adaptations of Shakespeare. In particular, the early examples help explain these filmmakers' preoccupation with anachronism, their sense that the matter of the past is reversible and manipulable, and their notion that Shakespeare's plays are particularly congenial to such manipulation. These preoccupations slant what Peter

Donaldson has called the "media allegory" in Baz Luhrmann's *William Shakespeare's Romeo + Juliet*, with its out-of-control culture of mass media and advertising (Donaldson 2002b: 62). Film and video technologies become the focus of a similar allegory of recording media in Almereyda's *Hamlet*. Both filmmakers subscribe to a non-nostalgic notion of memory as a cognitive and social skill or technique. Acts of memory, for them, serve as opportunities to assess the adequacy of different technologies in relation to present needs, not past actualities. Almereyda's Hamlet seems at first to personify the psychological costs and subjective impoverishment Nora attributes to modern media, when we encounter him absorbed in a melancholy session of video replay. In fact, Almereyda's film probes both the strengths and limitations of different memory technologies, including photography, film, video, and digital video. The film also serves to remind us that these media, like the earlier forms of artificial memory they remediate, are historically composite technologies that incorporate multiple stances towards remembering–technophilic, nostalgic, skeptical–often at the same time.

Almereyda's approach is different enough from other film-adaptations that it is worth marshaling a few examples for comparison. For adapters such as Branagh, the Shakespearean text functions as the material trace of lost experiences to be reconstructed as fully as possible, against the relentless forward rush of history. Barbara Hodgdon describes Branagh's *mise en scène* as a continual negotiation between the demands of audience accessibility and authenticity (Hodgdon 2001). His choice of source-text for debated line readings in *Hamlet* – Harold Jenkins's magisterial Arden edition – indicates Branagh's affiliation to the project of reconstruction. As several scholars have observed, this project is actually a double one: to reconstruct both a lost theatrical and a lost cinematic experience. Branagh's films explore the increasing difficulty of achieving the experience of immersion established so powerfully in Olivier's classic Shakespearean oeuvre (Hodgdon 2001). Olivier's adaptations seemed to answer the problems of editorial reconstruction with the seamlessness of classic continuity editing, restoring us to a fullness of experience not present in the partial text. At the same time, Olivier reveled in the new medium that made this renovation possible, to the point almost of exposing his technical resources. His cinematic daring is particularly evident in *Hamlet* (1948) when, in the famous Closet scene, the vertiginous sweep of Olivier's camera gradually reveals the mnemonic force of cinema, commanding its audience to an audition that returns the past to the present. By contrast to the early modern technologies the playtext describes, this scene emphasizes a supremely successful technical management of memory and emotion. Addressing the Ghost, Olivier's Hamlet directs his gaze not at a visible ghostly presence but at the camera, in a way that explicitly calls attention to the cinematic moment. First, he seems to assert the camera's ghostly oversight and prowess: "Look you how pale he glares! / His form and cause conjoin'd, preaching to stones, / Would make them capable." (3.4. 125–7). Then he wards off that force, still in the meta-cinematic mode, addressing the camera in the second person, "Do not look up on me," as if we and the camera alike have become the ghost that knows all, before he just as suddenly sunders that connection. For Branagh, the authority of this second-person address comes hard. Branagh understands himself to be addressing an audience that knows little, if anything, of Shakespeare and for whom the now unremarkable experience of cinematic immersion may only partly compensate for the archaism of the material (Lanier 2002a). The emblematic visual moment of his *Hamlet*, therefore, is the hall of mirrors, in which we watch Hamlet examine himself in his own reflections. The cinematic-screen-as-mirror may create a perfect simulacrum, but this series of reflected surfaces recedes into false depths. These compromise any sense that the camera can offer us access to Hamlet's inner life, to the Shakespearean past, or to an authentic exchange of emotion with either.

By contrast, for Luhrmann, Almereyda, and Julie Taymor, Shakespeare's plays serve as traces of the past that are recycled according to specific investments in the present. Taymor describes *Titus Andronicus* as a "complete . . . dissertation on violence" (Schechner 1999: 46). The play offers a systematic survey of knowledge about violence that anyone thinking about the topic right now will benefit from. Luhrmann and Almereyda come to their plays for similar reasons. Neither authenticity nor accessibility are the main concerns of these directors; conversely, the practice of "sifting and sorting" the knowledge of the past turns out to be fundamental to its cognitive and emotional utility for the present. Memory, simultaneously a cognitive and social phenomenon, is understood as the activity of tracing the past according to present interests, anxieties, and desires. As Frow observes: "rather than being the repetition of the physical traces of the past, [memory] is a construction of it under conditions and constraints determined by the present" (1997: 228).

For these filmmakers, as for Willis, accurate retrieval of the matter of the past is less important than its effective use. Accordingly, the technologies represented in their films are typically marked as belated, falling short of present needs. This is true of the older technologies of book and theater, and also of the modern modes of communication and transportation that proliferate in their hyper-modern, urban settings. Luhrmann and Almereyda layer technologies in a way that regularly feels anachronistic, altering the viewer's sense of distance from the modern *mise en scène* and from the Shakespearean text. It can be hard to tell which feels the most stylized and belated. The clash between the archaic language (delivered flatly) and the modern settings (delivered with visual energy) might suggest an aesthetic progressivism, as it clearly does for Taymor. But Luhrmann's use of a high-speed delivery service ("Post-Haste Dispatch") that arrives too late to give Romeo news of the Friar's ruse reverses the relation. Less obvious anachronisms can be just as telling. Absurdly, in a story that supposedly takes place in AD 2000, Almereyda's Hamlet transmits Claudius's message to England via floppy disk rather than email and relies on a payphone instead of a cellphone to complete his "interview" with Gertrude. In the first case, the choice is dramatically necessary. Yet the just-in-time economy of the web is wholly absent in the film, as is the continuous stream of communication made available by the cell-phone and text messaging.

All technologies in these Shakespearean worlds tend to lag behind our needs of them.[9] But nostalgia is not the only register in which the films address this problem. A brief example from Luhrmann's *Romeo + Juliet* reminds us that such lags are features to be reckoned with in most representational forms and practices, and always have been. Like Taymor, Luhrmann finds Shakespearean language and dramatic conventions readily available to his present interests. Indeed, they seem as available and current as the conventions of Australian Mardi Gras or the exuberant drag performances in *Priscilla Queen of the Desert* (Donaldson 2002b: 72). The matter of *Romeo and Juliet* communicates no more or less legibly in a global context than local Australian matter, and Luhrmann adapts Shakespeare in part because he's interested in the global transport of performance forms. He is surprisingly confident about the degree to which performance conventions remain legible across time and geopolitical boundaries. If the past is a foreign country, it's subject to the same challenges and opportunities of translation that apply to all cultural exchanges under globalism. Luhrmann's figure for such global translations is Shakespeare's "wooden O," stood up vertically, on end. The setting, a blasted-out cinema palace, introduces us to Romeo in the middle of a solitary experiment in love-melancholy (figure 3.5).

This blasted theater is a global conduit through which we receive conventional matter from far-away places. Romeo's stale Petrarchisms travel West as we look East through the center of a proscenium arch, into the rising sun. They hark forward in time as we listen back to their archaic silliness: "Why then, O brawling love! O loving hate! / O any thing, of nothing first create!" (1.1.186–2). Romeo's oxymorons set the stage for other conventional matter to pass through this setting: Mercutio's drag performance, the Western shoot-out in which he dies. The Petrarchan conventions are thin and outdated, but their belatedness makes them recyclable for Luhrmann as for Shakespeare. Romeo's musings are conveyed by multiple vehicles here: the modern

3.5 Wooden O

soundtrack, his handwriting, his notebook, the limousine, the theatrical setting. A longer clip would show us other modes of transport: TV screens, radio, more cars. To the extent that we recognize this setting as a vertical "wooden O," we are being asked to see these diverse vehicles not as anachronisms but as historically composite technologies, like the composite car described by Serres (1995: 45). As Petrarch is to Shakespeare, so Shakespeare is to Luhrmann: a source of commonplace conventions for interiority, to be reworked and reapplied in surprising ways. However, where the composite technologies of a car present themselves as seamlessly integrated – so well, indeed, that it can be hard to recognize their historical accretions – Romeo's Petrarchan toolkit for conjuring subjectivity emphasizes the very fact of borrowing.

The media allegory in Almereyda's *Hamlet* focuses on technologies of memory, particularly the ways that film and video mediate past experience, both for individuals and the community. Yet Almereyda is more concerned than Luhrmann with the trade-offs between different expressive tools. For Almereyda's Hamlet, the personal video is *the* technology of interiority among a variety of modern media, including telephones, television, photography, film, and so on. All but one of Hamlet's soliloquies are framed as video sequences that he has composed. As Hamlet dies at the end of the film, we see his life flash back in the same grainy black-and-white collage. Like Willis's visual prompts, Hamlet's videos create narratives of the past, not for the purpose of accurate retrieval but in response to present interests and desires. The formal features of film and video supply a cognitive grammar for the mind as it stores and recombines the traces of the past. Whereas for John Willis the constraints of memorial inscription governed the way in which ideas are stored and retrieved, Almereyda's key constraints are the framed screen

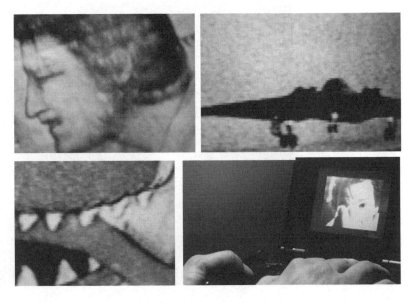

3.6 Video soliloquy

(film or video) and the conventions of continuity editing that create a continuous experience out of fragmented images. We see this in Hamlet's first soliloquy, which unfolds characteristically in a home video. Before the opening credits, we enter the film through a video collage that turns out to be what Hamlet watches as he works at his desk. While the audiotrack voices over his melancholy thoughts – "I have of late . . . lost all my mirth" – Hamlet's gestures link the work of his editing hands, moving on the track pad, with his mental experience (figure 3.6).

The clips Hamlet has spliced into this video look at first like what Pierre Nora would call the "sifted and sorted historical traces" of a lost past: Renaissance painting, military footage, cartoon monster. They seem like fragments of collective memory, a loose assortment of "pop images and simulacra" through which, as Fredric Jameson warns, we may be "condemned to seek History" in the nostalgic mode (Jameson 1991: 25; Frow 1997: 218). But what Almereyda sees in these screens is a composite vehicle like Luhrmann's Globe. And what Hamlet seeks in his videos is not history but a connection between collective experience and his own loss.

We are invited here to understand Hamlet's interiority in terms of the video record he manipulates (figure 3.7). The grainy, shimmery quality of the video image, and the way Hamlet addresses the camera in this video-within-the-film recall early video memoirs by Sadie Benning and others in the 1980s and 1990s that developed conventions for video soliloquy using a dated technology of their own, a toy camera called Pixelvision.[10] Hamlet rigs his Pixelvision camera to a digital recorder, adapting the older technology in a way that intensifies its original, radically personalized functions. The watery, shifting signature of his Pixelvision recordings echoes other imagined breaks through clear surfaces in the film, into private and protected space. When Ophelia later imagines herself

3.7 Video memoir

diving into the pool to escape Polonius's relentless toadying and exposure, the surface breaks into a similar screening, protective pattern of
bubbles. Yet the way Almereyda stages Hamlet's private interactions with
his videos reminds us that our *perception* of interiority depends on much
older technologies of self. Thus the next video soliloquy emphasizes the
composite technologies that transmit a shared past. Once again, we
watch Hamlet replay a home video of his parents, as he contemplates the
"weary, stale, flat and unprofitable" uses of this world. A medium shot
establishes Hamlet from behind, seated at his desk. Then the camera
reverses to a medium shot from the other side of the desk, and we see
Hamlet again, this time through a frame created by the two monitors and
the stack of books at the bottom of the screen (figure 3.8, first frame). The
books and monitors work together here to put Hamlet's inner life on
screen for us. Indeed, this window into his thoughts will expand in a
zoom to include the whole screen. The zoom reorients our attention to a
different set of frames as well. From foreground to background, our field
of view is defined by the two screens Hamlet sits between: the monitors
between the camera and his body, and the window behind him, with its
striped reflections, that serves as backdrop and double to the frame. As
the clip continues and the camera zooms in, Hamlet plays and replays
his father's image, offering us what will become a signature action for Old
Hamlet, as he brushes his hand across his temple and ear.

The emphasis of all these video soliloquies is Hamlet's editorial
process: there is no possibility of knowing the past here except through
captured images processed by the self. Yet the opportunity to process in
this intimate way makes these traces more than simulacra.[11] Hamlet
forges an authentic connection to the past, if not a perfect or unmediated one, and we know this because of the conventions of cinematic
reversal on which this connection depends. Two kinds of reversal are
displayed here. The first is the reversibility of video traces of the past:
rewound, edited, played back again by hand. These videos explore the

3.8 Editing video
memories: Hamlet's
inner life on screen

notion, critical to recent art-house filmmaking, of digital media as a
"haptic" technology that serves a sense of touch as well as sight.

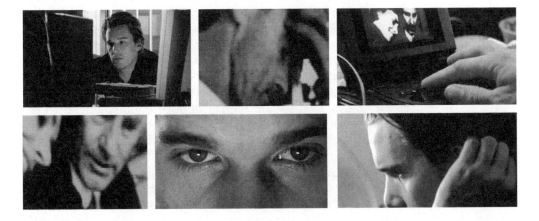

Almereyda offers the protected, psychic experience afforded by Hamlet's camera holding and by his editing as an analogy and extension to earlier modes of representation and storage. Shakespeare's Hamlet, like Willis's memorial subject, remembers according to the cognitive structures of "book and volume" and the theater; we know the ins and outs of his experience by watching him manipulate conventional matter – "trivial, fond saws" or a player's speech – in strategic ways. Similarly, Almereyda's memory arts depend on the representational constraints of film and video, assimilating and integrating the formal devices of other media. Notably, some of Hamlet's other speeches (such as one to Rosencrantz and Guildenstern) are assimilated into the mode of video soliloquy. And Hamlet puts his videos on pause frequently, turning moving images into digital stills, as if producing ephemeral photographs.

Our sense that Hamlet has an authentic memorial experience with these polychronic videos also depends, however, on a visual principle that is particularly cinematic. A second kind of reversal organizes the series of eye-line cuts in this soliloquy, cuts that come very close to the editing convention of shot/response shot, as we hear Hamlet's meditation over alternating shots of his face and the video he plays with. Shot/response shot sequences are a staple of continuity editing, often used to establish the fiction of intimate exchange. In classic cinema, the technique involves cuts that switch point of view back and forth between two characters in dialogue. One camera sets the scene, framing the characters in a specific location, typically at medium distance. A second and a third camera film the actors from opposite angles in close-up, staying on the same side of the actors as the first camera (and never crossing an imaginary line connecting the actors, called the "180-degree line"). The footage from these cameras is edited to show us first the pair together, then alternating, reverse-angle close-ups. We sit at person A's shoulder, watching person B react as A talks (as if we're seeing what A sees). Then we sit at person B's shoulder and watch A react as B replies. Shot/response shot is a cinematic trope that makes us feel party to an intimate exchange, creating the fiction that we can know both points of view simultaneously. Using this convention, for example, Olivier lets us know that Claudius suspects and hates Hamlet and that Hamlet requites the feelings. In sequences like this, alternating shots are "sutured" together so as to "seem to constitute a perfect whole," assuring the viewer that "his or her gaze suffers under no constraints" (Silverman 1988: 12).

Turning back to the editing sequence from Almereyda's film (figure 3.8), we can see Almereyda adapting this device and referencing its classic effects. First we see Hamlet through the monitors, then the scene reverses to the video he watches, which contains close-ups of his parents. It reverses again to a close shot of his eyes, and then again to the wider shot of his hand editing the video. In these tight, alternating shots we watch Hamlet react to the video, then see the video player (and by extension his parents' faces) respond to Hamlet's manipulation. Tellingly, as Hamlet replays and stops the images he internalizes his father's gesture, hand to the temple. As in classic shot/response shot, the camera stays on the same side of both figures; what would be the 180-degree line runs through the plane of the monitor screen. There is a kind of naturalized emotional transmission that happens in these reversals, intimate enough that Hamlet internalizes his father's gesture from shot to response shot. At this moment, digital video editing looks intensely akin to a handicraft, a medium of trained as well as spontaneous gesture passed on as organic experience.

Whereas the spectator in Willis's memory theater remains in a fixed optical relation to the matter stored in memory, the camera-work in classical shot/response shot moves us along a defined axis within the field of dramatic action. The conventions of cinema sustain this diffused, mobile viewing position for the remembering subject in Almereyda's film. Yet as the story unfolds, Almereyda's editing affords even greater play across the barrier of the past: the glass screen or wall through which the camera repeatedly moves along its defined axis. Indeed, in Hamlet's first encounter with the ghost, Old Hamlet appears easily out of this screen past. The camera crosses the screen barrier, taking the spectators over and then returning, bringing the ghost back through its plane with us (figure 3.9).

This sequence is gradual, and it is important to notice some of the differences between this shot arrangement and classical shot/response shot. As the actors cross each other, the camera switches not only point of view but also moves from one side of the *mise en scène* to the other, eventually tracking around to reverse position and taking us with it. As the scene begins, Hamlet wakes up to a phone ringing. The ghost appears on the **3.9** Shot / response balcony. Then, after a series of medium shots establish emotional connection shot: crossing the tion between the dead and the living, the ghost easily crosses the screen screen barrier barrier, the glass wall that had been a backdrop for the video soliloquy.

The dialogue that marks this crossing is the Ghost's command, "Mark me" and Hamlet's acquiescence, "I will." There is no apparent emotional barrier between father and son here, a fact underlined by the ghost's behavior as he tells of his death. In a rhyming shot the ghost repeats his gesture from the video (handkerchief to poisoned ear), then reaches to touch Hamlet in the same place, holding his head close. As the scene unfolds, the actors and camera circle until they have reversed positions from their opening arrangement. Hamlet and the ghost stand roughly where the camera had positioned the spectator as the scene opened. At the same time, the editing resolves into more classic arrangements of shot/response shot, with a less mobile camera. With the wall of memory technologies as backdrop – photographs, monitors, digital editor, even a film reel on the desk – the sequence hits its climax and they embrace.

This ghost (played with characteristic intensity by Sam Shepard) is tangible and emotionally available, though also intimidating. In crossing over into the affective field of a character whose morose introspectiveness and alienation from other people has already been established, the "ghost" violates the distance through which Hamlet's experiences have to this point been mediated. Formerly an absent presence that it was entirely within Hamlet's control to bring to life on his video monitor – to rewind, playback, fast forward, and freeze – this ghost claims the space between them. Indeed, he shrinks that space as he literally backs his smaller, bewildered son into a corner, commanding the space of the *mise en scène* and also what gets transacted within it. Rehearsing the process and pain of his murder, the ghost speaks with bitter precision and certainty, seeming to grow larger in power and purpose as Hamlet cowers before him, until the fervor of his embrace closes any remaining distance in a climactic two-shot.[12]

The shot/response shot structure repeats throughout the film, more often in the flexible mode of the first soliloquy than in the classical mode, moving both actors and spectators across the screen/surface boundary as we see here. Almereyda's conceit is that this crossing is the condition of intimacy between the self and others. Intimacy results from the projection of self simultaneously behind and in front of a screen, a projection that makes the self accessible because it provides a cognitive grammar for transmitting and internalizing multiple points of view. Yet for this Hamlet, as for Shakespeare's, the knowledge gained through editorial process is, by virtue of its very privacy, hard to transmit to others. The real conflict in the film and the source of Hamlet's melancholy is thus not the technical mediation of experience, but its social circulation. At first the easy circulation of public images seems to be precisely the problem. The private and autonomous record digital video makes possible appears as a necessary protection against the appropriation of memory technologies by large corporate systems. (A shot of a huge Panasonic screen launches the first video soliloquy.) The struggle over who controls the technologies of memory emerges as the opening credits roll, in the scene of a press conference where Claudius presides as the new CEO of Denmark Corporation. As it films the paparazzi filming Claudius's speech, Hamlet's camera serves as a "particular" rather than a "common" lens – betraying the oppositional stance Gertrude describes in 1.2.75, here restaged as dialogue on a city street at the press conference's conclusion:

> [*Queen*]. Thou know'st 'tis common, all that lives must die,
> Passing through nature to eternity.
> *Hamlet.* Ay, madam, it is common.
> Queen.   If it be,
> Why seems it so particular with thee?
>
>   (1.2.72–5)

In this public scene we are invited to see Hamlet's manipulations of his own video record as oppositional acts: a resistance to the official counter-memories of the corporate-media-advertising complex that swallowed his father.[13] The ghost's dissolve through the Pepsi machine, gateway to the underworld, captures the nature of this threat.

Hamlet's obsessive replays serve not to slow the rush of present into the past but to organize memory records for meditation and self-reflection. Of course, such meditation cannot be understood as fully private. For example, the opening sequence, "I have of late lost all my mirth," starts as news footage of the Gulf War (where television reportage was notoriously selective and one-sided), before cutting to the news conference in which Claudius (Kyle McLachlan) trumpets his triumphs over his opponents. Moreover, Hamlet gets the matter and inspiration for the "To be" speech from found footage taped from the TV. The soliloquy itself emerges in fragments (as if nodding to the different Folio and Quarto versions), and assumes its most familiar Folio form only through editing, interruption, and playback. This painstakingly assembled, "hand-crafted" version of Shakespeare's most famous set-speech, which our latter-day Hamlet memorially reconstructs and delivers while wandering through the aisles of a Blockbuster outlet, arguably emerges as the most "authentic" form of self-expression in Almereyda's film. Dislocated from the privileged recitative space and time reserved for it in conventional theatrical and filmic productions, it comes across not as an always already established speech-act (embedded in the memory theater of nearly every auditor and actor) but as the culmination of a long-sustained transaction between a character's personal preoccupations and his search for a mode of address answerable to them. Almereyda's audaciousness in transforming what has come to be the stiffest, most predictable moment in a *Hamlet* production into an emotionally charged channel of personal expression and clarified audition is doubly noteworthy given its setting. The speech is rehearsed in a space devoted to the commodification of film and personal experience alike. The Blockbuster outlet is a storage and delivery system that functions as a kind of encyclopedically organized, walk-in version of Willis's memory theater, but with the crucial difference that its contents are corporately selected and assembled in a one-size-fits-all manner for the individual consumer. Formatted to play back to us in such a setting, Hawke's delivery of the "To be" soliloquy as a form of private conversation in dialogue only with itself would seem to function as either a form of anachronism or anarchic resistance to the corporate monopoly exercised over all pre-scripted speech acts.[14]

As this comparison makes clear, Almereyda sees the editorial handling of Hamlet's video soliloquies as privatized in powerful ways. Video replay and collage serve to appropriate found footage from the media environment and recycle it for private audition. Yet the common grammar that makes such edited matter legible derives from a different medium. This fact emerges in the screening of the *Mousetrap* video, where it becomes clear that Hamlet has other uses for his collages than meditation and mourning. Hamlet edits his found footage in this video-within-the-film so as to expose the "real" interests behind Claudius's media show. In the process, he attempts to retrieve the memory of his mother's affection for his father from behind the counter-memory of her lust for his uncle. When Hamlet turns to the conventions of cinema in this way Almereyda introduces a different set of concerns than the problem of who controls modern technologies of remembering. Indeed, that concern turns out by the end of the film to be secondary to the problem of how well modern media technologies extend the social self: providing for intimacy with others as well as self-reflection, meeting the demands of occasion, as Willis understands memory to do. In order to trap his uncle, Hamlet needs a medium that serves collective audition: the arena of the screening room where he premiers *The Mousetrap* as a "film/video."

The found footage in *The Mousetrap* works differently from Hamlet's home videos: stitching together fragments of familiar images in a way that evokes a variety of earlier forms associated with the cinematic experiences of visual presence. These include sequences from silent films, stop-motion footage, advertising footage, and film pornography.[15] In stitching these sequences together, the film/video vividly evokes Bruce Conner's cinematic formalism, addressing the viewer aggressively in Conner's "second-person" mode, "reworking the already coded and manipulated cultural material of the movies" and peripheral media like advertising, in a way that reminds us of how these recordings came to be (Jenkins 1999: 187).[16]

Home video technologies remain so individuated (at the time of this writing and certainly at the time of filming) that we still have no idea if we can go around handing our version of the past to someone else – as Ophelia does her photographs – and expect it to be legible. By contrast, the *Mousetrap* generates some strong responses in Hamlet's on-screen audience, as some of the other imaging technologies in the film do (Ophelia's photographs for example). The *Mousetrap* hits its primary mark: Claudius. Yet like home videos and many "experimental" films, it may well bewilder spectators who are unacquainted with the private drama that bridges its associative leaps and shifts in format. All that may be legible to them is its "grotesque parody of Claudius's self-anointment before the mirror of the press" earlier in the film

(Lanier 2002b: 175) and the fact that Hamlet has offended Claudius. Indeed, the playtext *Mousetrap* may well be more socially legible than the *Mousetrap* video, rehearsing, as it does, scenes from a presumably extant play, *The Murder of Gonzago*, that bear obvious resemblances to the shifting configurations of the Danish royal family. Hamlet's contribution to this play (allegedly some 12–16 lines of added text) is, of course, famously unreadable; it is embedded in the text in a way that never expressly announces itself. By contrast, the imagery and found footage of the *Mousetrap* video are conspicuously self-reflexive. They constitute a rehearsal not of a play or action with which an attentive audience may be familiar, but of essentially the same matter – the "dramas" of a young man's preoccupation with scenes of domestic happiness and betrayal and of a secret murder – that Hamlet has been privately tracking and replaying throughout the film. This matter may not be legible to others in the way it is legible to him, or to us.

Apart from the "Monty Pythonesque images of the poisoning," "a perverse kiss clipped from the porn classic *Deep Throat*" (Hodgdon 2003b: 204), and "a gleefully sardonic bricolage of imagery culled from the mass media" (Lanier 2002b: 174), much of the *Mousetrap* video is comprised of black-and-white footage drawn from conventionally idealized representations of 1940s or 1950s American domestic life. What Hodgdon terms "home movies of a child's bedtime" (2003b: 204) substitute for the similarly directed footage of the home movies Hamlet screens earlier in the film. Had Hamlet wished to make his intentions or implications more legible or transparent to his audience, he had only to cull and edit imagery from his own memory theater, to which at least two members of that audience (Gertrude and Claudius) would also have easy access. Why doesn't he? And why does a young man as fluent as Hamlet is with so wide an array of video technologies offer up what seems more like a rough-cut than anything approaching a polished or finished product?

Almereyda's *Hamlet* is itself far from a perfect movie. But if we assume that everything in the film has its aim and intention, we may venture that the roughness and willful bad taste of the *Mousetrap* is consistent with the generational themes and grunge stylings of a film that pits the oppositional moods of Hamlet and Ophelia, Horatio and his girlfriend, Marcela, against the corporate slickness, lusts, and ambitions of Claudius, Gertrude, and Polonius. We don't need to know that Hawke modeled much of his performance on the inspiration of Kurt Cobain to see this.[17] As Lanier observes: "The video's style is . . . calculated to offend: pointedly crude, homemade, disjointed, campy, with its overwrought Tchaikovsky soundtrack, it roundly rejects the standards of bourgeois realism and high-gloss production. Most important, it is produced by Hamlet alone, created, we are to surmise, in solitude on his home media-workstation without the aid of visiting players or anyone else" (2002b: 175). We may also note that the *Mousetrap* video is closely linked to Hawke's casually idiosyncratic rendition of the "To be" soliloquy as a form of personal expression which (in Lanier's words) "rejects the corporate media system in which film and video elsewhere in the movie seem so inextricably implicated" (2002b: 175).

In an important essay that sought both to sum up and move beyond state-of-the-art Shakespeare-on-film criticism ca. 1993, Graham Holderness observed that "the most successful attempts to capture [the] elusive, shifting complexity of the Shakespeare text are to be found in the deconstructive experiments of 'underground' cinema" which "offer some degree of filmic equivalent to the modern theoretically activated Shakespearean text" (1993: 74). Lanier and others have noted "the contradictory position that Almereyda's own film seeks to occupy" (2002b: 177) and "the institutional double-bind faced by the contemporary Shakespeare filmmaker, who is confronted by the demand to produce a Shakespeare tailored to . . . [global media market] protocols epitomized by the action film" (2002b: 176). The video-within-the-film produced by this Hamlet – like Hawke's delivery of the "To be" speech against the backdrop of action-videos – negotiates such contradictions by confronting them head-on. Construed as an experiment in "underground" or *grunge* cinema, Hawke's *Mousetrap* presents itself in the anarchic, anything-oppositional-goes manner of the anti-globalist demonstrator or "play-it-like-you-don't-know-how" grunge band, whose message is legible enough to insiders but opaque, inchoate, or repellent to outsiders. It is a deliberate "rough-cut" that (again like Hawke's "To be" speech) conscientiously rejects the formal consolations of the well-mannered or well-crafted art-object. If Hamlet's goal is not to transcend mediating technologies but to inhabit them in a way that satisfies his need for self-expression and is transmissible enough to those who speak the same language, then the solution to the social and cognitive demands of memory technologies may just be the composite work-around of the inspired improviser or resourceful amateur.

Once the memory of Old Hamlet's death cycles through the shared venue of cinematic audition, its powerful affects may extend in turn to private modes of audition: the scene of Claudius, in his limo, repenting his rank offense in front of a small TV screen. For such purposes, Almereyda suggests, video allows us to receive and process content in intimate ways. Yet cinema provides the cognitive grammar that organizes that content in socially legible terms and produces it as shared knowledge. The claim is particularly clear in Hamlet's final moments. There video supplies the grainy, black-and-white final memories of Hamlet dying, products of intimate collection, sorting, and recollection. But those memories are also shots from the film: meaningful because conflated with and recycled through our cinematic audition. This is, of course, also the case with respect to Hamlet's film-within-the-film, which however jumbled or juvenile it may seem, plays back to us as plaintively as Ophelia's fantasized escape from her father. That fantasy, of course anticipates her "real" leap into the decorative pool later in the film. Though no one else *in* the film quite feels or hears the pain of its main characters, Almereyda makes certain that we do.

4 Colliding Time and Space in Taymor's *Titus*

An elaborately designed adaptation of *Titus Andronicus*, Julie Taymor's *Titus* (1999) is set in a spectacularly "virtual" version of the Eternal City, Rome, assembled out of the artifacts of 2000 years of Western culture. In this early revenge tragedy, Shakespeare had already synthesized fragments of history, myth, and invented tradition reaching back to rituals of human sacrifice (that were never practiced in ancient Rome) and forward to Rome's Germanic wars. But Taymor casts an even wider net of cultural reference and visual imagery over her adaptation. She fabricates a citational environment in which postmodern iconography and the oversized ambitions of fascist Italy superimpose themselves on ancient Rome's storied foundations and Shakespeare's play alike. *Titus* was filmed in sites as varied as a well-preserved Roman coliseum in Croatia and carefully assembled studio and outdoor sets at Fellini's famed Cinécittà. Yet it pays a disproportionate amount of visual and dramatic attention to a centerpiece of Fascist architecture: the monumental "stage-set" Mussolini commissioned to advance his efforts to model a modern Italian state on imperial Rome, now known as the "Colosseo Quadrato" or "square coliseum," in the EUR (Esposizione Universale Romana) quarter of Rome (figure 4.1).[1]

Taymor attends so closely to the "square coliseum" not only to link the authoritarian patterns of the 1930s to those of ancient Rome, but to work iconographic variations on them from the point of view of the present. (Peter Greenaway made similar use of this site in *The Belly of an Architect* [1987] and we find a related impulse in Philip Greenspun's photograph of the iconic Marilyn Monroe.)[2] Architecture and iconography are not the only media Taymor deploys to draw connections or dissolve differences between the modern and ancient worlds. She also exploits the anachronistic setting of Shakespeare's play – an indistinct time dominated by barbaric religious ritual, authoritarian militarism, and sexual excess – to produce the impression of atavistic resurgence by positioning her film at an indeterminate moment that crosses the ancient past with the post-apocalyptic future.[3]

Explaining why she superimposed the architectural excesses and authoritarian stylings of Mussolini's Italy on Shakespeare's own composite version of Rome, Taymor claims that "Modern Rome, built on the ruins of ancient Rome, offered the perfect stratification for the setting of the film. I wanted to blend and collide time, to create a singular period that juxtaposed elements of ancient barbaric ritual with

4.1A Colosseo Quadrato
in Greenaway

4.1B Colosseo Quadrato
in *Titus*

4.1C Colosseo
Marilyn Monroe

familiar, contemporary attitude and style" (Taymor 2000: 178). Taymor elaborates on these temporal collisions by contending that "the time of the film is from 1 to 2000 AD," and that "the film represents the last 2000 years of man's inhumanity to man" (DVD disc 1, Director's Commentary). Taken together, these comments effectively conflate the conceptual postmodernity Taymor brings to Shakespeare's *Titus Andronicus* with an approach to the play's content that is avowedly humanistic. In them, Taymor seeks to reconcile her commitment to a stylization that floats free of a specific ethical or political persuasion with a stance toward behaviors ("man's inhumanity to man") designed to engage our ethical interest and attention. Taymor's comments thus bring into focus contradictions that are defining features of her project and that make *Titus* both a powerful and troubling viewing experience.[4] Combining the affectless irony and sleek stylings of the contemporary cinematic, visual art, and theatrical avant-garde with the visual and auditory excess of a Hollywood blockbuster or horror film, *Titus* moralizes against violent and predatory behavior that it more often seems to revel in than revile (Burt 2002a: 312–13; McCandless 2002: 489).[5]

Like Fellini (who exerts as much influence on Taymor's cinematic imagination as does Shakespeare), Taymor has a quintessentially post-modern interest in pastiche, the practice of blending diverse artistic materials.[6] *Titus* not only blends and "collides" the architectural styles of ancient Rome and Mussolini's Rome, but juxtaposes these with other symbolic designs. The scarring of Tamora (Jessica Lange) and Aaron the Moor (Harry Lennix), for example, not only mark their ethnic difference from the "ancient" Romans but resonate with the contemporary vogue for tattoos and body art in a way that makes them seem a different, more compelling form of outsider. "Unmarked" Romans like Titus and his family are, by comparison, figured as solidly, even regressively, traditional. Taymor mixes such specifically weighted markers with designs drawn promiscuously from the domains of high art and popular culture that operate more loosely, as floating signifiers: they take on new meanings in each visual frame, call attention to the way they make meaning, and mean whatever a viewer decides they mean (Barthes 1977: 39). Indeed, *Titus* fabricates its idiosyncratic design concepts out of unusually mixed props, behaviors, and citational environments: horse-drawn chariots and tanks, swords and sports cars, human sacrifice and video games, captive Goths (the tribe) and heavy-metal "Goths," orgiastic sex and plastic baggies – the iconographic bric-a-brac of surrealist fantasies, American pop culture, transvestism, pornography, and the phantasmagoric film-imagery of Fellini.

As with any strong design initiative, particularly one as interested as hers is in symbolism, Taymor's risks reducing the film to an array of too prominent signs and markers. We may come away from it remembering only the outsized throne that makes Saturninus look like a spoiled boy and which, perhaps, plays too glibly with the Fascist associations of Alan Cumming's *Cabaret* look; the bleached hair and contemporary "Goth" looks of Tamora's androgynous sons; the color-coded costumes and backdrops; Lavinia's porcelain prettiness, which Taymor likens to that of Grace Kelly and later overlays with allusions to Marilyn Monroe and Degas's "Little Dancer, Aged Fourteen." Outside of the concept-addled New York art and theater scene where this convention is rooted, it may all seem too calculated and self-reflexive.[7]

Responses to the film that concentrate on its preoccupation with symbolic signs and markers, stylized sex, and violence, and the attention-getting "look" of its architectural settings, tend to see it as an extraordinarily beautiful but hollow cinematic shell, or worse (Burt 2002a: 295–300). These are important but partial observations that obscure the full range of uses to which Taymor puts *Titus Andronicus*. Taymor's dramatically sustained interpolations – both her explicit scenic additions to the playtext and her interventions in how that text gets cinematically expressed – do more than exploit blank spaces in the Shakespearean playtext to dramatic effect. They adapt Shakespearean stage-practice to the multi-mediated language of postmodern film-art and technology in a way that changes "the entire infrastructure of the art-form" (Grigely 1995: 100).[8] In what follows, therefore, we approach *Titus* as an opportunity for exploring the kinds of viewing and interpretative strategies called for by what gets "added to" a Shakespeare play in screen adaptations, concentrating on several strands of Taymor's allusions and interpolations.

In *Titus*, Taymor seeks a cinematic style poised somewhere between the immersive possibilities of experimental theater (think of her career-long use of masks, puppets, iconic movement, surreal and expressionist settings) on the one hand and of new media on the other.[9]

As Peter Donaldson has shown, *Titus* is one of many recent films that experiment with the visual and narrative codes of video gaming and virtual world-building (Donaldson 2006). We take our cue from this experimentation, approaching Taymor's allusive structures as interactive activities in which reception and adaptation are two sides of the same process. According to Donaldson, Taymor's virtual Rome resembles the play-spaces of interactive games, where the ethical spectator "is immersed in the story world, assumes a role within it, and is able to makes choices or intervene in ways that may alter the narrative's outcome" (2006: 457). But what happens when the film's allusive structures and the narrative in which they are embedded fail to signal clearly the choices or interventions this "ethical spectator" should make? And how "ethical" can one's choices be when Taymor's aim is to "unsettle" rather than relieve the spectator of uncertainty?

Allusion is of its very nature an artistic transaction controlled as much by audience as by artist. It is a highly unstable device precisely because it invites readers, viewers, or listeners to draw on "external" associations that may range from the widely shared to the highly idiosyncratic. It is likely, therefore, to produce varied, even contradictory responses (far more varied, indeed, than the highly routinized menus offered by interactive games). Accordingly, Taymor's free-floating allusiveness invites readings that are, to borrow Richard Burt's phrases, both "Shakespeare-centric" – concerned with what gets done *to* the play – and "Shakespeare-eccentric" – concerned with what gets accomplished *by means of* the play (Burt 2006). In this chapter we aim to balance Shakespeare-centric and -eccentric readings by following Taymor's allusions in the (sometimes contradictory) directions they take us and other critics. As we pursue these different interpretive paths, we seek to account for as wide as possible a range of reactions to Taymor's allusive imagery.

Stretching the limits of both Shakespeare-centric and -eccentric readings can be a lesson to the critic about what constitutes the externals and essentials of a work, whether it be a film or a playtext. A useful case in point is the bleached-and-black "Goth" look Taymor gives to Tamora's sons. Their leather and video games may seem as gratuitous as any design choice in the film. Yet the use of "Goth" to mark a subculture (in this case young, crude, and violent) calls attention to a Renaissance stereotype, the barbaric northerner, that is crucial to Shakespeare's play. In marking this stereotype, Taymor foregrounds ethnic divisions that might otherwise be invisible to modern audiences, who are more likely to register skin-color (in this case Moor vs European) as the primary sign of difference that matters, and to see the blond, northern Goths and dark-haired, southern Romans as uniformly "white." The extent to which *Titus* responds in this way to the inter-ethnic and anachronistic conjunctions of Moors, Goths, and Romans in Shakespeare's play reminds us, in turn, that we have not exited the circuit of ethnic rivalries, religious conflicts, and imperial anxieties that beset both his and our own contemporary political scene.

This political, or more strictly speaking, humanistic unconscious of *Titus* rises most obviously to the surface in its closing shots, when the walls that appear to enclose Titus's climactic bloody banquet suddenly dissolve and the dinner table is resituated in an unusually well-preserved provincial Roman coliseum in Croatia. The closing actions proceed before a silent audience of latter-day Croatians whose witnessing of this primal event constitutes an act of surrogation, "an ambivalent replaying" (Roach 1996: 2–3) of fraternal and tribal slaughters in the Balkans, which effectively bridges the distance between the year one and late 1998 when this scene was shot. It is here that Taymor stages her last, and for some, most questionable interpolation, having young Lucius (Osheen Jones) rescue Tamora and Aaron's son and carry him outside the walls of the coliseum – and, by extension, outside the bounds of a history that expands and contracts but offers neither relief nor escape from established patterns of mutual predation. That this action takes place as the elder Lucius (Angus Macfadyen) reiterates the play's last lines – an order to "throw [Tamora] forth to beasts and birds of prey" – explains both the utopian aspects of this final interpolation ("utopian" in that it gestures towards an ethos situated outside the bounds of history and any specific political persuasion) and why it might well be preferred to a more professedly "faithful" reiteration of the Shakespearean text.

The use of young Lucius as participant-witness throughout the film's unraveling is the most pronounced and sustained of the many "additions" Taymor makes to the playtext, and the one that has the most obvious ethical, if not quite political, valence. It is also the interpolation that has generated the most hostile reactions, even among avowedly postmodernist critics. It makes sense, therefore, to begin a discussion of Taymor's interpolations by focusing closely on the symbolic spaces through which Lucius moves and the different kinds of "ambivalent replaying" he models for the audience.

Recycling Rome

The Roman coliseum that frames the opening and closing moments of *Titus* is, like the settings of *Titus Andronicus*, a dislocated memory of Rome, weathered by different periods and uses. Indeed, the Romans of *Titus Andronicus* are not historically specific but composites blended and collided from different classical sources – Seneca, Ovid, Virgil – and different periods of Roman history.[10] Because our idea of "Rome" now regularly incorporates these many fragments of time and space (Rome as orgy, military power, and empire; Rome as both forum for civilized political debate and arena for barbaric entertainment) we may miss the explicit inventedness of this Shakespearean setting. Rome is not so much a specific location or city but an environment, a memory, and a set of texts for recycling.

Taymor's more dramatically sustained interpolations reiterate the playtext's indeterminate fracturing of time and space in a way that lets us see Rome in this way, as always relocated, translated, and reinvented. As we have observed in chapter 2, all works exist as multiple reiterations, enacted in new environments; each reiteration remakes and replaces the prior text in the series that constitutes the "work" (Grigely 1995: 99). Taymor's reiteration of Shakespeare's composite Rome foregrounds the essential ambivalences in this process by which classic texts are continually "unmade (as an object) and remade (as a text and as memory)" (Grigely 1995: 33). Taymor's particular interest involves the tensions internal to this process of surrogation, the way in which each performance aspires "both to embody and to replace" the text it performs (Roach 1996: 3). The coliseum in which the "real" action of the play begins evokes these different possibilities of performance: sometimes utopian, sometimes comic or farcical, and sometimes tragic in the ways they appropriate the authority of Rome. As Donaldson observes, this open-air enclosure evokes among other things: gladiatorial combat; Greek theater; the Globe theater; a World Wrestling Federation wrestling ring; European experimental theater dedicated to collapsing the "fourth wall;" "the many stadiums that have been used as sites for political detention, interrogation and execution in the last decades;" and "such simulated environments as historical video games or forms of interactive virtual cinema" (2006: 457).

The transitional figure with whom we move between these various surrogates of Rome, who is the focus of both uncanny and subversive reiteration, is the young Lucius. Taymor deploys Lucius in a manner that recalls Derek Jarman's use of the young Edward, the future Edward III, in his 1991 film-version of Marlowe's *Edward II*, a work to which Taymor's film seems deeply, if silently, indebted. As in the Jarman film, the Boy (in the persona of young Lucius) quietly shadows the actions and activities of the film's protagonists. Serving variously as companion, witness, interrogator, and mirror, he reflects the twists and turns of their fortunes, and the swings of their moods and attitudes. Taymor often positions young Lucius in purely visual patches of unscripted scenes where he functions less to advance the plot than to provide a reflection on it. In this he resembles Jarman's young Edward, who wanders outside the castle walls at night to silently witness a circle of naked men engaging in what looks like a rugby scrum. Also, like young Edward, young Lucius emerges at other times as an antidote or hybridized alternative to the manically vengeful energies that destroy both his family and their opponents. In a remarkably suggestive moment, for example, young Lucius enters a workshop that would appear to specialize in the manufacture of artfully contrived wooden prostheses, and returns with a pair of wooden hands that he gives to Lavinia (Laura Fraser). (Taymor assembled these props from a warehouse where dismantled carvings of saints and other figures employed in Neapolitan nativity scenes are stored between seasonal displays.) While the scene does little to advance the plot, it conveys young Lucius's active sympathy for his disabled cousin, which we will later see

4.2 Munch's "The Scream"; the Boy's silent scream

extended to Aaron's child, and an effort to compensate her for the lost "effects" of her hands. At the same time it provides an unsettling insight into how thriving an enterprise a prosthetics workshop might prove in a world so abundant in acts of arbitrary terror and mutilation.[11]

The composite figure of the Boy/Young Lucius is perhaps most striking for the way in which he crosses between fictional spaces, both deliberately and by acts of imagination. Those imaginative acts are not initially presented as restorative. In the dramatically unscripted "induction" to the film proper, we find the Boy playing with wild and destructive abandon in a kitchen filled with all manner of toy soldiers and model weaponry. His headgear, a paper bag "helmet," suggests his childish emulation of the "real" soldiers into whose orbit he will soon tumble. The helmet is also a mask, possibly an allusion to the child serial killer in John Carpenter's *Halloween* (1978; Donaldson 2006). Yet in Taymor's characteristic style none of these allusions remains stable. The helmeted figure quickly transforms from an agent of terror into an emblem of terror as the child presses his hands to his ears and the paper face crumples – a reference to Edvard Munch's "The Scream" (1893).

In the context of the film's ending, the Boy's abduction into the frighteningly "real" war-torn world of *Titus* to the ghostly applause of invisible spectators implies some broadly ethical plan that will effect a marked change in young Lucius himself – who, as he walks forth out of the film's frame, surely can no longer think innocently (or playfully) about man's inhumanity to man. Taymor observes that "the journey of the young boy from childhood innocence to passive witness and finally to knowledge, wisdom, compassion, and choice" operates as the film's "counterpoint to Shakespeare's dark tale of vengeance" (Taymor 2000: 185). Indeed, young Lucius functions as the virtual "eyes" of the film, and becomes the medium through which we ourselves witness, and may also decide to exit from, what the film constructs as history.[12] Taymor clearly conceives this final interpolation as a way of re-purposing what is otherwise resistant and unredeemable in Shakespeare's play – its apparent commitment to an honor culture that can see no response to injury but violence. Young Lucius's view of a way out must be clearer than ours, however,

since the camera follows his exit at a distance, zooming in with an excru-
ciating slowness that never quite catches up with him.

Yet any tidy narrative about the child's (and viewer's) maturation is
complicated by the way in which the induction reminds us that play (in
every sense of the word) is a kind of practice, rehearsal, imitation, and
preparation – an essential learning process for all human behaviors,
including violent ones. Initially, this child's "innocence" is also a state of
profoundly uncontrolled (perhaps traumatic?) mimesis of the TV that
illuminates this first scene and the violence that erupts from outside
into it. Taymor's setting of this scene in a generic 1950s-era kitchen,
where the Boy plays with "real" as opposed to "virtual" toy soldiers,
pointedly functions as another way of framing an alleged "age" of innocence as also one of violent rehearsal. It even suggests that young
Lucius's violent play may have generated the martial parade of the clay
soldiers in which he is now enveloped. As Donaldson observes, the
Boy's abduction into the performance space of the amphitheater,
where he is held aloft by his captor/rescuer like a trophy, underscores
his vulnerability to the violent entertainments in which he participates
– he is made vulnerable, here, in a way that resembles emerging forms
of "viewer decision" (2006: 461–2).

▓ Interpolation as Balancing Act ▓▓▓▓

This first interpolation alerts us that Taymor's additions will not only
fulfill the playtext by presenting what is unpresentable there; they will
offer a counter-narrative, and even critique, of destructively hierarchical and martial perspectives that the play (as an unusually lurid avatar
of Senecan revenge tragedy) fails to challenge. Indeed, another way of
conceptualizing the politics of Taymor's interpolations is to see them as
an attempt to bring a kind of clarifying balance to her representation of
the film's competing atrocities (as well as to the play's privileging of
Titus's patriarchal hold on our sympathies). Taymor's film clearly sides
with Titus's family in its struggle against Tamora and Saturninus, and
makes Titus appear (like Lear) a man more sinned against than sinning.
But it also attempts to balance the ledger of mutual recrimination and
vindictiveness. For example, in the first of what Taymor calls her "penny
arcade nightmares" (hereafter PANs), which function as both interpolations and extrapolations from the playtext, Taymor has Titus (Anthony
Hopkins) and Tamora (Jessica Lange) square off at the foot of the palace
stairs in a rigidly blocked face-off, while between and behind them fiery
images of the limbs and torso of Tamora's sacrificed son, Alarbus, shift
and blend into each other in a powerfully surreal manner.

This first PAN employs Alarbus's dismembered body mainly in the
interests of illustration, making it a bridge across which Titus and
Tamora will engage in a struggle-to-the-death. Later, however, a second
PAN appears to emanate from Titus's own guilty conscience, portray-
ing as it does "Titus's youngest son [Mutius] whom he himself rashly and

wrongly murdered . . . in the form of a sacrificial lamb, evoking the story of Abraham and Isaac" (Taymor 2000: 184). Here in particular we witness a more even-handed approach to the revenge motive than Shakespeare seems to be aiming at in the playtext, as Taymor extrapolates from Shakespeare's own silence on the subject ("the narrative," Taymor notes, "never brings up the event of Mutius' death once it is done") to claim for Titus a nagging "inner torment and guilt" that he does not appear to feel in Shakespeare's play (Taymor 2000: 1984; Burt 2002a: 310).

These PANs might appear to be flashbacks. Yet as David McCandless observes, "the ornate, static staginess of these images renders them implausible as post-traumatic flashbacks" (2002: 501). Clearly, they require another kind of classification, one that respects the terminology Taymor herself uses to describe them but that also references their arti-factual or manufactured quality. "Penny arcade" evokes the carniva-lesque atmosphere of a fair or beachside entertainment zone given over to casual meandering among games of chance, fortune tellers, tattoo parlors, and overstuffed displays of cheap prizes and merchandise. Yet Taymor's PANs also traffic in nightmare content and in icons drawn from the visual archives of high art and religion. Indeed, we consider them a visually overdetermined form of editorial intervention, a kind of expressionist collage that delivers a surplus of meaning. Although these PANs fasten on and replay recently staged events, they do so in a rad-ically displaced manner: scrambling the "post-traumatic" imagery presumably stored in the psyches of the remembering subjects and surrogating it to a series of iconographic metamorphoses beyond the capacity of these characters to generate on their own. The PANs reorganize the space of the screen into the cinematic equivalent of what Taymor calls an "ideograph." The term names the way visual artists add motion and "life" (in this case, images of bleeding, breathing, crying) to a symbolic collection of body parts and objects, arranging them so as to express an idea (Schechner 1999: 38). The PANs also resemble Renaissance emblems, a multimedia art-form composed of visual alle-gories, Latin mottoes, and English verse glosses. The meaning of an emblem comes from the interaction between its verbal and visual elements; their textual glosses tend to be highly meta-critical, making arguments about how this interaction should be interpreted. Taymor's PANs work in a similarly multi-mediated format that often includes text (e.g., the motto "Mutius" in figure 4.3) and they are equally meta-critical in their emphasis on the damage wrought by the conversion of persons into things – dead bodies, symbols, objects for the use of others.

Both spatially and temporally situated outside the "lived" dramatic reality of the characters, the PANs impinge less on *their* consciousness than they do on *ours*. They thus allow us to speculate freely on the rage Tamora feels but does not clearly show, and on the grief Titus shows but does not necessarily feel. In this respect, these two PANs answer difficulties scholars and students have regularly had with the play. Virtually every action the rigidly authoritarian Titus undertakes in the

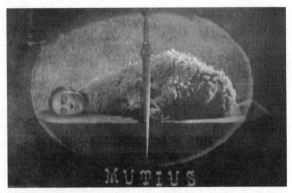

4.3 Renaissance emblem: Ixion's wheel; emblematic PAN

first movement seems obviously wrongheaded: electing Saturninus as Rome's emperor; allowing Saturninus to choose Lavinia for his wife; sacrificing Alarbus in the face of Tamora's passionate plea for mercy; executing his own son. Yet although voices in the text (in addition to Tamora's, those of the elder Lucius and Bassianus) identify these actions as errors, Shakespeare does not give Tamora's motive for revenge the same legitimacy with which he later invests Titus's claim. Taymor does. Moreover, she makes Titus's rejection of Tamora's plea seem so dismissively patronizing and coldly self-righteous that Tamora's answering indignation and contempt become far more humanly comprehensible than Titus's pietistically inflexible observance.[13] In this context, the rite of blood sacrifice, performed by the elder Lucius under Titus's supervision, seems like the ritualized exercise of a death-cult wedded to patriarchal authority. And though, like Shakespeare, Taymor soon positions her audience squarely on Titus's side, she never entirely lets us forget that both camps are, in their way, equally barbarous – equally fixated on the pursuit of agendas that, like the late civil wars and ethnic cleansings in the Balkans, admit to no constructively human or humane justification.

If the play *Titus Andronicus* provides no exit from the history of mutual predation, it does provide a fertile site for staging scenes of shocking cruelty and traumatic purgation, thereby offering the skilled postmodern practitioner a host of opportunities to display what we would all like to be saved from. On this account, Taymor has been roundly criticized for doing what she, as an unusually gifted manufacturer of stage-imagery, does better than virtually anyone else now at work in theater and film: that is, offer richly re-imagined representations of the already horrific subject matter lying in wait in the Shakespearean playtext. Much of this criticism has focused on her casting of Anthony Hopkins as Titus, a choice she allegedly made to exploit Hopkins's notoriety for his performance in the role of Hannibal Lecter in *Silence of the Lambs* (1993). As Richard Burt has argued:

> Because most audiences read backward from film to Shakespeare, Taymor's casting of Anthony Hopkins, given that Titus serves human

flesh at his banquet, will inevitably call to the minds of many review-
ers and other audiences the serial-killer cannibal, Hannibal Lecter.
The connection between Titus and Lecter is underlined by Hopkins'
quotation of his role in *Silence of the Lambs* when he sucks in his spit
before slitting Chiron and Demetrius's throats. (Burt, 2002a: 308)

Privileging the immediacy of pop-cultural allusiveness over other forms
of information, Burt renders most additional references to Titus in the
composite format, "Lecter/Titus" (Burt 2002a: 309), as if the two film
personae were effectively one. For Burt, the troubling effect of this over-
lay of popular reference with the network of allusions to Fascist Italy is
that it renders an alleged "anti-fascist as serial killer" (Burt 2002a:
305–10). Allusive structures are of course unstable in precisely this way.
Yet the memory of Hopkins-as-Lecter that superimposes itself on
Hopkins-as-Titus, an effect called "ghosting," needs to be read alongside
other performance echoes as well.[14] Some viewers may recall the
"ghosts" of Hopkins's other theatrical and filmic performances, such as
that of the diffident, life-denying butler in James Ivory's *The Remains of
the Day* (1993). The skill, authority, and *gravitas* an accomplished actor
like Hopkins brings to bear on the role of Titus, not to mention his
capacity to disappear into it at will, are equally powerful forms of information. The troubling effects of ghosting cannot be ignored. But they
operate within the context of a set of interpolations that, as we have
observed, systematically aim to balance the ledger of mutual transgres-
sion. As the character who publicly authorizes Saturninus's authoritarian rule, and presides over a death-cult devoted equally to honor and
patriarchal authority, Titus can hardly be said to be "anti-Fascist" in the
first place. And the film does not allow us to see his successive murders
as anything but a series of morally suspect solutions to conflict. For
Taymor, the key question seems to be whether there is any possibility for
resistance that is not also one of complicity. Donaldson's conclusion
that the film acknowledges a necessary complicity between its own
artistic resources and the cycle of violence is close to our understanding
of this problem. Taymor exposes this potential for complicity with terror
in the sequence from 3.1 that starts with Aaron's brilliantly improvisational request for Titus's hand and that ends with the delivery of his two
sons' heads, interpolated as a "real life" PAN.

Heads and Hands

This sequence begins when Aaron accosts Marcus, Titus, and Lucius as
they are returning home in the rain with the ravished and mutilated
Lavinia. (The umbrella that Aaron carries functions here as a cruel
contrast to the Andronici's naked exposure – to the elements and arbitrary violence alike.) The scene soon fastens on the darkly comedic
competition of Titus, Lucius, and Marcus (Colm Feore) over whose
hand will be cut, and the oddly conspiratorial interplay between Aaron
and Titus as Titus beats the others to the punch and Aaron drops the

4.4 Tableau of two heads and hand

"lopp'd" hand into a plastic baggy which he hangs on the mirror of his Maserati as he drives away. The brief, moving encounter between Titus and Lavinia that ensues, which functions like a bridge from one inconsolable injury to another, is followed by an interpolated Felliniesque scene in which the Clown (Dario Ambrosi) and his young, red-haired girl-assistant drive a motorcycle van into Titus's yard.[15] The two set out camp-stools for what looks to be an impromptu theatrical performance, and then, with an alacrity entirely at odds with the reluctant speech spoken by a compassionate messenger in the playtext, "discover" the heads of Titus's sons. These look eerily out from two large "specimen jars," while Titus's severed hand sits pillowed between them on a black velvet cushion like a rarefied piece of anatomical sculpture. (We wonder here about the effects on the infinitely suggestible Taymor of the recent British art-world vogue for the stylized representation of human and animal body parts.) The film lingers very briefly over this tableau, the composition managing to present both the bottled heads and pillowed hand and the stunned witnessing of the Andronici in one abruptly becalmed frame.

Apart from the highly stylized nature of this scene – which Taymor identifies as the first of her PANs that operates on the level of "stark reality" (2000: 184) – several significant substitutions, cuts, and additions are notable here. Taymor substitutes the rough-edged Clown for the play's compassionate Messenger; she cuts three of the latter's most sympathetic lines ("Thy grief their sports! thy resolution mock'd!/That woe is me to think upon thy woes/More than remembrance of my father's death" (3.1.238–40)); and she adds three harshly barked lines of Latin to the Clown's speech which few auditors would be able to decipher as speech, much less understand.[16] (They read in translation as "The aim of the law is to correct those it punishes, or make others better through the example of the sentence it inflicts, or else to remove evil so that the others can live more peacefully" (Taymor 2000: 107).)

These interpolations transform what may pass in the playtext as an inexplicable bout of arbitrary cruelty into an exercise of cleverly choreographed terror. Even the surviving residue of compassion in the lines Taymor retains from the Messenger's cropped speech is flattened: "Worthy Andronicus, ill art thou repaid/For that good hand thou sent'st the emperor./Here are the heads of thy two noble sons./And here's thy hand, in scorn to thee sent back" (3.1.234–7). The Clown delivers these lines in a detached Brechtian manner as if he is quoting something he, himself, has no stake in. (Characterization is similarly discontinuous here: the role of the Clown is assumed by the figure who "rescues" young Lucius from his exploding kitchen in the film's opening shot, while his young assistant is played by the girl who appears as the trumpet-blowing angel of mercy in the second PAN.) Such slippages or disconnects indicate that the same appropriative drive that animates Taymor's interpolations informs her rendering of the playtext. In this case, for example, the Clown's flat line-reading pointedly unsettles the relationship between what the words say and how they mean. The sympathy that the excised messenger felt for Titus is, as it were, put into quotation marks. It is cited (or re-cited) but not really stated or delivered. It haunts but no longer inhabits its scene of inscription.

In the aftershock of the Clown's horrific delivery, the film jarringly resumes dialogue directly drawn from the playtext, which makes no provision for so sustained or stylized a presentation of the heads of Titus's sons. A revealing consequence of this transition is how slow and stodgy the dramatic interactions of Titus's family seem, so out of keeping with the pace, panache, and black humor of the interpolated material. This is one of several moments in Taymor's film that highlight the virtues and limitations of different representational practices as the multi-layered cross-cuttings of cinema and the more measured, single-framed focus of theater "collide" with one another. The sequence that begins with Aaron's entrance is remarkably fast paced. It starts with Aaron's arrival being glimpsed from an upstairs window of Titus's house by the ubiquitous young Lucius, functioning both as "our eyes" and as the object of our (and Aaron's) gaze. The action speeds up as Titus trustingly responds to Aaron's misleading offer of mercy, with the camera making quick cuts between the wrangling Titus, Marcus, and Lucius before leading us forward into Titus's kitchen. There the beautifully composed, hanging bodies of fowl complement Titus's laying of his hand on the chopping block as Aaron chooses between a pair of poultry scissors and a meat cleaver in playfully silent collaboration with Titus. The frenetically distorted mix of Elliot Goldenthal's jazzy carnival music attends Aaron's quick-paced departure, executed in a face-on tracking shot as Aaron speaks directly into the camera on his return to his Maserati. The same music accompanies the Clown's arrival, evoking a carnivalesque mood that suddenly dissolves upon the display of the severed heads and hand, then devolves to a drama that seems to have no more than a second serving of lamentation to speak for it. The somber mood results not just from the tragic turn of circumstance, but from the cessation of the frenetically comedic camera-work and editing sustained through the hand-cutting scene. Indeed, it might be said that until or unless Titus and his family themselves begin to generate the kind of manic energy and resourcefulness exercised by Aaron and the Clown in these scenes, they will remain victims of their attachment to older, primarily rhetorical modes of expression and representation.

This embrace of the surreal, improvisational, and absurd begins apace when Titus responds to Marcus's mournful speech by laughing, and then calmly supervises his family's collection of the bottled heads and pedestaled hand, ordering Lavinia to "Bear thou my hand, sweet wench, between thy teeth" (3.1.265, 282). Lavinia's effort here both highlights her own and Titus's loss of "effect" and agency, and signals the beginning of their resurgence. Importantly, that transition begins in their manipulation of the symbols that dominate Roman politics in the play: the heads and hands that figure martial and political authority. When Lavinia carries Titus's hand offstage, and later when she writes with a stick, she redefines her mouth as a grasping part in a way that complicates its earlier identification with the passive bubbling fountain of the scene of her rape. Taking up the severed hand as a supplement to her lost tongue, Lavinia begins to convert herself from a figure of dismemberment into a figure of agency (Rowe 1999: 78). Taymor seems to confirm this sense of gathering agency in the ensuing interpolation where Lucius, motivated by sympathy for Lavinia's plight, retrieves the pair of wooden hands to serve as prostheses for his aunt. While these hands do nothing practical for Lavinia, her donning of them prepares us for the empowerment Lavinia and the other Andronici will feel once the identities of her ravishers are made known and Titus begins (however uncertainly) to make motions towards revenge.

The question of Lavinia's and Titus's renewed agency is sufficiently crucial to Taymor's re-apportionment of the play's dramatic energy to deserve closer scrutiny. The first consequence visited on the Andronici by the violence of Tamora's sons and the villainous manipulations of Aaron is a disabling passivity that employs rhetoric as its preferred mode of expression. We hear this especially in Marcus's overextended "discovery" speech in 2.3, bearing witness to the ravished Lavinia, but also in the moving but ineffectual speech Titus delivers as much to himself as to the Roman senators in what Taymor presents as her "Crossroads" scene (the first half of 3.1 in the playtext). Rhetoric is, of course, the primary dramatic and expressive medium of Shakespeare's play. Marcus and Titus "unpack [their hearts] with words" because that is all they can do under the circumstances. What they require to move to the level of action are scenes of suffering so intense that words formally ordered into elaborate rhetorical displays will no longer serve: or, as Taymor would have it, scenes that bring the shock of disordered perceptions into the orbit of "lived" dramatic experience. Such scenes, provided by Taymor's third and fourth PANs, free the Andronici from the closed circuit of lamentation and resituate them in a dramatic mode more consistent with the playfully ironic, manically purposive, and intensely sardonic style that has heretofore been the stock-in-trade of Aaron. In the process, the improvisational authority that has solely been Aaron's to command (on the basis of his dramatic energy, cunning, and imagin-ation) slowly migrates into the compass of the Andronici themselves.

Recall that Taymor categorizes the scene begun by the arrival of the Clown and his assistant as another of her five penny arcade nightmares, but distinguishes this one from all but the last on the basis of its "stark reality." As Taymor observes:

> Unlike the other P.A.N.s, which were abstract or symbolic representa-
> tions of an event or psychic state, this P.A.N. is actually happening.
> This "still life" P.A.N. signals the turn in the play where the nightmares
> are now reality and madness can be confused with sanity. Order has
> been replaced with chaos and the road to justice is paved with
> revenge. (Taymor 2000: 185)

Although we are at this point still quite far from the moment when Titus will take effectual action against his enemies, Taymor's interpolation turns what seems in the playtext an entirely arbitrary exercise of cruelty on Aaron's part into something much more purposeful and premedi-tated. However, instead of driving Titus into a deeper state of despair, this nightmare display has the effect of reorienting his response to his enemies. Marcus responds to the display of heads and hand in much the way he responds to the display of the mutilated Lavinia; he calls for Titus to "die," to "rend" off his hair, to "gnaw" his other hand, and "to storm," that is, to display his grief in all the prescribed manners of histrionic expression (Roach 1993). But Titus, in what Jonathan Bate terms "the play's pivotal indecorum," *laughs* and then turns the occa-sion of their grief into an opportunity to re-order and reconstitute the dismembered family (Bate 2000: 204 n. 265). He first stares into the faces of "these two heads [which] do seem to speak to me" and charge him with the imperative to revenge. Then he has his remaining family members "circle [him] about," as he places "his palm on either the head or heart of each one of them" (Taymor 2000: 109). Finally, he allots to each duties that range from Lavinia taking his hand in her mouth to Lucius raising an army of the Goths against Saturninus.

The ritualized nature of this scene echoes with crucial differences the earlier scene at the family mausoleum, as we watch the remaining Andronici gather together dismembered parts of their familial body as a first stage towards reinventing their relationship both to themselves and to the Roman state. Though much that they do or say from this point forward will remain ineffectual, and virtually all that Titus does will generate the pity and skepticism of the more rational Marcus, a corner has been turned in Taymor's representation of their plight that will fill them with some of the same anarchic energy and force hereto-fore invested primarily in Aaron and, to a lesser extent, in Tamora and her sons.

▨ Ovidian Cinema ▨

The fourth of Taymor's PANs, in which Lavinia writes the names of her attackers in the sand with a stick, is perhaps the film's most powerful and ambiguous interpolation. It is also the one that most explicitly addresses the complicity of art with violence – an insight delivered by the intertext that has exerted enormous influence on Taymor's work throughout her career, that is, Ovid's tales of serial violence in the service of power, *The Metamorphoses*. This long, narrative poem relates more than two hundred classical myths, stories of various humans bodily transformed by the gods. The theme of these stories is the inevitability of entropy or change, for both individuals and civilizations (Troy, Rome), but Ovid leaves it to the reader to interpret the consequences, opportunities, and costs of transformation. As in the playtext, this influential classical text appears in the film as a source, a prop, a key to the action (Titus and Marcus draw on several Ovidian stories to decode Lavinia's signs), and an occasion for improvisation. *The Metamorphoses* was to Renaissance writers what Shakespeare's play is to Taymor, a "universe of knowledge" collected in one place (James 2003: 346). Sensational, violent, and sometimes erotic, the poem was also understood by commentators, translators, and imitators as a profoundly political work – though there was hardly a consensus about the morals this fluid, ambiguous narrative might be seen to endorse (James 2003). Like Taymor's film, Ovid's poem was notorious for being sensually and aesthetically powerful but morally undefinable, so complexly allusive as to be irreducible to a single, coherent moral or message.

Allusions to a number of Ovid's tales abound in *Titus Andronicus*, sometimes as passing references but more often in the ways characters explain and justify their experiences. Tereus's brutal rape and silencing of Philomel, and the terrible culinary revenge exacted by his wife, Philomel's sister, Procne, is source and referent for one of the primary plots of this play. The Andronici men regularly draw this connection to explain what has happened to Lavinia ("sure, some Tereus hath deflow'red thee," 2.4.26). Yet the Ovidian story that may matter more to Taymor is the story of Daphne. A quick summary is helpful for understanding its full resonance for the film and the way it organizes this PAN in particular. Pursued by a rapacious Apollo (the patron god of art and letters), the reluctant Daphne flees to her father, the river god Peneus, who to protect her transforms her into a laurel tree. Catching her just before the transformation is complete – her hair and hands turned to branches, while her heart still "panted in th' unfinish'd part" – Apollo vows he will have her, if not as his love then as his emblem, a trophy of sorts.[17] Breaking off a branch, he makes himself a laurel crown and announces it will henceforth become the symbol of triumph, in war and in the arts. For conservative Renaissance commentators, as Heather James explains, Daphne's transformation was regularly interpreted as a reward; she "reposes in her laurel form, welcoming the honor granted to

4.5 Lavinia
as Daphne

her for revering virginity" (2003: 348). For writers such as Shakespeare, however, the ambivalent, uncomfortably erotic and resistant aspects of her story become an occasion for subversive accounts of the silencing of creative voice, particularly female voice. Daphne's physical distress even at the moment of transformation serves as a reminder of the objectifying violence of art as it makes persons into symbols, whether in the service of pleasure or political power (Enterline 1997). For a highly stylized artist of symbols, such as Taymor, Daphne's story encodes the ever-present dangers of complicity with this objectification.

Taymor introduces the Daphne motif obliquely, with the sound of Alarbus's panting torso in the first PAN. The torso is a metamorphic figure: half-transformed by mutilation into a sign and precedent for Tamora's revenge, resembling the iconic torsos of classical sculpture. The agitated gasps on the soundtrack insist on its humanity and testify to individual pain – underscoring its confused status as both object and subject and emphasizing the cost of this metamorphosis. The Daphne motif becomes shockingly explicit when we first see Lavinia after her rape. Shot mostly from below, she is posed on a stump (a visual pun for the laurel and for dismemberment), at the marshy edge of a river. The black twigs are artfully bound to her bloody wrists and her straggles of black hair echo the pleading shapes of dead branches around her (figure 4.5).

The wooden hands that young Lucius later provides develop this motif. Donaldson notes that Lucius picks them up in a "rhyming shot" that suggests the compensatory power of art to "answer" his earlier violent handling of the action figures (2006). Yet that shot also rhymes with Lavinia's own, helpless gestures as she rotates first her twigged stumps (in the post-rape scene) and later the hands themselves (called, in the DVD title, "Prosthetic Branches"). Because these prostheses seem to have been carved as the hands of saints, and because they serve to express *Titus*'s meanings as much or more than her own, they remain ambiguous interpolations: part compensatory tools, part reminder of Lavinia's conversion into a figure or sign, a symbol of martyred innocence and "pattern, president, and lively warrant" of the moral authority of the Andronici (5.3.44).

4.6 Doe-girl and Tiger-boys

Taymor's fourth PAN elaborates these ideas and connects the Daphne motif indexically with a number of other, ambiguous, visual allusions. In "Lavinia's Sorrows Printed Plain" we watch as (in Taymor's words) "a bolt of electric shock seems to run through [Lavinia's] body" which prompts the intercutting of her "ferocious writing in the sand" with "a bombardment of surreal images of her rape and dismemberment" (Taymor 2000: 117). These images reproduce the scene of her ravishment in broadly symbolic terms; Lavinia is figured as an innocent "doe-girl" (visually fulfilling the metaphors of hunting and pursuit that mark her plot-line in the playtext) trying to ward off the rabid attack of "tiger-boys" Chiron (Jonathan Rhys Meyers) and Demetrius (Matthew Rhys) (figure 4.6).

4.7 Little Dancer and Marilyn Monroe

The three figures are arranged in the familiar triptych structure that characterizes most of the PANs: with aggressors posed opposite each other on the sides and the pleading figure of their victim posed vulnerably on a pedestal in the center. Screen overlays of dead branches in the background reprise the tree puns from the post-rape scene and anchor this PAN in the moment of Lavinia's writing, where intercut shots from below frame her head against a tree-filled sky. The triptych layout of the PAN makes more sense in this Ovidian context. We can see it as a two-dimensional version of the first-person, surround space grammar Taymor adapts from virtual story spaces.[18] The figure at the center thus serves as the crossroads of different allusive readings, alternate paths of interaction viewers follow as they make meaning from a discursively unstable collage of images. We might also see the triptych structure as a triumphal one, composed of arcs (the leaping tigers) and columns (the statue-like centerpieces; the huge, mask-like flanking faces).

These overlays and the digital collage that gives Lavinia hooves provide a powerful cinematic correlative for the terrible metamorphoses that beset Ovid's famous characters. We see Lavinia through the branches of her transformation both as a symbolic figure and as a character undergoing a powerful internal experience. For Shakespeare's characters, Ovid's stories organize ways of thinking, planning, and experiencing the world. So it is plausible here to see this iconography as belonging at least in part to the inner life of Lavinia-the-character, as the DVD chapter title "Lavinia's Sorrows" implies: these are the received materials of culture that she thinks with and recycles as she writes her experience. As Taymor remarks, "I devised the concept of the 'Penny Arcade Nightmares' to portray the inner landscapes of the mind as affected by the external actions. . . . They depict, in abstract collages, fragments of memory, the unfathomable layers of a violent event, the metamorphic flux of the human, animal, and the divine" (2000: 183).

Yet, as with the Alarbus PAN, the iconography of this nightmare is clearly also external to character, meant not to unfold her inner life but to call attention to the way in which Western culture destructively recycles the Daphne/Lavinia story. Thus the PAN surrogates Daphne – seeks satisfactory modern stand-ins for her – with a culturally promiscuous set of modern allusions. The figure of Lavinia sculpturally displayed on a columned pedestal alludes to Degas's "Little Dancer, Aged Fourteen" (1880–1). That statue's "physiognomy, oddly tilted up and thrust forward" in a manner that could well "express a sense of strain or suffering, reflecting her effort to maintain an awkward posture," was disapprovingly construed by Degas's public as a form of preening, which "mingled with it a vaguely sensual yearning, especially in the half-closed eyes" (Czestochowski and Pingeot 2002: 51–2).[19] Lavinia's pose also quotes, in a decidedly more anxious and ambiguous fashion, the erotic abandon of Marilyn Monroe allowing a draft of air to puff up her summery dress in *The Seven-Year Itch* (1955) (Lehmann 2002a: 274–75; Burt 2002a: 315).

These allusions prompt troubling questions regarding what exactly Taymor wants us to draw from such iconically crossed references. Are we supposed to be turned on or turned off by the fact that what alluringly lifts Lavinia's skirts is radically unlike the desired draft of air in which Monroe's skirt bellows? And which Monroe, of the many idealized figures of twentieth-century American femininity, is being evoked? After all, Monroe is another compound cultural icon, like Lavinia, whose story recombines not only Daphne, nor only Philomel, Lucrece, and other Ovidian objects of desire, but all these figures at once and none of them exactly.[20] Surrogates always fall short of or exceed the figures they replace, generating such troubling mismatches. But in doing so they also keep alive the network of cultural meanings and relations that attach to their avatars. The perverse eroticism evoked by the Monroe and Degas dancer allusions evoke the essential cultural dynamics of Daphne's story: the destructive, symbolic conversion of the female body in the service of erotic pleasure, artistic triumph, commercial success, masculine control, or political authority. As with the Daphne story, the silent agitation of the female figure placed at the center of this story, transformed into a work of art (as her position on the fluted pedestal implies), insists on the cost of silenced voices (especially female voices). It is important to remember here that we do not learn about "Lavinia's sorrows" from these images. "Printed plain" on the sandy ground are only two names, Chiron and Demetrius; Lavinia's experience remains inaccessible, a blank space onto which the Andronici, Taymor, and we inscribe our own meanings, in variously tragic, triumphal, and subversive ways.

That this inscription of meaning is an objectifying and ultimately violent process is Ovid's theme and also Taymor's. It clarifies the brilliant necessity of Degas's ballerina and Monroe as surrogates. The substitution of pedestal for stump is the final transformation in a series that begins with a living figure and ends in a monument. For Taymor's purposes it does not matter if anyone remembers that the discomfort generated by this confluence of ideas was once invested in Ovid's Daphne. It is sufficient if we feel the discomfort enough to begin to reflect critically on our own processes of reception and recognize the violence of objectification not as an ancient barbarism but as a function of the workings of our own culture.

Violent Reversals

The action that generates or is co-generative with this nightmare – that is, Lavinia's resolute embrace of the stick that enables her writing in the sand – is considerably less ambiguous than the Ovidian visuals, at least at first. The "ferocious" nature of Lavinia's writing serves as an incommensurate but effectual answer to the ferocious attack on her by Chiron and Demetrius, and underwrites the energy and resolve with which Marcus and Titus engage in yet another ritual vow of revenge, this one aimed against "these traitorous Goths." Lavinia's extra-dramatic reliving of her ravishment and mutilation appears to operate on her with the force of primal therapy, as she transforms the trauma of memory into a cathartic expression of renewed agency. Indeed, the long, angular marks in the sand seem to answer rather than echo the branches in the sky behind her, reconfiguring Daphne's transformation, suggesting that for this moment Lavinia is author and agent as much as object of the story. This scene does not so much replay as recycle Ovid's story of Tereus's rape of Philomela with some crucial variations. As in Shakespeare's play, Marcus models a way of writing using his mouth that supersedes Philomel's visual illustration of the scene of her rape and mutilation in the weaving she fabricates and sends to her sister, Procne. But Taymor's Lavinia innovates further (in a gesture not provided by Shakespeare) when she refuses to take the stick's vividly phallic handle in her mouth, and braces it with her shoulder instead. This triumph of traumatically charged writing over illustration is, in turn, visually "overwritten" by the stunning Ovidian collages Taymor seems to draw out of Lavinia's unconscious, but actually embroiders through the medium of advanced computer technology.

These adaptations of Ovidian intertext prompt the first effort on the part of Titus – successor to and substitute for Ovid's ferocious Procne – to meet terror with terror as he sends young Lucius over to the apartment of Chiron and Demetrius to deliver a bundle of "archaic weapons from the dark ages" laced with an apt quotation from Horace (Taymor 2000: 121). We use the word "terror" to describe this action because however ineffectual the gesture may seem, it marks the first time that Titus becomes master of the kind of activated dramatic irony that has heretofore been exclusively Aaron's medium of manipulation and control. The term also suits the panicked response Titus's second exercise – showering the imperial palace with letters of complaint to the gods – elicits from Saturninus. Taymor choreographs this scene (4.3) with a carnivalesque panache that makes Titus seem more divinely inspired artist than madman as he assembles his followers, moving from house to house, with young Lucius pulling a red Radio Flyer wagon filled with tools and weapons. Although in Shakespeare Titus's extended family participates in his exploits solely to "feed" the "humour" of a "noble uncle thus distract" (4.3.26), Taymor presents the action in a manner that belies the family's misgivings and the pathos that normally attends this scene in production. She emphasizes the pleasure and solidarity the Andronici experience in the act itself, and she provides us with direct access to the immediate effect the shower of arrows has on Saturninus and his decadent court. Thus instead of enduring the comparatively static Clown and pigeons scene that follows the discharge of arrows in the playtext, we watch as the camera follows the arrows' flight into a Felliniesque scene of orgy and banqueting where they descend like a siege of avenging angels.

We soon catch up with the elided playtext in a sequence that again surrogates something new to something textually established, as news of the shower of arrows awakens Saturninus, who has been contentedly sleeping, naked as a baby, on the breast of his wife-mother. At this point, Taymor plays dramatically fast and loose both with the text and with our expectations of "reality" as the night-time arrows that find Saturninus asleep, push him from his bed, into a dressing gown, out to a courtyard brimming with daylight, and then fully dressed into the Senate chamber in a montage of six cleverly edited tracking shots. The abruptness with which Saturninus moves from child-like calm to hysterical abandon is made to appear the direct result of an action that could not seem more ineffectual, but which transforms Titus into the aggressor and Saturninus into prey.

The effectual terror Titus and his cohorts unleash – and go on to burnish considerably as the film unfolds – suggestively resonates with two scenes that flank it which concentrate on Aaron. In the first of these, Aaron removes himself from the contention between the Andronici and Saturninus by dedicating himself to the survival of his newborn child, an act cued by his shocking murder of the nurse who functioned as intermediary between Aaron and Tamora. This act is performed with a suddenness and resolve that recalls, but departs from, Titus's earlier murder of his son Mutius by making Aaron seem a far more purposeful than reactive figure. Taymor elaborates on this contrast by having Aaron, after being taken captive by Lucius, exercise an impressive degree of control over what his captors can do with him. In both scenes we watch Aaron casually exceed the limit of behaviors that seem reasonable, turning his associates and enemies into the same kind of awestruck witnesses that we all eventually become as we witness Titus's own gathering assurance and empowerment.

Although Taymor presents the dialogue of this scene in full fidelity to the text of 5.1, her direction and filming of it forcefully elaborate on the disproportion of line-assignments in the scene: Aaron gets 20 lines for every one line uttered by Lucius. Jonathan Bate's edition of the play has stage-directions that read *A Goth brings a ladder, which Aaron is made to climb* and, later, *to climb down*, but offers no prompts for actions undertaken during Aaron's interrogation. By contrast in *Titus*, Harry Lennix's Aaron pridefully sustains a vicious blow from Lucius for every self-congratulatory claim he makes: "I trained/I wrote/I played." Then he climbs the ladder himself and places the noose around his own neck, before unexpectedly removing it in order to leap down upon the unsuspecting Lucius. In each instance, Taymor cues the crafty aggressor in Aaron to rise against his newly established status as victim and captive; this makes the characteristically aggressive Lucius seem increasingly ineffectual, to the point of implicitly acknowledging Aaron's unconquerable spirit. When we join to this Aaron's earlier (and successful) effort to have Lucius swear, "To save my boy, to nourish and bring him up" (5.1.84), we may well register a more deeply (and darkly) ironic mingling of the roles of villain and victim than the playtext alone would encourage. That mingled role anticipates (and possibly conditions) Titus's own erratic evolution from rigorous militarist to Job-like victim to cold-blooded butcher to "homicidal merry prankster" (McCandless 2002: 492). As the film's momentum shifts in Titus's favor, and he develops an Aaron-like command over his enemies and cinematic resources alike, the certainty that we are about to surfeit on another course of ultra-violence qualifies the pleasure we may also feel as Titus ambles around the banquet table in white chef's attire, to serve up his pasty of crushed bones and blood to Tamora and Saturninus.

Our status as "ethical spectators" is challenged more pointedly in this closing movement than it is at any other moment of the film. Lacking the improvisatory genius supplied by Aaron, Tamora and her sons virtually fall into Titus's lap as he parodically models Jacques-Louis David's iconic painting of "The Death of Marat" (1793) while making childish sketches of his enemies in his bath. The coolness and efficiency with which Titus takes advantage of this opportunity would no doubt garner Aaron's professional approval. It clearly strikes Taymor's artistic fancy as well as she cuts from the phantasmagoric mode of her fifth PAN (which includes allusions to everything from the Statue of Liberty to Blind Justice to *The Rocky Horror Picture Show* (1975)) to an even campier style that evokes David Lynch and the everyday terrors of American suburban life in films such as *Blue Velvet* (1986). As Titus's human meat-pies cool in the breeze, who really chafes at the certainty that a fully earned act of retribution is about to ensue? Our fairly assured complicity in approving Titus's designs is, however, given a rude check by the quietly maniacal manner with which Taymor has Titus break the passive Lavinia's neck, as if she were more wounded sparrow than human being. And the further elisions and interpolations Taymor makes in her filming of the last section of 5.3 make it even harder to sustain an unalloyed regard for Titus, who arguably becomes at this moment more "psycho-killer" than

4.8 Lucius walks out of history

prankster, perhaps even retrospectively clarifying for us the "cruel irre-ligious piety" of his devotion to a death-cult devoted to honor.[21]

Taymor dissociates our sympathies from Titus in these closing scenes in several ways. She cuts close to 30 lines of moving farewells to the dead Titus spoken in the playtext by Marcus, Lucius, and, most crucially, by young Lucius – who, in Shakespeare's text, wishes that he, himself, were dead "so you [that is, Titus] did live again" (5.3.173). She maintains the elder Lucius's closing condemnation of the "beastly" and pitiless Tamora, who by this point seems no more beastly or pitiless than Titus himself. And she gives young Lucius the crucial final direct-ive to take up Aaron's child and carry him away through the once-closed gates of history into what appears to be a new dawn. In this way, Taymor affiliates the offspring of the ravenous Moor and Goth with a character who, in this surrogation of *Titus Andronicus*, has supplanted his grand-father as *our* stand-in, witness, and point of reference.

In his new gentleness, Lucius has discernibly learned things that his father and grandfather could not teach him. Whereas the young Lucius of the playtext promises to do everything in his power to emulate the fallen Titus, the young Lucius of the film's ending prom-ises to differentiate himself from the patriarchal mold of his grandfa-ther and father alike. As noted above, Aaron and Titus have, by this point, become oddly paired sharers in the manic theatrical energy that, in this film, signals agency and command. By contrast, Aaron's child and Titus's grandson are paired at the end in a very different form of agency. That new form of agency involves a determined effort to move outside the frame of the filmic *mise en scène* (composed of long-established artifacts, allusions, patterns of violence) and thus out of what that film has represented as "the last 2000 years of man's inhumanity to man."

Taymor draws our eye to Lucius's movement outside the frame of the film's *mise en scène* in a very deliberate way. Having exhausted all that the playtext can say for itself, she interpolates an ending that takes us on a slow-motion tour of several successive forms of artistic and dramatic framing. In the first still, the camera frames Lucius leaving the coliseum in a "realistic" long shot, as he heads towards one of the arches of the surrounding arcade. His departure, after the last spoken line of the play, is heralded by the counterpoint cries of a baby and the shrieks of birds. These sounds dissolve into the sound of bells, blending into Elliot Goldenthal's elegiac score. In the second still, the realistic structure of the arcade seems to have dropped away or been removed, replaced by a backlit proscenium-arch stage. Although Lucius still seems to be walking on solid ground towards a theatrical sky that recedes beyond him, the rectangular frame contained within the larger film frame also suggests that he may be walking towards, or into, the screen of a movie theater. In the third and fourth stills, Lucius has journeyed so far that this internal theatrical frame has dissolved, as has the illusion of an essentially theatrical backdrop: the horizon seems to stretch beyond the frame on both sides in a full realization of the endlessness and "continual newness" of CinemaScopic space (Cohen 1998: 273). While he seems a tangible, if increasingly "cinematized", presence in the third still, in the fourth the reddish hue of the sunrise seems to seep through him as if the light and landscape are more real than he is. And whereas Lucius's tall figure fills the center of the frame in the third still (a medium shot that literally enlarges him), by the time we arrive at the fourth he seems to have taken several strides beyond our reach, becoming ever more remote, at the point of vanishing into cinematic space. In the last frame, however, the impression of Lucius's dissolution is arrested by the freezing of the entire image, in the manner of a carefully posed photograph.

This artful freeze of the dissolving image of Lucius carrying a second child into a cine-mediated dawn serves as a strong aesthetic and dramatic counter to the violent and frenetically paced way in which we were first introduced to Lucius in the film's induction. Young Lucius remains a figure of transport between fictional worlds, but here he is the agent rather than the object of that movement. This freeze also radically alters the terms of our engagement with a film that throughout seemed wedded to an aesthetic and ethics of uncertain signification. Although the politics of this gesture may no doubt be construed as "soft" and hardly an effectual answer to the horrors that the film puts on display, it operates as the most sustained and sustaining of Taymor's postmodern interpolations, offering an undeniable ethical (and aesthetic) counterpoint to the continuous predation the elder Lucius proclaims at play's end.

▒ The Door in the Sky ▒

Several influential interpreters of Taymor's film take a more skeptical approach to this interpolated ending than the one we offer here. We quote them at length because the issues they raise are compelling and because it is the nature of allusive reading to travel along different associative axes. Indeed, the richer the context in which a film may be approached, the more diverse, even contradictory, the readings evoked. Taymor's tampering with the ending of Shakespeare's play has evoked hostile reaction among even avowedly postmodern critical practitioners. Richard Burt concedes that the "early violence, including the opening scene of the boy playing with his war toys, throws Lucius's later pacifism into bold relief"; but he also observes that in a "schlocky" moment "worthy of a 'Kids Raising Kids' episode of Rikki Lake," young Lucius "walks with the baby out of the arena into a sunrise much as the boy Eliot carried the alien E.T. when they rode together on a bike off into the sky in Spielberg's *E.T.*" (Burt 2002a: 311). David McCandless takes a similarly double-edged stance towards the film's ending. McCandless first observes, "This climactic rejection of violence constitutes the film's final decisive instance of trauma management. In exiting the Colosseum, Young Lucius breaks the cycle of violence that the stage-production portrayed as unbreakable. To the extent that the boy's violent play called the world of violence into being, his absence from it signifies its collapse" (2002: 509). However, McCandless also claims that Young Lucius's walk into a "computer generated sunrise" is a "wish-fulfillment fantasy [that is] uncomfortably comparable to a 'Hollywood Happy Ending'" (2002: 510). What might be seen as a genuine release from trauma for the character appears more ambivalently as an invented, "quasi-therapeutic," even false vision of safety for the audience (2002: 510).[22]

We take seriously such reservations about both the ending and Taymor's explanation of its operation as a "counterpoint to Shakespeare's dark tale of vengeance" (Taymor 2000: 185). Yet we also see Taymor's decision as contextually linked to certain artistic tendencies of the last 15 years or so that complicate any simple opposition of fantasy-wish-fulfillment with realism (particularly in cinema, where the two are impossible to separate, as Burt and McCandless remind us). We offer in conclusion examples from two artists who seek similar alternatives to what we have, *pace* Taymor, identified as "history," or, in her words, as "the last 2000 years of man's inhumanity to man."

One of the most defensible examples of this tendency to seek narrative "ways out" is the alternate, or double, ending that Derek Jarman appends to his 1991 film-version of *Edward II*. In the film's fantasy of escape (and resistance both to Marlowe's play and history alike), Edward's designated executioner, Lightborne, casts his hot poker away and embraces Edward as a lover. Jarman supplies footage of the play's ending as well (having Lightborne drive a hot poker up Edward's anus),

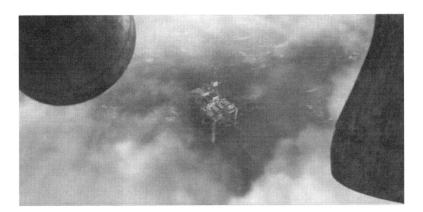

4.9 Von Trier's triptych: Expressionist bells

but intercuts the two in a way that privileges neither – thereby providing his audience with a double perspective. One perspective articulates the past; the other articulates the "best-case" present or, at worst, anticipated future. To a critical reader, Jarman's apparent "decision to delegate Edward's actual execution to the province of nightmare . . . magically elides the very relation between past and present oppressions that he otherwise seeks to document" (Cartelli 1998: 220). Yet Jarman's provision of what is, after all, only a possible ending (and not the most plausible one) also suggests he is "unwilling to allow a too powerful imaging of the material oppression of homosexuals to carry over into the present without simultaneously providing a way out" (Cartelli 1998: 220). In this enterprise, Jarman could have found a powerful ally in Tony Kushner, whose "gay fantasia on national themes," *Angels in America: Part One; Millenium Approaches*, would generate a second part, *Perestroika*, in which its presumably doomed protagonist, Prior Walter, is allowed to outlive the same AIDS virus that took Jarman's life.

However, even if we grant such politically charged antecedents the authority to flaunt realism in this way, what authorizes Taymor's attempt to release Shakespeare's "dark tale of vengeance" from the grip of darkness? How do we differentiate her "Hollywood Happy Ending" from the happy ending Nahum Tate appended to *King Lear* 200-odd years ago? We do so not by reproducing Tate's argument that he was simply naturalizing (that is, restoring a natural perspective to) the unnaturally horrid prospects Shakespeare was compelling his audiences (and readers) to swallow. Instead, we do the opposite, and accept the artificiality of Taymor's "computer-generated sunrise" as an admittedly strained solution to – but needed departure from – the seemingly insoluble problem of mutually predation. That said, there are surely cognate humanist impulses in Tate's and Taymor's decision to turn brutal stories to new purposes. As Jarman might say, why take on such a "musty play" in the first place if you don't intend to "violate it"?

Victoria Nelson offers a somewhat different take on the problem in her brilliant account of the Lars von Trier film, *Breaking the Waves* (1996), which ends with the ringing of enormous heavenly bells (visible to the film viewer from on high no less) that confirm the "holiness" of the "sacrifice" performed by the film's sexual martyr, Bess. To abbreviate her argument, Nelson seeks to rescue the ending of von Trier's film from detractors who find in it "an unholy alliance of 1940s movie kitsch with organized religion" (Nelson 2001: 229). She does so by claiming that, absent "the metaphysical level on which the bells operate . . . *Breaking the Waves* would be just another example of the sort of art Westerners have happily consumed for a hundred and fifty years: social realism shading into modernism that steadfastly upholds a rational-empirical worldview" (Nelson 2001: 229). And she concludes:

> To the adherents of this sensibility, the demand for "realism" is as narrow and two dimensional as the bells are to detractors of *Breaking the Waves*. In New Expressionist terms, the bells represent a Shakespearean ending in which the moral order has been restored by a message from those inner areas of reality coincident with a transcendental reality we do not experience with our five senses – and it is a defiant message in the face of all sensible judgment as rendered by the well-intentioned, both within the film and in the audience. (Nelson 2001: 230)

Taymor would no doubt discern some slippage between Nelson's effort to recuperate the space of the spiritual or uncanny for Western art and her own effort to generate – "as if redemption were a possibility" (2000: 185) – an ethical alternative to the very different kind of "Shakespearean ending" with which she was contending in *Titus*. For Taymor, the *idea of a possibility* – of release, escape, redemption – is about as far as it gets. However, the solution she arrives at through the medium of young Lucius uncannily echoes von Trier's conclusion, as the soundtrack dissolves from the cries of infants, to the shriek of birds of prey, to peals of bells. When Taymor briefly quotes Edvard Munch's "The Scream" (1897) in the opening scene of *Titus*, the gesture connects her project with the earliest aims of Expressionism: to represent feelings, emotions, reactions to the world, rather than the world itself. Young Lucius's departure into a cinematic sunrise invites us to think along the vector of this aesthetic. Whereas the terrified figure in Munch's painting turns its back to a burning sky, this figure turns to face it: daring it, risking it. This reframing gesture suggests that while the world does not change – indeed, remains full of dehumanizing violence – one's stance in relation to it can change. The figure of exit is important, then, not because such exits exist as such or are being offered (that would be compensatory reassurance) but because they can be imagined. In Nelson's words, such reframing gestures mark "the moment when we become completely conscious of the boundaries of the worldview we have comfortably inhabited for several centuries that is also, inevitably, the moment we abandon it: we see the door in the sky, and we walk through it" (Nelson 2001: 23).

5 Vernacular Shakespeare

The adaptations explored in this chapter operate in a different vein of cultural reference and technical sophistication than the comparatively "high-style" remediations of *Hamlet* and *Titus Andronicus* on which we have focused thus far. Julie Taymor's subject is nothing less than "the last 2000 years of man's inhumanity to man," and the art-forms and iconography through which that inhumanity has been represented. Michael Almereyda's is a play to which Western culture has regularly returned over the course of 400 years to stage the conflict between the always unsatisfied desire for presence and certainty and the technologies that mediate that desire. By contrast, the "subject" of a film like Al Pacino's *Looking for Richard* could be said to be adaptation itself, particularly the adaptation of Shakespeare to "the movies," as that term is commonly understood in the vernacular surround of American popular culture.

Several obstacles have long stood in the way of Shakespeare meeting America "on equal terms" at the movies. In her article "Welcoming Shakespeare into the Caliban Family" (1996) culture critic Margo Jefferson identifies the first of these as a problem of language:

> Shakespeare must meet America at the movies, and on equal terms. Combative, experimental and mutually seductive, whether in a mass-culture smash or a quirky art house "docudrama" like Al Pacino's current "Looking for Richard." . . . Shakespeare must adjust to city street and suburban mall English, constantly reinflected by different regions, neighborhoods, races, ethnicities and classes. (1996: C11, 16)

No matter how vividly present the architecture of a cinematic Venice or Verona may seem, characters speaking Shakespearean verse (particularly in the classic British acting tradition) may sound stuffy and mannered, if not downright foreign to modern American audiences. Moreover, the passage implies, a film fully invested in that language reflects a world of unequals: on the one hand an educated elite who inherit the difficult language as their own; on the other, those urban and suburban speakers from "different regions, neighborhoods, races, ethnicities" who do not. In this chapter we explore several recent films that set out in different ways to redesign Shakespearean language to echo the pacing and rhythms, the sounds and stylings, of the American street. At the same time, we explore the different vocabulary required for talking about adaptations that may be deeply engaged with a playtext or some part of it, without being conventionally "faithful" to it.

Both the abrasive rhythms and duller textures of American urban and suburban life are put to work in such films as Gus Van Sant's *My Own Private Idaho* (1991), William Reilly's *Men of Respect* (1990), James Gavin Bedford's *The Street King* (aka *King Rikki*) (2002), Al Pacino's *Looking for Richard* (1996), and especially Billy Morrissette's *Scotland, PA* (2001). What links these films is their effort not just to make Shakespeare viable in the popular marketplace but to find a way of translating Shakespeare into a specifically American cinematic vernacular. This involves a transformative approach to spoken language in its own right as well as a transformation or compression of stage-dialogue into cinematic image or gesture. But vernacular translation also means different things for each of the filmmakers in question. For Morrissette it involves a sustained reckoning with the competing vernaculars of music, radio, and television. For Van Sant, it occasions the "translation" or transposition of Shakespeare into American English paraphrase, most effectively in the sequence when his Prince Hal figure, Scott Favor (Keanu Reeves), rejects Bob Pigeon (William Richert), his vagabond "Falstaff" surrogate. The deployment of Shakespeare in *Idaho* is also signaled by a movement out of the speech patterns of the street, into the high style of blank verse directly culled from Shakespeare's *Henriad*. In these instances, Shakespeare is superimposed on the matter of the street in the estranging manner that Brecht highlighted movements from ordinary speech to songs. This privileging of Shakespeare-derived language differentiates *Idaho* from *Men of Respect* and *The Street King*, which translate Shakespeare into "mafiaspeak" and "spanglish," respectively, and rely upon clever citational strategies and visual substitutions to mark their respective debts to – and difference from – *Macbeth* and *Richard III*.[1] In Pacino's film, Shakespeare's language is, for the most part, "done straight." But Pacino also invites large incursions of urban American speech patterns, compresses long speeches into shorter ensembles of speech-actions, and unmoors entire passages in order to restructure our experience of the play.

▣ Shakespeare and the Street: *Looking for Richard* ▨

Looking for Richard begins portentously with the tolling of a church bell, punctuating a wintry view of bare trees and a Gothic-spired church as a British-accented actor's voice speaks lines from *The Tempest* that will be reprised at the end. The church view fades into that of a New York brown-brick apartment house rising above a schoolyard where a boy shoots baskets. Pacino wanders aimlessly into the frame, dressed in black and wearing a baseball cap turned backwards on his head. The montage fades back to the church, to fingers flipping through the pages of a Shakespearean playtext, then again to the playground where

Pacino turns to notice the camera as the speech concludes. At this point the film proper abruptly begins: an animated indoor scene which finds Pacino in company with his associates beginning their interrogation of Shakespeare's *Richard III*. Two aspects of this preface are noteworthy: (1) the artful dissolving of the English pastoral scene into American urban space, which is mediated by the speaking voice of Prospero and the black-and-white pages of the playtext (as well as the contrast they make with the colorful but artless graffiti on the wall of the apartment building); and (2) the craftily conceived "look" of Pacino as he shambles aimlessly into our gaze wearing the immediately recognizable signs of adolescent sloth and studied indifference. Old world beauty, serious- ness, and decorum are juxtaposed against the relaxed and sloppy standards of a new world which, as this first scene develops, speaks in a lively, contentious patter as the struggle to assemble a common or consensus understanding of the Shakespearean playtext takes shape.

Although his approach to *Richard III* is avowedly "docudramatic," what Pacino documents in the most compelling moments of his film is how much more dramatic Shakespeare can be made by "penetrating into what at every moment the text is about," and how film itself may be better positioned than theater to bring the truth of the speaking voice to the surface. These insights belong to Peter Brook, one of the few British authorities in the film whose pronouncements are not violated by a knowing smirk or jump-cut. According to Brook, American actors can achieve this speaking voice as long as they stop being "obsessed with a British way of regarding text" – that is, as a kind of musical score – and embrace the sustained exploration of character and motivation that has been a hallmark of American acting since the high-tide period of "the Method" and New York's Actors Studio.[2] Brook elaborates this point at length in a clearly privileged moment in Pacino's film, claiming that:

> Every actor knows that the quieter he speaks, the closer he can be to himself. And when you play Shakespeare in close up in a film and have a mike and can really speak the verse as quietly as this [Brook demon- strates as he speaks], you are not going against the grain of verse but are going in the right direction because you are really allowing the verse to be a man speaking his inner world.

While it is unclear whether Pacino "quotes" Brook merely to articulate a position to which he has already committed himself, Brook's state- ments bring into focus two prevailing concerns of Pacino's project. First, they underline its Americanness, which is apparent not only in the acting choices and speech patterns of Pacino and his cast, but also in their alternating anxiety and hostility toward the authority of British acting, scholarship, and behavior. (All the scholarly talking heads in the film are uncoincidentally British.) Second, they emphasize Pacino's commitment to a conspicuously cinematic (and "Method"-oriented) dissolving of the distance between word and feeling as a way of getting at the truth of experience.[3]

Pacino's film combines an unusual blend of humility and deference to Shakespeare with confidence, nay arrogance, regarding the ability of actors, particularly *American* actors, to seize possession of a play to which they claim to contribute an energy and "truth" that escapes the capacity of scholars and other kinds of actors to deliver. The claim Pacino makes is conveyed with both conviction and a discernible measure of irony. He is well aware (we think) of his own lack of authority as either scholar or well-trained speaker of the verse. But he also wants to persuade us that the playing-space Shakespeare left behind has been vacated or, what amounts to the same thing, has been ineffectively filled by a theatrical and scholarly establishment that operates more as a heritage industry than as a creative force that can bring anything close to Shakespeare's originary power to dramatic production. This consideration is dramatically realized in a scene played more for its farcical than serious potential: when Pacino and his sidekick Frederic Kimball pay a surprise visit to the Shakespeare birthplace. There they find, to their manifest unsurprise, that no one is home – and that, moreover, the beds are too small and the rooms too threadbare and narrow to have housed so august a presence as the Bard.

One way of reading this scene is to see the visit as a pilgrimage that involves a sincere effort both of understanding and veneration (Lawson 2000: 45). But the casually irreverent tone Pacino and Kimball adopt persuades us to see it as what in the streets of New York would be called a "goof:" a form of acting out and acting up premised on a studied state of unseriousness, aimed at demystifying the very idea that one could hope to find Shakespeare in such a setting. In this setting of Bardic veneration, Pacino constructs himself as a seriously playful and playfully serious seeker-of-truth: inviting his own ejection from the Shakespeare birthplace by men he casts in the role of proprietary caretakers, exercising a curatorial control over a Shakespeare made to seem more at home in a museum than in the open air or street. When Kimball and Pacino find themselves back outside, Kimball (middle-aged, casually dressed) offers a closing comment, "What a bummer." The gesture brings what Pacino elsewhere labels "the quest" further into the circuit of an adolescent's "excellent adventure," bumptiously but earnestly pursued by a seemingly ageless American Don and his Sancho-like sidekick.

Pacino's related preoccupation with dissolving the distance between word and feeling emerges in the New York based, man-in-the-street interviews he conducts and in the contrast they make with the British, scholar-in-the-study sequences. It also emerges in other contrasts Pacino stages between actors and scholar-experts. The privileging of feeling over word, directness over rhetorical display, is most powerfully evoked in a statement Pacino elicits from an anonymous panhandler, who claims to derive from Shakespeare the message, "If we *felt* what we said, we'd say less and mean more." This assertion is dramatically linked to a carefully edited comment by Vanessa Redgrave, who assesses the evolution of 400 years of British political culture in terms of an ever-widening gap between word and feeling. Together, the two judgments suggest that the antidote to this dissociation is waiting in the humble confines of the American street, where passion may still be said to speak directly. Redgrave's intervention is largely presented in voice-over: as indirect commentary on the just-concluded, passionate implosions of Estelle Parsons's Queen Margaret (in a staged "rehearsal" of *Richard III*, 1.3) and as a kind of vocal bridge or caption for yet another give-and-take discussion between Pacino and his actor-associates. As such, Redgrave's message – "The music, literally, I mean the music, and the thoughts and the concepts and the feelings have not been divorced from the words and in England you've had centuries in which word has literally been divorced from truth and that's a problem for us actors" – seems to gesture in two directions at once. It points back to the expressive immediacy of Queen Margaret's utterance and forward to the ongoing quest for truth pursued by Pacino and his band of American brothers (and sisters), a quest underwritten by its grounding in the expressive immediacy of the street as embodied by the panhandler's commentary.[4]

Although the panhandler's statement brings a street-savvy urgency to Redgrave's magisterial pronouncement, it is hard to see how Shakespeare – a playwright given to sustained rhetorical flourishes, verbal *excess* and studied ambiguity – can be said to advance the idea of saying less but meaning more. What does advance this idea is Pacino's performative spin on *Richard III* which, though it mainly proceeds through a series of intense discussions and filmed rehearsals in theatrically defined spaces, is decidedly cinematic and not at all consistent with the American theater's often slavish devotion to the full Shakespearean script.[5] In the best moments of his film Pacino does not seek to "stage" Shakespeare as much as to restructure our experience of the play; he does this by maximizing the dramatic potential of individual moments in the playtext, and by eliding equally significant scenes and speeches that fail to translate into the medium of film. This is especially the case in the Lady Anne scene and in the scene in which Richard debates the arrest of Clarence and wrangles with his enemies, which Pacino intercuts with images of King Edward writhing on his bed. Pacino and his colleagues speak – and inhabit – their lines as well as one would like. But it is Pacino's preference for physicality and for fracturing the linear "screen" of text-based interpretation (by means of close-ups, jump-cuts, montage, and other cinematic devices) that most effectively delivers the "truth" of these scenes.

This is not something Pacino arrives at spontaneously, without discussion or careful preparation. The "truth" in the case of the Lady Anne scene is the sum of its evolving parts. We watch Pacino assemble these parts: from his casting choice (he asks for an actress young enough to make Lady Anne's vulnerability to Richard credible) to his sensitive probing of why, apart from her youth, Anne would be vulnerable to Richard (she has no sponsor or protector in the royal court). As the sequence unfolds, Pacino again intercuts commentary and conversation with superimpositions and fades of full-dress rehearsals and more casual walk-throughs, privileging all the while his sampling of facial tics, sounds, lines, and gestures. Crouching in dark corners of the film-frame, he tries on scowls, limps, and line-readings that all but announce "An actor prepares," at once striving and refusing to make a seamless transformation from Hollywood celebrity to Shakespearean character.[6] As the scene goes forward, we witness both the intensity with which Pacino abandons himself to the character of Richard and the unusually erotic charge Pacino brings to an encounter that may test an audience's capacity to abandon disbelief. The sequence is further enriched by film's capacity to allow a camera to focus and circle in close-up on their figures to the exclusion of all else in the frame. (This tight focus affirms Brook's point that film allows actors to speak their lines with an intimacy the stage does not usually afford.) Given how closely Pacino draws the viewer in, it is both shocking and exhilarating to witness how, upon Lady Anne's withdrawal, Pacino reduces an actor's dream of a 36-line speech to three lines. He turns the *caesura* in the third line – "I'll have her, but I will not keep her long" – into an occasion for gleefully triumphant laughter that combines with the swinging of his riding-crop overhead to make action eloquence.

Saying less and meaning more thus translates – at least in Pacino's filming of the early scenes of the playtext – into an aesthetic that shows off the power of American acting styles. Those styles prefer gesture over word, the body over the head, and suit film's capacity to deliver (in howsoever stylized a way) the pressure and fullness of experience, the tenor and immediacy (if not the "truth") of the street. It is no coincidence that the film flattens out when Pacino reverts to playtext chronology and conventional filmic realism in the closing battle scenes with Richmond. In these scenes, *Looking for Richard* moves far from the American street that was, in many respects, its inspiration, and just as far from the rough-ness and immediacy of the play's earlier scenes. Those earlier scenes were distinctive in a number of ways: filmed in "found" playing spaces and rehearsal studios, they seemed the product of intense, often contentious, debate and made potent use of montage to show us things that do not literally "speak" in the playtext (King Edward's writhing on his bed, Queen Elizabeth's passionate embrace of his corpse). In the end, Pacino gets caught up in the seductions of conventional cinematic display and falls prey to the temptation to "open up" the play to the presumptive freedoms of out-of-doors color, light, and panoramic spaces. In so doing he loses touch with what Neil Sinyard describes as the liberties of "fragmentation, enhanced by a montage that leaps about in time and place with a mobility that only cinema can manage" (Sinyard 2000: 70). Pacino's reprising of Prospero's lines on the fading of "this insubstantial pageant" at film's end is dramatically effective, but at simi-lar cost. The decision imposes a sense of polish, refinement, and closure on a film otherwise committed to the power of process, accident, and the passion and inspiration of actors themselves as they *unmake* established ways of understanding *Richard III*.

▓ **Accents Unknown:** *The Street King* ▓▓▓▓▓▓

James Gavin Bedford's *The Street King* substitutes a site-specific and ethnically hybridized American vernacular for Shakespearean language: channeling *Richard III* to fit the rhythms of *chicano* gang subculture in Southern California (specifically, east Los Angeles), and the cinematic and televisual conventions that characteristically represent them. Unlike *Men of Respect*, a mechanical, point-by-point paraphrase of *Macbeth* in terms of a New York mafia subculture, *The Street King* wears its Shakespearean pedigree lightly, gesturing rather than deferring to the plot-line of *Richard III*. The film certainly grounds itself on the play: employing Spanish equivalents for the names of Shakespeare's primary characters; dramatizing the drive to power of younger brother Rikki (played by Jon Seda as more hunk than hunchback), who engineers the demise of older brothers Jorge and Eduardo, the current "king' of the Ortega gang. Yet viewers unfamiliar with the playtext might be hard pressed to notice the Shakespeare connection, so seamlessly does the film conform to the established conventions of the ethnic gang/drug subculture genre of films such as Martin Scorsese's *Goodfellas* (1990) or the Brian De Palma remake of *Scarface* (1983). *The Street King* stands in relation to *Richard III* in the same way that the spray-painting of Shakespeare's image stands in relation to the reproduction of the Droeshout portrait that first appears on the *barrio* wall in the film's opening credits (figure 5.1). As we witness this progressive defacement (by a hand that refashions Shakespeare's image through the addition of a goatee, shades, red bandanna, beauty mark, and large cross earring), we are disarmed of any expectation that a film which announces itself as "based on *The Tragedy of King Richard III*" will deliver something other than an ironic masquerade of that transaction.

Indeed, the film's strategy throughout is more parodic and citational than assimilative. It dips into selected passages of *Richard III* without attempting to swallow the play whole, providing a series of filmic substitutions and displacements for what the playtext supplies. For filmgoers who know the play by heart, some new level of interpretive significance may be mined as we watch the "good cop" who fills the role of Richmond become the "bad cop" at the film's end. His conversion suggests an equivalence between presumed legitimacy and criminality when he reiterates the words "plata" and "plomo" (silver and lead, or bribes and bullets) which appear on either side of the restructured portrait of Shakespeare in the film's prologue. Yet new interpretations of the play may be only incidental to *The Street King's* citational strategies. The film's substitutions more often merely reward the knowing viewer with a double (largely parodic) perspective on the action that will remain unavailable to filmgoers unprepared to read the Shakespearean signs and signals.

Some of the more successful effects of this kind involve Rikki's daring visit to the wake of his old friend Alejandro (the film's stand-in for the

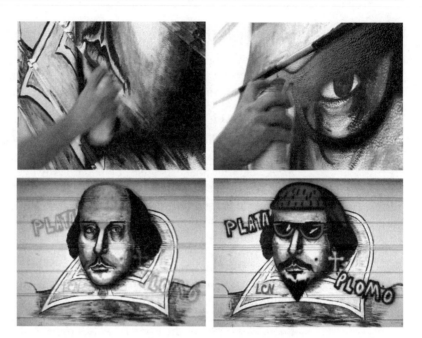

5.1 Barrio Bard

murdered Edward, Prince of Wales). He purportedly undertakes this visit to retrieve a piece of Alejandro's mother's famous lemon cake to share with his buddies, but uses it to make a date with Alejandro's surviving girlfriend, Anita (the film's stand-in for Lady Anne). Swearing oaths to his innocence in the more-sincere-than-thou manner of Richard Duke of Gloucester, after having conspicuously plucked a red rose from a funerary bouquet, Rikki emerges unscathed, cake in hand, anticipating his meeting with Anita, where his production of the same knife he used to kill Alejandro proves entirely convincing. Pressing the knife into his workout-hardened stomach until it draws blood, Rikki transforms Richard's act of theatrical daring into an entirely contemporary and ethnically specific display of *macho* vanity and endurance. *The Street King* deploys the dramatically cued strategy of direct address to the camera considerably more often than Shakespeare has Richard deliver asides or soliloquies. Yet in this instance the 36-line bravura speech that Pacino reduces to "I'll have her but I will not keep her long" is even more efficiently translated into a few winks of conversational bravado followed up a moment later by a wryly narrated clip of Anita's visit to a tattoo parlor, where she has the elaborately wrought name of Alejandro painfully erased and replaced with that of her new object of devotion, Rikki. Of a piece with the vigorous misogyny that animates the film, the scene nonetheless acutely realizes the vanity that makes Lady Anne believe in Richard's love while providing a culturally specific application to the mores and practices of the East Los Angeles gang subculture.

This is not the only time that Bedford renovates the plot of *Richard III* in a timely and inventive manner instead of attempting to reproduce it.

Alejandro forever.

5.2 Alejandro forever?

For example, rather than have Rikki's brother, Eduardo, die of an unnamed illness as does Edward IV in Shakespeare's play, Bedford's script has Rikki cut Eduardo's cocaine with a foreign substance and later disguise himself as a physician in order to channel air into Eduardo's IV tube. The byplay gives Rikki an added occasion to demonstrate his ruthlessness and resourcefulness and the film another opportunity to advertise its ironic take on the iconic original. Here as elsewhere in *The Street King* – when, for example, Rikki announces that "You gotta think global for the twenty-first century" upon his short-lived ascension to the position of *jefe* or king of the Ortega family – expansive irony distinguishes Bedford's effort to translate *Richard III* into the idiom of the American street. This irony is less self-reflexive than Pacino's wry undercutting of his quest for Method-based emotional truth. Yet Bedford's transposition of Shakespeare's English history play to fit the contours of the *barrio* clearly echoes Pacino's translation of the same play into an American vernacular of gesture, action, and speech, and Van Sant's site-specific rewriting of the *Henriad*. It also brings Shakespeare back to the future of nineteenth-century Shakespearean burlesques, when irreverence first began to displace deference in American treatments of the Bard (Cartelli 1999: 29).

Media Vernaculars: Listening to *Scotland, PA*

> To me Shakespeare is like James Brown. . . . Shakespeare is someone to be appropriated and sampled.
>
> Oscar Kightley[7]

No recent Shakespeare film or spin-off treats Shakespeare as irreverently, or with as much deference to American popular culture, as does Billy Morrissette's *Scotland, PA*. Yet unlike other recent screen *Macbeths* (such as the dogged *Men of Respect*) *Scotland, PA* is engaged less in updating the play within a popular and marketable genre-niche than in backdating it. *Macbeth*, it turns out, provides a way to look back on the rise of popular, consumer culture. Mass media features prominently in both the story the film tells and in the way it backdates *Macbeth*: 1970s films, television, and radio provide the audio-visual vernaculars into which it translates Shakespeare's play. Like *The Street King, Scotland, PA* maintains a remarkably close relationship to the playtext throughout this process of translation. In doing so, it helps expand our vocabulary for talking about the ways films that do not aim to revive Shakespeare handle their source material.

Van Sant's and Bedford's films variously sink into, pass through, paraphrase, and allude to the playtexts they recycle and renovate. Morrissette's film provides an example of three other modes of renovation. It "riffs" on and "samples" *Macbeth*.[8] And it reproduces the structure of Shakespeare's language when not using the language itself. *Scotland, PA* also focuses our attention on soundtrack in a way that helps stretch our thinking about these different modes of translation. Although film is a multi-track medium that includes dynamic sound and also print (credits, subtitles, words printed on objects within the *mise en scène*), critics are often sidetracked by image versus text debates. Thus we may forget that Shakespearean language happens as much or more in the soundtracks of a film as it does in the image-track. And in a number of ways, the vocabulary of sound quotation may be better suited to the kinds of adaptation going on in Shakespeare films than print-based vocabulary.

Before exploring these concerns, we need to sketch the story *Scotland, PA* tells about the rise of mass culture. The film resituates the tragedy of *Macbeth* in the economically depressed confines of central Pennsylvania, in the post-Vietnam era. It maps the play's cultural divisions between barbaric northern Scots and civilizable, Anglicized Scots onto the conflict between a stalled-out culture of small-town losers – personified in Joe "Mac" McBeth (James LeGros) and his deer-hunting buddies – and a counter-culture of hippies, rockers, and New Age vegetarians. The counter-culture is personified most suggestively in the person of Lieutenant McDuff (Christopher Walken), an outsider to Scotland, who plays meditation tapes in his pea-green Audi. Working dead-end jobs at "Duncan's" burger joint, frustrated by their lack of opportunity, Mac and his wife Pat (Maura Tierney) seek to escape into management by killing the owner and taking over the business. The barely submerged plot of Macbeth's rise to power unfolds as the two renovate the restaurant, emboldened by a prophecy heralding transformative new business practices, such as a drive-thru service window. This prophecy is delivered by a creepy trio of stoners (somewhat anachronistically called "hippies" in the cast list), played by Andy Dick, Timothy "Speed" Levitch, and Amy Smart.

As with other low-budget Shakespeare spin-offs, such as *Men of Respect* and *The Street King*, the cast is largely drawn either from unknowns and B-list TV actors (Maura Tierney and James Rebhorn here, Jon Seda in *The Street King*) or from established character actors doing star-turns in low-profile vehicles (Christopher Walken here, John Turturro in *Respect*). The film's setting, characterizations, pratfalls, and send-ups owe as much to the comedic conventions of gross-out films such as John Landis's *Animal House* (1978) as they do to TV shows like

McCloud and *Colombo*. Drinking, eating, lecherousness, rock music, fag-jokes, and sight gags dominate (especially the first half of) the film. Broad comedic liberties are taken with minor characters (the stoner witches, Malcolm and Donald) and with unprecedented add-ons (the sun-tanning guy and his burnt-to-a-crisp son). There is a sense that these conventions are totally in charge of what once was *Macbeth* – until, that is, the play's relentless plot and constrained field of action reassert themselves in the second half.

Part of the appeal of the film is certainly its campy, gross-out sensibility: Duncan murdered in the Fryolator, Pat's lopped-off hand in its oven mitt. Yet as Lauren Shohet has shown, the gross-outs in *Scotland, PA* carry undercurrents of the demystifying disgust evoked by Eric Schlosser's *Fast Food Nation* (2001). Where the play harks forward to the coming of James I to the English throne, the film foreshadows the dominion of the consumer economy, a king of burgers and entrepreneurial aristocracy supplanting medieval monarchs. Shakespeare's "supernatural solicitings" are re-imagined here as the inexorable rise of the fast-food industry. The questions of agency that dominate *Macbeth* and make its supernatural effects genuinely spooky – did Macbeth, the witches, or Lady Macbeth first spark the impulse to take over the throne? – are remapped onto anxieties about unskilled workers being permanently left behind by the rapid emergence of that economy. Like Van Sant, Pacino, and Bedford, Morrisette intensifies our attachment to his Shakespearean anti-heroes by emphasizing the complacency of characters such as Malcolm and Donalbain who, like *Idaho's* Scott Favor, inherit family wealth. Their wealth distinguishes them from those who must hustle for a living or rely on illegitimate means of advancement: Mac and Pat, *Idaho's* Mike Waters, *The Street King's* Rikki, and Pacino's Richard. Thus, when the moral framework of *Macbeth* resurfaces in *Scotland, PA* it does so in class terms. We watch Pat treat the help as badly as Duncan and Doug treated her, and we witness the McBeths' sudden prosperity turn to a private hell of anxiety. We can hear the pull of *Macbeth's* plot assert itself at the Grand Opening celebration, where the McBeths' dysfunctions are broadcast in language remarkably close to that of the banquet scene (3.4), the corresponding turning point in the play.

Like *Macbeth*, *Scotland, PA* and its characters are haunted by its future, the audience's ambivalent present. That future is not incidentally a global future, in which the intrusion of the fast-food industry into rural and urban communities alike has become a dominant symbol of the evils of globalization. Where Shakespeare's play provides for Malcolm's return to the throne, Morrissette's film provides the equivocal triumph not of individuals but of an industry. McDuff, not Malcolm, takes over the restaurant, remodeling it a second time as the "Home of the Garden Burger." Three decades of fast-food menus later, we can see what a disaster this particular entrepreneurial dream is likely to be for him. Glossing the play's final scene in terms of competing business models, rather than competing models of kingship and nation, the film uses repetition to pose questions about the costs and benefits of new modes of business. Which version of the local (if any) will triumph in a global economy?

The real irony of this final remodeling is that, given his counter-cultural/New Age tastes, McDuff is possessed by entrepreneurial dreams in the first place. (Walken establishes this with marvelously understated hints of covetousness and admiration for the burger joint.) McDuff's drives appear oppositional: his remarks about the killing potential of greasy food identify him as a prototypical Green Party environmentalist. Yet his desires turn out to be remarkably conventional. One way to understand McDuff's appetite for business is to see it as the remodeling of his oppositional drives in the image of Mac's by the invisible hand of capital, a process that can only end in tragedy for McDuff. But tragic and parodic impulses intersect here in more complex ways . The Garden Burger will surely be a disaster in McDuff's time. However, vegetarianism is now a billion-dollar industry. And the film's class-mediated gravitation into the moral vortex of *Macbeth* makes it clear where our sympathies should lie. In the final reckoning, the meat-free (i.e. "not born of woman"), educated, professional, and law-abiding McDuff earns his new reign of vegetarianism by biting the hand that feeds him. By contrast, the greedy, over-sexed, under-educated, under-achieving McBeths are cruelly and comically punished for their transgressions. The innocent (largely) endure and the audience can see in McDuff a virtuous forebear of alternative lifestyles that now thrive.

It is not entirely clear whether the anti-establishment counter-authority of alternative lifestyles represented by McDuff can change the establishment in a real way. But the hindsight allowed by the film helps us see clearly that this is how the establishment renews itself – by adopting anti-establishment counter-authority as its own. The film also helps us see that this assimilation is neither complete nor unilateral. Mac will never confess, McDuff will not eat meat except in self-defense, and burger chains now serve vegetarian food. Convention and the process of conventionalizing – being made over according to an established formula or script – are the central dramatic preoccupations of *Scotland, PA*. Yet the film, like the play, sees the exchanges between received forms and those who perform them as a feedback loop, not as a process of absolute possession.

At different moments in Shakespeare's *Macbeth* we hear summaries of Renaissance ideas about a good king, a tyrant, a repentant murderer, and so on; the characters embrace, reject, or adapt these normative ideas for themselves. In a similar vein, *Scotland, PA* rehearses mid-century American ideas about economic success ("don't you think she deserves better?"), satisfaction ("we *rock!*"), and good taste. Indeed, the aspect of the play that seems most to interest the film is the way in which it dramatizes individual encounters with dominant fictions about success. This point is brought home by the addition of a detective to investigate Macbeth's crimes. Detectives as a fictional class are purely instrumental narrative devices: ideological tools, empty of all drives except those of the order it is their function to restore. But in American popular culture, detectives also register the romantic dream of agency: the ability to negotiate a system and yet remain integral, sincere, oneself, which we code as "character." *Scotland, PA*, smartly, returns that instrumentality to all its characters. All are tragicomically subject to cultural scripts (and the fantasies of power that attend them) to the same degree. All are engaged in negotiating some script as their central actions. Walken especially builds this struggle into the way he "scores" his lines as an actor, establishing McDuff's motives and back-story. Among the many moments worth pausing over is a (no-doubt Walken-initiated) reference by Lieutenant McDuff to his earlier career as a dancer during his interview with Donald. The reference both points back to a more creative past and anticipates his later career-change from officious detective to health-food entrepreneur, thereby indicating less a fixed character than an individual fluidly moving from one role to another as an actor does.

In *Macbeth*, we become aware of the cultural scripts characters play out and negotiate through shifts of genre or gestures towards familiar fictional devices. The source material reworked in Shakespeare's play is generically varied, borrowed from classical drama, contemporary prose history, the preoccupations of the court, and the latest fad in popular print. Thus the play restages stories from Tudor chronicles to the tune of popular murder pamphlets and mixes in a comic porter from late-medieval cycle plays with Jacobean witches who sing. A long tradition of stage burlesques has been alive to this pastiche, or mix of genres, in *Macbeth*. With the exception of *Scotland, PA*, modern film-adaptations have largely missed it.

The campy aesthetic of *Scotland, PA* foregrounds the ways that it retransmits culturally charged matter, marking every action or behavior as already conventional, even when it seems to be freshly invented. The stylings, sounds, and narrative conventions of 1970s television and radio do the most aesthetic work in these terms, by aggressively backdating the story. Morrisette's period details are lush, even extravagant: polyester pant-suits; shag haircuts; "Rock Blocks" playing Three Dog Night and Bad Company on the radio; black-and-white TV. Almost everyone drives Camaros. Almost everyone is underemployed. We are meant to see and hear the 1970s in a double sense, here. Visually and aurally alluring, it is also as archaic and formulaic as a tragedy of medieval kings. And when the film combines this period material with Shakespearean matter it does so to underscore their shared archaism and conventionality.

McDuff makes an especially good example of this kind of recombination. Walken's primary source is Peter Falk's Columbo, the detective in an enormously popular show of that title. Walken borrows Falk's deadpan delivery and canny misdirection. And Morrisette's screenplay borrows an important narrative device from the show. The constant reference to an absent Mrs Columbo, who never appeared on the scene, is reprised in Walken's comments about "Mrs McDuff," which reconfigure Lady Macduff's doomed fate. The film combines the two intertexts, Shakespeare play and TV serial, quite wittily. When Mac makes a snide comment about "all the little McDuffs" anyone who has read the play in high school will recognize the implied threat. Yet for Columbo, such references would be nothing more than a verbal gambit, designed to put his quarry off balance.

More than anything, then, this mix of allusions points us to the thin apparatus of inherited forms, reminding us that character is a function of story and verbal gesture. One consequence of such intertextual playfulness is that we see how radically Mac's dramatic possibilities are curtailed by comparison to those available to Shakespeare's Macbeth. There will be no true pleasure for him to experience, no real horrors to perpetuate, no heroic national scene for his action.[9] The narrative possibilities offered in this re-imagined 1970s are far more limited; we might even think of them as depressed. The three hippies underscore this point when they briefly bare the apparatus of adaptation, as if they are newly inventing, then rejecting, and then reconsidering the pertinence of the *Macbeth* script to modern life. "I know, Mac should kill McDuff's entire family!" Hippie # 2 (Levitch) offers brightly. "Oh that'd work *great* . . . about a thousand years ago!" scoffs Hippie # 3 (Dick), "You can't just go around killing everyone." "Or can you . . . ?" invites Hippie # 1 (Smart). The question of scripted outcomes points in several directions here, not only to Shakespeare's medieval Scotland but to the police serial. Killing everyone who knows anything is exactly the sort of tired solution that the bad guys in *Columbo* resort to, just before they are caught. The same strategy figures in contemporary events such as the mass killings orchestrated by Charles Manson and his "family," which famously inform the bloody Roman Polanski film-version of *Macbeth* released in 1971 and compared to which this parody seems very tame indeed.[10]

Drawing genealogical connections between Renaissance tragedy and detective serials, in this way, *Scotland, PA* might be read as a comic lament to the decay of culture: even bad guys had bigger stages in the past. This kind of reading – emphasizing the film's interest in the commodification of experience – would be in keeping with other recent "genre" adaptations of Shakespearean tragedy, such as Almereyda's noir *Hamlet* or the mafia *Macbeth, Men of Respect*. Those films, Douglas Lanier has argued, deploy screen Shakespeare as a form of social critique of the way in which cultural material (such as Shakespeare's plays) is appropriated by mass industries like Hollywood (2002b).

Morrissette's adaptation has a related, but finally different, set of interests. The film is less concerned to convey the pathos of interpellation – the melancholy recognition that we are shaped by discursive and social structures that conform to a dominant ideology. It is more concerned with assessing the costs and benefits of a recycling process that it sees as an essential feature of culture. To be sure, the film ironically acknowledges the increasing homogenization of consumer experience: whether it be the new practice of "eating out" or the standardized emotions purveyed by radio station playlists, under the cover of stirring, hard-rock backbeats. Yet it never allows the costs of that homogenization to register as truly tragic, even when it turns out that the practice of "eating out" originates in murder. Indeed, the film makes fun of the tragic view of interpellation, asking us to see the scripting of experience as a kind of consumption, digestion, the only way in which any inheritance – including Shakespeare – continues to live. Accordingly, Morrissette's innovation here is not – as in Luhrmann's film – to put Shakespearean material into *mise en scène*, in the form of brand names and advertising (fragments of Shakespeare absorbed and repurposed by corporate America). Instead, he uses the story and language of *Macbeth* to model the *circulation* of conventional material within a consumer economy. Mass media serves as much as Shakespeare as this film's touchstone – even the hippie witches amuse themselves by parroting lines from popular commercials. So we turn now to look closely at three scenes that foreground the different ways *Scotland, PA* translates the playtext into the vernaculars of film, television, and radio.

Scene I: Duncan's in slow motion We begin, appropriately, with the food fight, a mock-heroic version of the battle described in the early scenes of *Macbeth*. For those familiar with the play, the scene alerts us that Morrissette is engaged not in revival but in parodic translation and even close reading. Set in Duncan's greasy spoon, the food fight establishes Mac's status in the film in the same way the soldier's description of the battle establishes Macbeth's status in the play. The sequence dramatically homes in on the equivocal phrase, "Valor's minion," describing Macbeth's ruthless triumph over the rebel Macdonwald (1.2.19) in Shakespeare's play. "Minion" is an equivocal word, meaning both "darling" and something less positive like "boytoy," or male favorite. As Harry Berger has observed, this phrase foreshadows a host of later concerns: the question of what constitutes true manliness; the notion that even in triumph Macbeth will nevertheless remain subordinate; the fear that favoritism, not desert, might govern the workings of the court – a worry repeated at Malcolm's restoration, when like his father, the new King creates a host of new titles for his lords ([1980] 1997).

Morrissette emphasizes the equivocal messages in this phrase by providing visual and aural equivalents for them. As the food-fight escalates, Mac vaults the counter and throws the instigators bodily out the door. Quotes from Beethoven's 7th symphony rise magisterially in the score as Mac leaps into action. At the same time, the camera and diegetic audio slip into a slow-motion sequence that signifies "Heroic Action" is taking place. But the goofy slow-motion sound of Mac's voice grates against the score and, together with the fundamentally trivial

5.3 Mac jumping the life to come?

situation, deflates those tired action conventions. After we return to normal speed and Mac acknowledges the general applause, all that awaits him is the short-order grill. The distorted sequence and sound remind us that even when he seems to be acting most effectively Mac cannot "jump the life to come" (1.7.7). Later, when Duncan promotes him to Assistant Manager (conferring the coveted title of Manager on his unwilling rocker son Malcolm) this disappointment simply recapitulates what the slow motion established. Mac's problem is a failure to progress.

The slow-motion sequence plays on the Shakespearean phrase, taking it in new directions, improvising freely and sometimes with heavy distortion, but always returning to that central theme. What is happening here is a kind of audio-visual *riffing* on the phrase "valor's minion" in the context of familiar action conventions. We borrow the term riffing from the common practice of quotation in jazz and rock music, which involves alluding to and innovating on *riffs* (melodic ideas, usually in the form of short, repeated phrases) from earlier songs. Played on a single instrument, often bass or rhythm guitar, riffs provide the underlying structure for improvisation in a new composition. Unlike print quotations, most musical quotations are unlabelled. For this reason, riffing seems especially suited to describing the dynamic and variable ways in which Shakespearean matter registers with screen audiences. When we hear something familiar in a musical riff, that familiarity may locate itself anywhere along a continuum, from explicit citation, to intertextual conversation, to echo. Or, given the wide circulation of many standard riffs, such borrowings may register simply as stock material, as the mixed-genre effects of the "valor's minion" sequence do.

The inventiveness of a riff lies not so much in the selection of a particular passage or source – the body of material to draw on is well established as with the way in which it is played on or elaborated. While riffing may sound like extempore art, the practice is as highly codified as Renaissance verse. As Albert Murray observes:

> When they are effective, riffs always seem as spontaneous as if they were improvised in the heat of the performance. So much so that riffing is sometimes regarded as being synonymous with improvisation. But such is not always the case by any means. Not only are riffs as much a part of some arrangements and orchestrations as

the lead melody, but many consist of nothing more than stock phrases, quotations from some familiar melody, or even clichés that just happen to be popular at the moment. (Murray 1976: 96)

Shakespearean language stands in precisely this relation to the screenplay and action in *Scotland, PA*. It offers musical and dramatic ideas that the film riffs on in ways that are more and less recognizable, depending on the listener's familiarity with the source, yet are meant to sound spontaneous – even when those riffs hold closely to the play-text (as they often surprisingly do in this film). Like musical riffs, Shakespearean riffs do their artistic work in films whether they are recognized or not. For the most part the verbal riffs this film performs are unlabelled. So, for example, when Pat tells Mac "It's done. Can't be undone" – a line that particularly worried Morrissette, as he notes in the DVD commentary – the familiarity of the phrase has more to do with the way it has been absorbed into contemporary idiom (as "what's done is done") than with its Shakespearean coinage.

The screenplay of *Scotland, PA* dips in and out of explicit intertextual reference both to Shakespeare's playtext and to other popular and high-culture matter in this way, weaving it together in a mode that is sometimes ironic, sometimes comic. But in several key scenes Morrissette wants us to hear this kind of riffing as genuinely occult. The very absorbency of popular culture, as it recycles earlier material and reproduces it as convention, is the source of Scotland's uncanny.

Scene 2: Spell at the midway   As a verbal mode, riffing belongs partic-ularly, it turns out, to the witches. Their power to absorb and recast earlier material is established before the credits roll, in the opening sequence at the midway. Sound cues – composed of foley effects, dialogue, and musical score – organize this sequence, bridging several shifts in location. These sounds carry us from a long-distance shot to medium shot, then from this "real" scene to a recorded scene from a TV show, and then back to the "real" of Scotland. What starts us on this journey – the first sound we hear – is the reverberating thunk of an industrial switch echoing in a large open space, as the lights go out on a midway at night. The camera had been trained at a distance on the lit circle of the Ferris wheel. We learn we have leapt forward (blindly, in the dark) because of the sounds that follow: stoned giggles of hippies with the munchies, miked in medium close-up. As they riff on the opening lines of the play, the hippies tune our ears from echo to double enten-dre and irony: "The fowl was foul. . . . " "The Fair was fair. . . . " "Shhhh! She's having a spell!" "Oh God, *so* dramatic." The wordplay comes across more clearly than the visuals, though we have glimpses of the caretaker leaving and the trio sharing their fried chicken.

Under the lingering associations of the phrases "having a spell" and "*so* dramatic" the scene shifts to an extended montage from the popular 1970s detective show *McCloud* and the credits roll. Emerging from the murky colors of the fair into black and white this montage

5.4 Disestablishing sequence in *Scotland, PA*

partly returns us from the dark. But we are still somehow spell-stopped, conjured into this new medium – as we can tell again from the score, which has a particular, carnival sound that connects back to the midway. Anton Sanko's jazzy accordion composition plays over the *McCloud* montage, punctuating Denis Weaver's impossible stunts on a helicopter as he captures a quasi-corporate bad guy (note the suit and briefcase). The montage closes with a cut to Duncan's burger joint, still in black-and-white. This long shot (what will become the establishing shot of the next scene) resolves from black and white into color on the final chord and the printed credit to Shakespeare.

"Having a spell," the witch's phrase that ushers in this montage and names the shift in medium, means feeling queasy and disoriented (because you ate bad chicken). But it also means conjuring and exposing the fictional apparatus that renders lived experience. This Brechtian break in the form is designed to make us notice mediation taking place. Like the credit sequences in Luhrmann's *Romeo + Juliet* and Almereyda's *Hamlet*, this disestablishing sequence emphasizes not only the mediated nature of what is to follow (editing, camera-work, color) but the mixed nature of the media in question, which will recombine elements of drama, TV, and film. The resolve to color suggests not that we have exited the televisual world conjured by the witches – with its impossible heights of masculinity and mobility – but simply that the lights have turned back on in a contiguous space. The world of the film is scripted by the televisual, mediated in an occult way that will itself become the subject of the unfolding story. Moreover, the sequence suggests, the occult may be inseparable from the workings of reference as such. If we have at least read *Macbeth* in high school (the audience that Morrissette describes in his DVD commentary), we are likely to hear the echo of the famous opening lines of the play, with their doublings and inversions. Even without having watched many detective shows in the 1970s we may still recognize the signature graininess as a marker of a shift to video and the staginess of the chase scene, with its predictable closure, as a feature of the action genre.

Television clearly has uncanny effects on the characters in *Scotland, PA*. As Shohet observes, real policing lurches to a halt when the enthralling Denis Weaver hits the TV screen at Scotland's police station

(2004: 190). But the opening sequence prepares us to notice such hypnotic effects and view them ironically. Indeed, if the conventions of Hollywood cinema depend on an aesthetic of seamlessness, in which sound reinforces our sense that the event is "for me," lacking any barriers to immersion and understanding (Altman 1992), then what the audiotrack offers "for us" in this opening sequence seems to be a qualified distance. Sanko's theme tunes our ears not only to the film's campy aesthetic, but to the ironic listening position that the soundtrack will provide throughout the film. When the slow-motion sound effects grate against Beethoven's 7th Symphony, disrupting our sense of aural realism, we are already prepared for that distance. Later, when the music track turns to the machismo of Bad Company and Three Dog Night, it performs what is by now a very old audio convention for matching feature song to visual narrative. We share (hear) Mac's fantasy in the music track ("Oh, I was born with a 6-gun in my hand") even as we see him objectively in the *mise en scène*, wandering the midway at night. We may notice how poor the match is between the tough-guy persona of the song and Mac's aimless wandering. If so, that dramatic irony assures us that we know his inner self better than he does.

Yet the cumulative effects of this disestablishing sequence are less comfortable – and less about privileged audience knowledge – than the notion of dramatic irony usually implies. While the *McCloud* montage plays, we are invited to recognize ourselves being acted on (conjured or hailed) by televisual representation in a way that does not fully release us from its spell.[11] In what is clearly a moment of media allegory, the greater cultural potency and reach of television is invoked here: what scholars since the 1950s have described as its "extension of the perceived environment," a form of "going places" without expending energy or resources.[12] Moreover, television arguably interpellates its audience more thoroughly than does film because it traffics to a much greater extent in repetition. "Repeats" of episodes from shows such as *McCloud* now circulate endlessly, perhaps infinitely, on cable TV. Through their repeated catchphrases and jingles, TV commercials in particular are made to adhere to both the conscious and unconscious life of the viewer and thus enter into everyday conversation. Even the hippie witches can't get the repeated call of "Anthony, Anthony" from an old Prince Spaghetti commercial out of their heads.

Yet because the processed nature of the representation is exposed in this sequence (cinema briefly trumping the televisual), self-reflection and even some measure of control seem possible in the act of reception. It is not so much that we are being hailed as being invited to adopt and adapt what the convention offers us, and to recognize ourselves doing so. The truly eerie quality of this process is that we choose that possession as much as we are chosen by it. The absolutely normative quality of this process is that we can find campy (self-aware) pleasure in choice and refusal: the kind of pleasure we might get in imitating voice-overs of *Animal Planet*, for example, or in the punchline commentaries in *Calvin and Hobbes*, or even in watching Macbeth refuse to play the part that Macdonwald earlier starred in (made popular in Elizabethan murder pamphlets) of the repentant sinner.

The aesthetics of this credit sequence, then, belong to the world of recombination and sampling evoked by Oscar Kightley, in the epigraph above, in which listeners and consumers of recorded material may become makers and recording machines become instruments. Morrissette samples *McCloud* the way late-twentieth-century musicians sample earlier compositions. Sampling is a technical art that involves extracting elements of a sound recording (often rhythm track, sometimes just a single unit of sound) and recombining them with other material in ways that let us hear the original sound differently. The excerpted montage from *McCloud* works in this way: it provides familiar visual rhythms (as if it were a James Brown bass-line) over which Sanko remixes new melody. Where riffing concentrates artistic energy on the way a familiar idea is borrowed and elaborated, sampling concentrates artistic energy on the process of selection, extraction, and reuse of recorded material. In this case, Sanko's music has the effect of estranging the familiar rhythms of compressed time in the action montage. Its witty, squeaky, commentary estranges in the mode of Kurt Weill, making the montage and its later imitations in the film itself seem like a puppet show.[13]

This discussion may seem to have traveled fairly far from the problem of Shakespearean language on screen, as it passed from sound effects through riffing and sampling. However, both techniques provide a formal vocabulary that helps us understand better how carefully Morrissette and his artistic directors have listened to *Macbeth*. For all its supernatural apparatus, the truly eerie qualities of the play have to do with its verbal echoes – echoes the audience hears but the characters do not. From the moment that the witches' words come out of Macbeth's mouth ("so foul and fair a day I have not seen" 1.3.38), ideas, intentions, and feelings slip contagiously across subjects and possess them in a way that cannot be described by clear lines of agency, cause, and guilt, but that nevertheless has profound consequences. The truly eerie qualities of the film – and also its pleasures – have less to do with visual effects than with the way in which phrases, ideas, and feelings echo and cross-contaminate in its soundscape. Consider how phrases from Macbeth's famous "sound and fury" speech are parodically recycled for New Age consumption on the self-help tape McDuff listens to in his car: "Tomorrow is tomorrow, tomorrow is not today, etc." Riffing and sampling are the arts of the echo, in *Scotland, PA*, that alert us to the slippage of ideas and feelings across the subjects of commercial mass media.

Scene 3: Prophecy and Rock Block   It is not just that Morrissette's screenplay samples and riffs on passages of playtext. The interactions between dialogue, diegetic music, and non-diegetic music are governed by the repetitions, equivocation, and drift that characterize language in *Macbeth*. The verbal patterns borrowed from the play can be heard especially clearly when the hippies hail Macbeth, interrupting his night-time wanderings to tell his fortune. The hippies begin by deconstructing the title of the play in alternating voices. "Mac!" "Beth!" "Beth!" "Mac!" "Fleetwood Mac!" "Macramé!" "I *love* macramé. . . ." Their exchange runs along the chiastic patterns of the Witches' opening lines: words and ideas come in pairs, then repeat in reverse order. Like the Witches, the hippies speak in clichés, a fact they call explicit attention to. When Mac asks how they know his name, they equivocate: "You mean your name really is Mac? I thought we were just saying it like you say it . . . like 'Watch your step, Mac!,' 'Up yours, Mac!,' 'Fuck you, Mac!' " Reducing the name to its component phonemes, their free association simultaneously empties those sounds of signification and loads them with excessive affect, promiscuously attracting new meanings and new mouths: "Love the one you're with" "(love the one you're with)." This reduction also brings the remote and formal titles of Scottish feudal culture down to local, colloquial scale. Indeed, the hippies' colloquialisms seem a kind of verbal inventory of a culture that has leveled social distinctions and lost any memory of its patronymics. "Mac," the prefix that signifies "son of", is reduced to an epithet (Shohet 2004: 191–2).

As in Shakespeare's play, verbal repetition is the mark of the uncanny movement of language, as it speaks the subjects who appear to be speaking it. The source and vehicle of that movement is commercial media, as the quotations that make up this dialogue suggest. We hear the names of bands, fads, the refrain from a CSNY anthem, and fragments of what sound like insurance ads.[14] When Hippie # 1 tells Mac's fortune, this ventriloquism becomes explicit. Dubbed androgynously in different voices (including Mac's), her prophecy is a verbal collage of fragments from contemporary songs and television and radio commercials (and parodically recalls the famous moment when a demon's voice emerges from the swiveling head of a possessed girl in William Friedkin's *The Exorcist* (1973)). All the fragments involve the signature pattern of doubling and at least one employs echo ("Anthonyyy! Anthonyyyy"). Material that we might expect to find in a hit soundtrack cross-contaminates with dialogue here, as if sending up the convention that non-diegetic music glosses the inner life of the characters on screen: "Even though you ain't got money, she's *so* in love with you honey. Don't you think you deserve better? Don't you think [Mac's voice] *she* deserves better?"[15]

The overall effect of this speech mode is to suggest that every utterance (and feeling and idea) emerges as a repetition of prior utterances and the experience can run the gamut from verbal play to possession to stupor. Where the Witches' earlier spell conjured television, this one conjures radio as the medium that broadcasts conventional matter. As the scene closes, it turns our attention to the way in which radio delivers sound and sentiment "for us" and under that spell, produces listeners as

5.5 Spinning like a record

consuming subjects. As Mac succumbs to the multiple disorienting effects of the evening – the carnival ride, the prophecy, alcohol, marijuana, and the late hour – the camera closes in on his face. His eyes roll up and the audiotrack drops everything but non-diegetic music, Bad Company's "Feel Like Making Love." The miking sounds close, the volume loud: like a good stereo turned up high in your room – but not the dingy room where the camera cuts to, as Mac wakes, and flashes back to the spinning carnival ride. Is he still possessed by the prophecy? Dissolving from music track to diegetic sound the song continues, playing over a series of cross-cut scenes organized around the theme of listening. As the sequence unfolds, the volume drops and loses resonance, re-establishing its source in various radios in the background. Downstairs Malcolm fights with his father. Upstairs, Donald mourns in youthful gay melancholy, listening to Janis Ian with his headphones on. Mac and Pat plot their rise in the burger joint and begin to mess around on their bed, playing "New Manager/Bad Counter Girl" (figure 5.6).

It comes as no surprise to find the McBeths' erotic life so scripted by economic immobility. The real twist in these cross-cut scenes is the gradual convergence of diverse emotions under the spell of the radio: a spell marked by audio dissolves that collapse the distance between music track and diegetic track, referential sounds and symbolic ones, real and ideal. The same song, turned up in each space, promises transformed circumstances to each individual. It releases Malcolm from impotent rebellion (he cranks up the radios in every room); it frees Donald from isolated melancholy; and it promises the McBeths a way out of the dead-end of recession. But the actual transformations are eerily the same. Malcolm's rage and Mac's orgasm both expire. They do so, ironically, in the recognition that the station has shifted to non-commercial mode, playing several songs from the same album in succession (in this case, a third Bad Company song, "Shooting Star"). "Rock Block" is now a promotional phrase but it originally described the ubiquitous practice of original programming by local disc jockeys (playing several songs in a row from the same record allows for coffee breaks). The coinage marks the practice as residual, in the process of being overtaken by bulk advertising, playlists, and other homogenizing effects of conglomeration.[16]

5.6 Rock Block

This scene gives us one of the film's darkest views of interpellation by modern media but also its happiest nostalgic buzz. If we step back for a moment to think about the nostalgia being offered, we can see – in the passionate blasting of Bad Company on an old stereo – a remembered moment when three aspects of our media-scape that are now totalized, à la McDonalds, were the once-separate vernaculars of film, TV, and radio. Looking back to this moment, when each is fully emerged and yet on the cusp of consolidation, *Scotland, PA* offers a genealogy of our present – of the invention of MTV, with its feature-song narratives, no less than the invention of the drive-thru. In this media archeology of our own present we visit an imagined youth, in which separate media powers – that have since come together, like Scotland and England – had an independent life and clearly differentiated claim on our attention. Shakespeare's *Macbeth* sponsors that look back and also reminds us that this genealogy is a fiction addressed less to the past than to the anxieties and desires of the present, as all genealogies are.[17] This particular genealogy answers to two pressing concerns of the present: it is crafted at a moment when the old structures of authority (media and food industries) are again in productive ferment and when, in part because of this ferment, the prospect of mass, absolutist consolidation appears especially fearful. In this context, the film's insistent parody (even as the old moral framework of *Macbeth* resurfaces) can be obliquely reassuring. For it suggests that our own moment of absolutist fears may be only a mistaken fantasy of authority dreamed at an earlier stage. We may be called to restage it, but the possession will be far from perfect or complete.

In a subtle but important substitution of governing symbols, the film figures this shift from a tragic to a parodic view of historical change (and cultural transmission) by replacing the Ferris wheel with a different ride. The "Rock Block" sequence began (as the film did) with that figure of vertical, cyclical change, evoking the pattern of rise and fall that governs *Macbeth*. The ride Mac gets on, however – the nauseating ride where the Witches tell his future – rotates horizontally, like a record on a turntable (the device that sponsored disc jockeys, Rock Blocks, and, of course, sampling as a technical art). The substitution of flat spin for vertical rotation evokes the leveled social scene in *Scotland, PA*. It also suggests a different model of historical change, understood not in terms of tragic fall and restoration but in terms of cyclical substitution and return.

6 Channeling *Othello*

- televisuality
- surrogation
- character function and effect
- voice-over
- race and performance

As innovative and as risk-taking as recent film-versions of *Hamlet, Titus Andronicus,* and *Macbeth* have been, no Shakespeare play has been adapted to the screen as provocatively as *Othello* has in the last twenty years. Janet Suzman and Oliver Parker directed highly eroticized film-versions of *Othello* in 1988 and 1995, respectively, the former challenging the proscriptions against cross-racial "mixing" of South African apartheid, the latter pitting Laurence Fishburne's sexually magnetic Othello against Kenneth Branagh's brilliant but brittle Iago. More recently, Tim Blake Nelson has reset the play in a South Carolina prep school (*O*, 2001) and, in the shadow of a series of American school shootings, has used it to analyze teen violence (Semenza 2005). The same year brought Geoffrey Sax's and Andrew Davies's inspired televisual reformatting of *Othello* as a racially charged British police procedural. In these films, Shakespeare's Moor becomes less "all wheeling stranger" than talented insider, privileged as much for his gifts as for his character and reputation. In his transit from South African to African-American to black Londoner, Othello grows increasingly adept at navigating social milieus still coded "white" and at finding ways to make his mark on them. But each production's fidelity to Shakespeare's plot, which requires the gifted black protagonist to devolve once again to murder, locks these films into a storyline that suggests racial stereotypes are inevitably self-fulfilling. In different ways, each prompts the question: *can Othello* be successfully updated? And what would success mean if it could?

▨ A Negative Myth? ▨

We have come some way from the days when Othello was (literally) a white man. Indeed, Laurence Olivier's black-face performance of Othello (1965, dir. Stuart Burge), marks one of the last times the role was played on film by a prominent white actor, Anthony Hopkins's portrayal of a tawny-complexioned Moor in the1981 BBC TV-film (dir. Jonathan Miller) supplying the exception that proves the rule.[1] But even black actors who measure their professional standing by playing Othello arguably perform the role in black-face, insofar as they are compelled to rehearse pre-scripted and stereotyped notions of black male identity (Hill 1984: 40; Daileader 2000: 184–5). These notions have changed over time.[2] But to say that they have also evolved would be to trust that what

Celia Daileader (2000) has classified as "Othellophilia" has fully separated itself (or can ever separate itself) from the "Othellophobia" that
has discouraged some prominent black actors from taking the Othello
test, and prompted the Nigerian writer Ben Okri to claim that *Othello*
serves as "a negative myth for black people in the West" (1987: 564). The
"black person's response to Othello" is, according to Okri, considerably
"more secret, and much more anguished, than can be imagined" (1987:
618). Or should be, as the British actor Hugh Quarshie suggests in
describing "his resistance to [a] role, which he sees as reinforcing racist
stereotypes" (Daileader 2000: 185; Quarshie 1999).

As secret or as anguished as their response to Othello might be, a
number of prominent modern black actors have, nonetheless, chosen
to take on the part. They have done so despite the fact, as Daileader and
Barbara Hodgdon suggest, that in taking it on they allow themselves to
become conduits for an array of latter-day stereotypes about black
male sexuality and black male violence superimposed on presumably
outdated but enduring stereotypes about "relapses into primitivism
under stress" (Neill 1989: 393).[3] We might think of the relationship
between the ongoing circulation of these stereotypes and this vexed
role as a form of "channeling:" performances of Othello "channel" a
prevailing racial construction as much as they do a dramatic persona.

What other patterns of change do we find in these films and how
should we assess their success? A conspicuous aspect of the four
Othellos referred to above is their double focus on black male sexuality
and on the erotic responsiveness of the Desdemonas in question. Much
of this may be attributed to the marketing concerns and stylistic
conventions of the contemporary film industry. After all, even recent
film-versions of *Hamlet* supply audiences with flashback scenes showing Hamlet and Ophelia enjoying intimacies that are never alluded to in
the playtext. But as Daileader notes of stage productions of *Othello*, the
repeated focus on the black male body in different stages of arousal and
undress is matched by a comparative indifference to the bodies of the
aroused Desdemonas in question (2000: 196). This shift of attention to
Othello's body would seem to cut against the grain of mainstream film
conventions, which tend to display the female body as liberally as
possible, often at the expense of the male's. Yet these conventions
generally make exceptions for the prominent display of the *black*
male's body, which the camera fastens on with the same frequency,
intensity, and erotic fascination that it lavishes upon women's bodies in
mainstream films.[4] Think of Wesley Snipes's tattooed chest in *Blade*
(dir. Stephen Norrington, 1998), Denzel Washington lounging in tank
top and suspenders in *Devil in a Blue Dress* (dir. Carl Franklin, 1995), or
the soft focus on Washington's supposedly prison-trained torso in *He
Got Game* (dir. Spike Lee, 1998) and *The Hurricane* (dir. Norman
Jewison, 1999).

A second characteristic worth noting is the devolving age of the four
Othellos in question: John Kani, Laurence Fishburne, Eamonn Walker,

and Mekhi Pfifer. Whereas Kani, in the Suzman film, has entered the same "vale of years" as Shakespeare's middle-aged Othello, Fishburne seems a burnished thirty-something, the statuesque Walker considerably younger, and Pfifer is supposed to be all of 17. This tendency may again be attributed (particularly in the case of *O*) to the filmmakers' desire to cater to the youth market; or it may be explained by consistency with related plot rearrangements. Yet the change throws not only the black male's sexuality, but also his energy, beauty, and virility into bolder relief. Cast in the subject-position of sexually magnetic lover and husband, the Othello in question also becomes the not-so-obscure object of audience desire, and often of the desires of the film's Iago or Iago-surrogate.

Rejuvenating Othello has additional implications. While it casts his sexuality in bolder relief, it also dissolves the anxiety the "originary" Othello is made to feel about being unequal to Desdemona's youth, thereby putting added pressure on the anxiety he continues to feel about being black. In the Suzman and Parker productions, which deploy the formal language of the playtext and are set in a clearly demarcated historical past, this anxiety is largely understated, though made apparent in a number of displaced ways. In the Sax and Nelson updatings, spoken in colloquial British and American English "paraphrase", respectively, anxiety about race and how race inflects sexual relations is foregrounded. That anxiety repeatedly finds its way into the new material (both scripted dialogue and cinematography) added to the playtext by their writers and directors. Although race clearly matters in all four films, it is made to matter considerably more when the Othello in question no longer can blame his wife's disaffection on his age, his eroded sexual attractiveness, or a lifelong career as a soldier that has diminished his domestic skills.

This erotically charged objectification of the black male body has other consequences in these films. One is to strengthen the already dramatically privileged point of view of Iago, or more correctly, the dramatic function the character named Iago fulfills. Shakespeare's play ostensibly identifies the Iago-function as an abnormal behavior performed by a perversely motivated individual whom the audience is encouraged to despise. Yet when that behavior is reproduced in countless stage-productions and "restored" or reinvented in films that provide powerful substitutions for Iago's dramatically privileged asides, it may be said to take on the sponsorship of the producing parties – and to take in the audience, in the sense that it re-anchors "an invisible network of allegiances, interests, and resistances" attached to race and the display of race in Western culture (Schechner 1985: 36; Roach 1996: 27, 39). Othello's devolution from singular character to racial construction is, in these terms, an *effect* of his falling prey to a *function* that satisfies the larger cultural imperative that it dramatically channels. Now that the Othello-effect is almost always colored black – and hence "naturalized" in a way that a performance in black-face is not – while the Iago-function is colored white, we are compelled to see this trans-action as more racially charged than ever.

Whether conducted on stage or on film, contemporary perform-ances of *Othello* are haunted less by the play's theatrical or cinematic history than they are by the crises in racial relations we see staged daily: not only in our tabloids and on TV, but in our secondary schools and workplaces, in local and national debates about affirmative action, capital punishment, and even spousal abuse. An obvious example is Janet Suzman's film-version of her conscientiously "progressive" stage-production of *Othello* first performed in 1985 at Johannesburg's Market Theater. Consistent with its anti-apartheid agenda, both the film's and play's Iago-functions are performed as virulently racist: the embodi-ment of an embattled extremist bias reasserting its prerogatives. Its Othello-effect, in turn, is embodied by an actor (John Kani) who cut his teeth on the anti-apartheid plays of Athol Fugard and later courted danger by openly embracing his Desdemona in this production. Sax's and Davies's ITV *Othello* directly alludes to a more circumscribed crisis in British racial relations provoked by the 1993 beating-death of a young black man recounted in another ITV film, *The Murder of Stephen Lawrence* (dir. Paul Greengrass, 1999). The two productions were linked as companion-pieces when PBS broadcast the films on successive Sunday evenings (January 21 and 28, 2002) on Masterpiece Theater (Hodgdon 2003a: 94–5). Davies's brilliant script sustains this connec-tion by updating Shakespeare's play in the popular format of the police-procedural. Yet the film's avowed good intentions are subverted in telling ways, as the black male body (and the concomitant disintegra-tion of the black male mind) come in for prominent display when the film predictably culminates in the black Othello killing his white wife.

Black male subjectivity and the black male body are not the only enti-ties objectified in this otherwise estimable updating. For example, when confronted by John Othello's jealousy in a moment of amorous self-revelation, John's wife, the polished, educated, freelance writer Dessie (Keeley Hawes), describes herself as a "blank sheet waiting" for her husband to write on. This phrase, carrying such a long history of feminist critique, generates immediate dissonance, particularly since the scene marks her avowal as true devotion. As Hodgdon writes, "Dessie's words" depict her as a "shadow function in a narrative where, consistently, it is men who shape her identity and articulate her past" (2003a: 97). Is Dessie, then (and by extension Shakespeare's Desdemona), no more than a negotiable piece of cultural capital symp-tomatic of the male drive for possession? What name can we give to this chronic omission? And what do we make of the fact that so much that we know or can learn of John and Dessie is channeled through the suspect but seductive agency of Ben Jago, the name Sax and Davies give to their Iago-function? We turn now to look more closely at this film: a compelling adaptation in its own right but also an eloquent illustra-tion of the ways *Othello* remains haunted by its own cultural history.

▓ *Othello* as Police Drama: Geoffrey Sax's ITV *Othello* ▓

About a third of the way into the ITV *Othello*, Ben Jago (Christopher Eccleston) learns that he has been passed over for promotion to commissioner of the London Metropolitan police force in favor of John Othello and propels himself into a hallway with histrionic abandon. There, in a brilliantly edited montage of face-on tracking shots and direct address to the camera, he releases all the pent-up rage and resentment he has carefully suppressed while carving a path to what he assumed would be a richly deserved promotion. Jago's point of view as candid informant and confidant of the audience (to whom he repeatedly speaks in the film's version of Iago's theatrical asides) has been privileged throughout. But it has to this point been characterized by a knowing wink and oily charm that make him hard to resist but also "characteristically" unreadable. We are pretty sure what he wants, yet knowing the story as we (think we) do, we also assume that he will get caught out in the end, and won't make much of a fuss when he does. As Jago spits out his rage and venom – crying "I could howl like a dog," claiming "It should have been ME!" and, in a mocking, ventriloquized version of John Othello's voice, proclaiming "I'm just a token handsome nigger" – his passion spills out of him in a manner so raw and revealing it would make Shakespeare's Iago blanch.

Discomfiting as it may seem, Ben Jago's fury arguably becomes a charged source of viewer engagement here, the scene's vertiginous camera-work serving as the appealing but disorienting signature of our surrender to the Iago-function. Jago has his hand on the controls of most of the forensic and disciplinary technologies of the film: the secret recording that compromises the first commissioner; the computer through which he sends disguised racist threats to John and Dessie; the tape-recorder that he deploys like a musical instrument to solicit confessions; and the fake "DNA" test that appears to confirm Dessie's adultery. All these tools help him manipulate the emotions of others, as he generates sudden lurches and reversals of affect of the kind that take place in this hallway. Indeed, as the camera spins and up-ends in this scene it reproduces a way of "being there" that Jago claims specifically as the condition for sympathy – ours with him and his with everyone else. "I've been there," he tells us, a refrain that assures we all share the experience of Aristotelian reversal, "whirling down into some dark pit ass over tit." The camera-work and editing here and elsewhere in the film seem designed to pull the audience into this disorienting sense of vertigo and into complicity with Jago. We are invited in this way to sympathize less with him than with his alternately controlled and uncontrolled fury as he carries out the Iago-function.

In Shakespeare's play, Iago's resentment at Othello's promotion of Cassio as lieutenant has a double focus: envy of the gentlemanly Cassio and vindictiveness against Othello. That focus leads first to the plot that eventuates in Cassio's degrading (and Iago's appointment to his place) and then to the destruction of Othello's marriage. By contrast, the ITV *Othello* pivots on the prominently displayed *failure* of Ben Jago's plot to succeed to the position of the discredited commissioner and on John Othello's appointment to a position that even we are led to believe he may not entirely deserve. Though it is hard to pinpoint exactly where Ben Jago fits into Britain's class and social structure, it is clear enough that he has, like John Othello, come up through the ranks and is uniformly considered a savvy and accomplished administrator. As such, he is ill-prepared to suffer the promotion of someone he has mentored – much less an officer "of color" for whom his friendship seems grounded more in physical attraction than in intellectual respect. For a film whose most graphic effects focus on the fatal, unprovoked, and unpunished beating of a black suspect by four white policemen (three of whom are presented as confirmed racists), the scope given to Ben Jago's rage seems unusually broad. That rage is granted the same rationale as the otherwise unmotivated violence of the racist policemen and the racist comment Jago elicits from the (soon-to-be) degraded police commissioner: that is, resentment of the presumed privileges and undeserved sympathy British minorities enjoy thanks to the hypocritical ministrations of upper-crust Labour Party liberals. This is not to suggest that the ITV *Othello* is complicit with, or speaks on behalf of, this source of race-based resentment. It does, however, indicate how much at odds the film's channeling of dramatic and imaginative energy may be with what one takes (indeed, what *it* takes) to be its express aims or designs.[5]

Whereas the play's Iago is caught out in the end and vows "never to speak word more," Ben Jago remains our primary interpreter throughout this retelling of *Othello*. This becomes clear early on in the film. As the opening credits roll, the camera slowly brings into focus an indeterminate moment in time through an extreme close-up on the eyes of the sleeping Dessie. The camera moves down to her lips then shifts briefly to the eyes and face of her seemingly adoring lover, John Othello, who entwines his black fingers through her white ones. Close as they are, the lovers seem separated by the mystery of Dessie's dream-speech, pitched just below the level of intelligibility. Her muttering, evidence of a mysterious inner life, seems to entrance John. But it will return to haunt him – and the film – as the story unfolds. The film proper doesn't actually begin until the unspecified presentness of this intimate scene abruptly slips into a similarly unspecified past as the screen shifts focus to the narrating presence of Ben Jago. He sits in the back seat of a car, wearing the uniform of a highly placed police official, and tells us (speaking directly to the camera) that "It was about 'luv' . . . don't talk to me about race, politics, stuff like that." Coming so quickly after the confusion of Dessie's cryptic dream-speech, his pronouncement cuts through that auditory puzzle with the ring of clarifying authority.

The specific form Jago's authority takes requires analysis since it will recur throughout the film in various permutations. Jago's modes of address are marked cinematically as privileged: direct, intimate asides and voice-over, what some consider "the most dominant and dominating of all vocal positionings in cinema" (Donaldson 2003: 110). Some aspects of his commentaries, however, qualify that dominant position. Hodgdon, for one, contends that the "sneering, slightly nasty tone" in this opening scene undermines his credibility (2003a: 96). It matters here that the voice-over belongs to a specific, presumably biased, person.[6] Kaja Silverman distinguishes different kinds of film voice-over in precisely these terms, embodied and disembodied. Conceding that voice-over sustains its position of dominance when it is "disembodied," that is, when it "superimposes itself 'on top' of the diegesis" and remains "inaccessible to the gaze of either the cinematic apparatus or the viewing subject," Silverman claims that "it loses its power with every corporeal encroachment, from a regional accent or idiosyncratic 'grain' to definitive localization in the image" (1988: 49). Silverman's observations do not tell the whole story, however, since they draw only on film traditions – and classic ones at that. Jago's voice-overs hark back to other performance traditions as well. For example, his intimate access to the viewer in the form of direct address, knowing winks, confessions, and so on, has its dramatic roots in the many *asides* Shakespeare scripted for Iago, derived in turn from the older performance conventions of the medieval Vice figure. In theatrical terms, embodiment constitutes no more or less a source of authority from one character to another. Moreover, as the next scene of political machinations makes clear, Jago's voice-overs owe as much to the televisual asides Andrew Davies developed for the character of Francis Urquhart (played with a similar oily charm by Ian Richardson) in the 1990 BBC political thriller *House of Cards*. That serial developed a specific conceit for asides, construing them as a political tool: a form of access Urquhart doled out equally to the audience and to those who helped in his rise to power. The protean quality of Jago's asides may also owe something to the parodic voice-overs in contemporary films such as *Trainspotting* (1996) and *The Butcher Boy* (1997).[7]

That Jago commands (however uncertainly) so much narrative authority, and may even control a system of audience rewards, should alert anyone familiar with the plot of Shakespeare's play to an implied change of ending. The destabilization of what we think we already know about *Othello* continues apace as we next witness what, chronologically, is the "real" beginning of the film, in a now "past" filmic event conveyed to us in a dramatic present. This is a fast and furiously filmed police raid on a London housing estate which eventuates in the beating and killing of a black suspect whose otherwise indeterminate features surface only long enough to distinguish him from the still unidentified black man we saw in the earlier shot (whom we may take to be "Othello"). The film cuts back here to Ben, now dressed in black-tie and casually inviting us to serve as his invisible escort at a banquet convening at the same time that the police raid is rapidly devolving into a riot.

The two intercut events begin to collide when the character we have just been formally introduced to as John Othello, protégé of Assistant Commissioner Ben Jago in the London Metropolitan police hierarchy, is called away by his beeper to attend to the riot.

The banquet scenario reveals the extent to which the film's prevailing point of view is tied to that of Ben Jago and helps recontextualize the play in terms of the racial problems that beset both the public and private face of the Metropolitan police force ("the Met"). As Jago cleverly traps the current police commissioner into making a racist statement in the men's room, which is recorded by a confederate planted there for the purpose, he seems to be paving the way to his own imminent promotion. But his decision to play the race-card redounds against him when we see, in the next extended sequence, John Othello singlehandedly putting down the cross-cut riot in an act of seemingly selfless courage and bravado. The double scandal of the police murder of a young black man and the commissioner's own perceived racism prompts the prime minister (in an act of oily opportunism visible to anyone apart from John Othello) to promote John to the commissioner's position, thereby making the foiled Ben Jago subordinate to his former protégé and provoking the sustained expression of rage described above.

In Shakespeare's play, Othello is always already established as the Venetian state's celebrity general. Possibly a former mercenary, but in the "now" of the play's production a military leader of proven merit and magnificence, he is the one and only man capable of defending Cyprus against the Turks. In the ITV film, and particularly as performed by Eamonn Walker (known to viewers of HBO's *Oz* as the charismatic and intellectually self-assured Kareem Said), he is similarly presented as a man of rare parts and principled integrity. He is also the one black face in a sea of white police officials listening to a speech that calls for the recruitment and promotion of more black and Asian officers: a factor that no doubt explains why he is the only official summoned to contend with the riot. John is also revealingly presented as a powerful physical specimen: so tall, young, muscular, and handsome that he could well be called beautiful. In a clever substitution for the eloquent manner in which Othello subdues Brabantio and his confederates in the first act of Shakespeare's play, and later disarms further resistance to his marriage to Desdemona, the solitary John Othello strides forth from behind the glass doors of the entrance to the now besieged housing estate and takes command of an increasingly dire situation. He begins with the simultaneously modest and proud statement, "Brothers and Sisters – My name is John Othello. I was *born* here. I grew up on these streets. I went to *school* here" (figure 6.1).

Shot from several angles in the manner of a jumpy but stylized on-the-spot newscast – the most effective shots being directed from behind the rioters, which illumine him in the refracted glare of Molotov cocktails, burning police cars, and spotlights cast by hovering police

6.1 "My name is John Othello"

6.2 "We must have justice under the law"

helicopters – John ignores the advice of other (white) officers to with-hold the fact that the black suspect, Billy Coates, died on the way to hospital. Predictably, this news arouses another series of loud protests and explosions. Rather than retreat, John instead calls attention to the TV cameras that are recording the action and admonishes the rioters not to conform to established stereotypes by behaving like "ignorant fools" but to repossess themselves of their dignity. Again he identifies himself as one of them: "We just want justice. We must have justice under the law. Justice under the law" (figure 6.2). This shot is not only recorded by the cameras in question but also reproduced on the front pages of the next day's tabloid, juxtaposed with an image of the now degraded, former commissioner.

When John returns from his public triumph to the glowing privatized space of his and Dessie's bed, one of the rewards that await him is a gift that oddly resonates with the already cultivated impression of John's racialized celebrity. As John reluctantly accepts from Dessie, and tries on, a golden-colored silk robe, he tries to cover his embarrassment by saying "I always think of silk as being a girl thing." We learn soon enough that the robe functions in the film as an updated substitution for the handkerchief Othello gives to Desdemona, an apt vehicle for Ben Jago's fake DNA testing of semen secretions. But as John reluctantly dons it, looking like an exotic African prince, echoes of the "noble Moor" of Shakespeare's play are everywhere apparent, from the arches of the bed to the wooden frame of a medieval painting hanging on their wall. As Dessie contends that the "look" John assumes in this golden robe is "absolutely you," one feels prompted to ask if the "look" he had before – in shirt and tie, or a moment later, with his shirt off – is as much *him* as this one is. And what makes John so uncomfortable at the prospect of wearing the robe in the first place? Does he really think wearing silk is "a girl thing?" Or is he savvy enough to suspect that the woman in whom he has invested more of himself than he is comfort-able with has begun to exoticize him, to see him less as the man who was "born here" and "went to school here" than as an extravagant stranger?

6.3 "Absolutely you"

The immediate corollary to Dessie's gift of the robe is the prime minister's "gift" of "the Met" to John a few scenes later. As a translation of the handkerchief, the robe invokes anxieties of performance and inauthenticity that a handkerchief does not – while still serving as the trace of sex. Similarly, the Downing Street scene pointedly recontextualizes the established command of Othello in Shakespeare's play in terms of the notorious interpenetration of politics and public relations in England during the three Blair administrations. Indeed, the ITV film intimates that John Othello's appointment as commissioner itself constitutes a kind of borrowed robe – or at best, implied consent to perform public idealism in black face and voice.

The precedent for the Downing Street scene is an offstage event in Shakespeare's *Othello*: Othello's appointment of Cassio, instead of Iago, as his lieutenant for reasons that, Iago alleges, have more to do with Cassio's social standing than with his qualifications. Davies no doubt took this cue in order to bring the play into the domain of a world in which factors having to do with public relations even more conspicuously supersede practical considerations. One could, of course, "read" the events that transpire in this scene more positively, as (what the Prime Minister terms) a bold statement "about the kind of Britain we want our children to grow up in," inspired by his intuitive grasp of John Othello's absolute rightness for the position. But even John questions the prime minister's motives. And though the interchange concludes with John's assured confirmation of his abilities – "I know my own worth" – the entire scenario is informed by how it will play to a public in need of assurance of the Met's capacity to bring its renegade officers to justice. As John candidly admits that he never thought his abilities would be recognized so soon, the prime minister turns to his advisors and says "Isn't he great?" making his pleasure at discovering this diamond-in-the-rough seem as much a triumph of public theater as an inspired appointment.

The problem here is not so much John's administrative qualifications as his insufficient wariness about the opportunism and cynicism of a system more focused on immediate effects than on the sustained

6.4 "You clever big black bastard"

commitment to "justice under the law" that he has vowed to deliver. Surprised as he is by the prime minister's sudden offer – "We want to offer you the Met. Are you on for it?" – John also seems insufficiently suspicious of the motivations of men who can make such offers as casually as if they were inviting him to play a round of tennis. Another problem is the extent to which John's now confirmed sense of his own worth makes him blinder to his own limitations, one of which is the trust he places in Ben Jago. When, in the next scene, John informs Ben of his promotion, Ben is surely not the only auditor who wonders how (if he is really as principled as he claims) John could accept it so quickly, or how he can now assume so patronizing a tone towards his former mentor. In contrast to the knowing wink Ben passed us behind the back of the Commissioner, Ben's expression here is a strained study of anger, shock, despair, and frustration combined (figure 6.4). It makes John's repeated solicitude, "I know you wanted this job, but you are too good a man for envy," not only seem doubly patronizing but deeply mistaken.

When Ben Jago rushes out and engages in the sustained bout of histrionics described above, three additional aspects of his performance command our attention. The first is the plaintive question he asks when he reaches the street, "How can I love you now?" The second involves his somewhat abashed, self-reflexive comment, "Well, well, what a passionate performance," as he straightens his tie and acknowledges our presence. The third concerns the recovery of his poise and good spirits as he offers what seems to be a counter-intuitive response to the apparent failure of his plans, "Shame, really, he's a good man," and turns directly back to the camera to say, "Cheer up. Do you like sex?" Disturbed by the fact that it is John who will profit from his clever plot against the former commissioner, Ben sees the extent to which his ambition and desire now operate at cross-purposes, and temporarily "loses it." Once he returns to "himself," he reassumes a subject-position from whose vantage point "passion" again operates at the level of "performance," as part of his *function* as opposed to his affect. Addressing the camera as if it were both an empathetic "us" and a mirror of his projective narcissism, Ben offers "cheer up," as if his disappointment were our own. To help us on our way, he has the temerity to pre-empt our answer to his "Do you like sex?" question by transporting us into the domain of a sex scene in which, fully dressed, he manually brings Lulu (the film's substitute Emilia) to climax. In this respect and others, Ben reminds us that though he, himself, may occasionally lose control, he is still the figure who has been pleasuring us by pulling the strings of what we may come to see as a hijacked version of *Othello* from first frame to last.[8]

▨ Othello as Prime Suspect ▨

The notion that Ben is in control is, of course, an impression that the producers of the ITV *Othello* have chosen to cultivate. Yet the film also embeds the Iago-function in a generic context that naturalizes his professional behavior. The film is styled in the manner of a high-minded police drama like *Prime Suspect* (Granada TV/ITV; 1991–2003), which focuses its plots on investigations complicated by the efforts of women, blacks, and gays to claim the respect that is due them in a changing British social hierarchy. Indeed, a hallmark of that series, to which this *Othello* clearly draws connections, is the fraught climate of competition and sympathy between subordinate officers representing such marginalized groups. The professional lives these officers lead and those of the criminals they pursue display common symptoms of exclusion. This generic context establishes a topical layer of mediation that is thickened by the interventions of a dubiously motivated, centralized authority, making tokenism simultaneously a route to advancement and an obstacle to success.

In this respect, Ben Jago may be as much an effect as a function of the topicality of the genre superimposed here on the matter of *Othello*. His triumph in the end is itself an effect of the political system's correction of its self-styled "brave experiment." Having attempted to make room for the exceptional black outsider, who was allowed to skip "a couple of rungs" on the promotion ladder, the system ultimately reverts to form, congratulating itself for its openness at the very moment it regretfully closes ranks. A structure of authority that is continuous with Ben's casual but mannered style and mode of address allows him to melt back into a system that ultimately awards him the position he has been seeking all along. The dramatic irony that attends this reversal is the product of a more powerful institutional irony that translates the torture about to be meted out to Iago at the end of *Othello* into the rewards that await Ben Jago. The implicitly racist and openly sexist observations that the prime minister and his advisor avail themselves of at film's end collaborate with Ben's closing assertion: "It was 'luv,' simple as that, not race, not politics." These dismissals mystify the situation in a manner clearly intended, first, to arouse our resistance and then, when no alternative reading emerges, gently put it to rest in the cradle of established social and dramatic conventions.

So much for how the tragedy of the Moor of Venice is recontextualized as a headline for a failed experiment in public relations. Yet the collaboration of the generic conventions of British television with the film's institutional setting in retailing Shakespeare's tragedy may also help us clarify some of the difficulties we raised at the beginning of this chapter, about the underlying misogyny of a narrative that makes the Desdemona-figure a "blank sheet" for the inscriptions of others ("my wife," posh girl, battered wife, "a handful"). This problem in turn helps us reassess the forces acting through the Iago-function, which depend not only on the cultural status of Shakespeare for authority, but on the specific forms of visual and auditory pleasure film itself offers. As a medium, film has the capacity to deliver what the stage, for the most part, cannot: a densely elaborated *mise en scène* in which an entire city may serve as setting: a setting which can be made available to the viewer from any number of angles and can be selectively cut in pieces and sutured together through the power of montage. In several of the other films we have discussed (particularly, *William Shakespeare's Romeo + Juliet* and Almereyda's *Hamlet*), directors "thicken" their filmic accounts of Shakespeare in a broadly allusive, citational manner, so that it can be said that their very *mise en scène* is littered with, or haunted by, the ghosts of Shakespeares past. In this way, the films "open up" the play in question to embrace the trappings of a richly detailed material world. They also put the play (and other earlier films based on it) into a state of fairly transparent surrogation to its latest avatar or incarnation. We do not necessarily think of the countless other times we have witnessed a character named Romeo climb up to Juliet's balcony (or window or fire escape) as we watch Leonardo DiCaprio make his pitch to Juliet in Luhrmann's film. But Luhrmann has generated so pervasive a citational environment for his film that it's hard to read any such gesture in a decontextualized way.

Although the ITV *Othello* also wears its intertextual heart on its televisual sleeve, the visual space it inhabits seems considerably flatter than the more cinematically resonant settings that Lurhmann and Almereyda generate for their similarly updated reproductions of *Romeo and Juliet* and *Hamlet*. This sense of flattening is abetted by the film's immersion in a contemporary setting that bears only the most incidental similarities to the *mise en scène* of Shakespeare's *Othello*; by its substitution of contemporary language for Shakespeare's verse; and by its channeling through the largely disenchanted medium of TV, where the only ghosts that haunt it are echoes from the police procedurals and political thrillers that it mines. Indeed, the conventional intimacy of the televisual mode of address collaborates with the film's privileging of Ben Jago's "asides," which, rather than being spoken in hushed tones from a corner of the stage, are delivered with a face-on immediacy that fills the screen. As a TV film that mines the conventions and pacing of the high-toned police drama, the ITV *Othello* also traffics heavily in topical interests, so much so that its substitutions take on a life of their own and occasionally become unmoored from their referential roots in the Shakespearean playtext.

This is not to suggest that the film floats entirely free from its moorings in Shakespeare. As flatly contemporary as it sometimes seems – with its tony clubs, private rooms in expensive restaurants, luxury flats, gritty housing estates, posh swimming pools – the film gains considerable density, depth, and intertextual resonance when it fastens on the watchfulness and sensitivity of John Othello. In many of these instances, the general disenchantment of the film's *mise en scène* is countered by a scopic haunting of decidedly racial (if not exactly racist) proportions. As noted above, our first sighting of John Othello is of a handsome face and liquid eyes tenderly focused on Dessie, who seems as much the extraordinary object of John's affection as she is of his desire. The next private moment they share is when Dessie gives John the silken robe, a gesture that should resonate with viewers knowing enough either to associate it with the play's handkerchief, or to see it as a sign of recurring exoticization. In their third meeting on screen, we see them totally immersed in each other on the morning of their wedding; however, this celebratory scene ends on a note of foreboding, as John introduces Dessie to the soon-to-be-suspect Michael Cass with an enthusiasm that seems hard to sustain: "This is my *wife*" (the italics hardly do justice to the sheer sense of pride and awe Eamonn Walker brings to the word). This moment prefaces several later instances when John confesses to Ben how he spies on her while she sleeps (in part because he's afraid of the negligible role he may play in her dreams) and how the excess of affection he has for her "scares" him (because it makes him feel "as if [he is] at her mercy"). Each of these admissions serves as an effectual gloss on similar admissions Othello makes to Iago. In the eyes and ears of the knowing viewer, that connection may haunt the scene of John's latter-day pronouncements. The main difference is that in the play Othello's anxiety is presented as a symptom of his age, exclusively military experience, and, ultimately, his race. In the film it seems to proceed from a less specific source of emotional vulnerability.

Initially, when the specter of the old play threatens to penetrate the glass walls within which most of John's encounters with Dessie take place, the mutual affection of smart, articulate, thoroughly modern Londoners tends to lay the ghost low. Drawing on the recent convention of casting actors closely matched in age in *Othello* productions, the ITV film cultivates the impression that John and Dessie are perfectly matched in virtually every way that matters: in beauty, taste, temperament, and desire. But by planting early on, on Eamonn Walker's expressive face and in the viewer's mind, a pronounced fear of emotional over-investment, and having the naively trusting John Othello mistakenly choose Ben Jago as the father-confessor of his anxieties, the Sax/Davies collaboration also finds a way to match this Othello's uncertainties with the insecurities of an older Othello who worries about his age, background, and race. Although there is no specific moment when John echoes Othello's anxious rumination that begins "Haply, for I am black" (3.3.279), the film foregrounds the *effect* of John's blackness from first image to last. Moreover, it finds both coded and overt ways to indicate the connection between his emotional insecurities and what being a black man continues to entail not only in Tony Blair's England but in the scopic economy of the contemporary TV and cine-mediated public relations apparatus.

The film begins to distance John from Dessie by twice making him seem a suspicious (and suspect) voyeur, looking up at the opaque windows of their flat from the vantage point of the reflecting pools at his feet. The reflecting pools provide the perfect medium for John to screen his anxious projections, one of which displays the naked bodies of Dessie and Michael Cass reaching out to him or to each other. The figure of a desiring but silent Dessie, in particular, serves as the screen opposite to the real but impenetrable Dessie of John's obsessions. Yet the anxieties about that unknowable Dessie return here with the image of a mutually desiring Michael Cass. The extent to which Michael's arms also seem to reach out to John correlates in suggestive ways both with Iago's recounting of the night he spent sleeping beside the dreamily aroused Cassio in Shakespeare's play and with the homoerotic undertow of the series of poolside conversations John has with Ben. These exchanges could have been shot anywhere. That they are set at a palatial private pool where John regularly swims laps no doubt suits the "young professional" *mise en scène* in which most of the film takes place. But the setting was also clearly chosen to display the power and perfection of John's body: a factor that alerts us to the complicity of the filmmakers in trafficking in contemporary stereotypes about the sexuality of black men. In the two poolside scenes which involve the fully clothed Ben Jago, the uxorious white man ministers to John in the way that a side-man ministers to a boxer. The crucial difference is that as he rubs John's shoulders in the first of these scenes Ben's theme is the probable promiscuity of John's wife, and in the second it is the fabricated DNA "proof" that she has had sex with Michael Cass. The visual and dramatic stress in both scenes fastens on the fully dressed white man/mind exercising his/its mastery of the all-but-naked black body in a manner that directly evokes the early scenes of the film in which the naked Billy Coates is beaten to death by other fully dressed white men for having had the temerity to wag his penis in their direction.

The two poolside exchanges that focus on Ben's arousal and confirmation of John's suspicions frame four more dramatically eventful scenes, each of which has its analogue in Shakespeare's *Othello*, but which all pull the film into disturbingly contemporary racial terrain. Although the first of these scenes draws liberally on matter taken from the third and fourth acts of the playtext, it elaborates on them to considerable topical effect. Set in a private room in a Moorish-themed restaurant at a moment when relations between John and Dessie have become frayed by jealousy and distrust, the dinner scene prompts John to step out of his delegated role as licensed exotic to bring the history of his racial positioning out into the open. As the dinner conversation turns to a visit made by Dessie and John to his grandparents' home in St Lucia, John first waxes nostalgic, evoking the image of a prelapsarian Caliban as he recalls an old gardener named Joshua who knew "every inch of that island." He soon turns, however, to bitterly anatomizing the postlapsarian condition of "Blacks waiting on whites, just like they did in the old days on the plantations. . . . That's what St Lucia's all about, St Lucia, Grenada, Barbados, all of those places. Your people brought my people over there to work and die as slaves on your plantations."

John's contentious depiction of social conditions on the islands seems designed to pull his complacent interlocutors up short, as if he is seeking historical justification for his growing disillusionment with his marriage and his gathering belief that his emotional investment in Dessie has been betrayed. His reply recontextualizes both the Moorish medievalism of the restaurant and that of their apartment: revealing the latter as the potential spoil of conquest and raising the specter of Dessie as a spoiled collector of trophies. (She "has an eye," Jago insinuates; posh girls like collecting elegant things.) Because this scene devolves on anger and violence, we may forget how particularly repellent Dessie and Lulu (Rachael Stirling) – well-intentioned upper-crust liberals who might well have never harbored a prejudicial thought – find John's comment about *his* people working as slaves on *their* plantations, as if the prosperity enjoyed by one gifted black man in Britain were enough to put both history and bitter memories permanently to rest. Indeed, their defensiveness has the effect of mystifying racial conflict by shifting the cultural field of reference backwards, from riots at London housing estates to mountains rising out of the Caribbean to an orientalized North Africa of noble Moors dressed in silken robes. Ben counters with a more telling response to John's seemingly unprompted playing of the race-card, "You haven't done too badly for yourself," thereby re-evoking the resentment against race-based initiatives of the degraded police commissioner (and possibly of other members of England's middle- and lower-classes).

If the restaurant scene offers disturbing insight into how thin the line between accommodation and resentment can be on both sides of the racial divide, the next scenes pose ever more disturbing questions about the representational aims of the film itself. As John physically assaults Dessie to the coarse tune of "Tell me the truth, bitch," drives her from their flat, and then proceeds to turn it upside down as he growls and curses (and as the camera literally turns itself and him upside down), we may know that we are in the dramatic terrain of the play's fourth act where similar things happen. But we may also feel that the filmmakers are mining some pernicious stereotypes to make their dramatic points felt. Indeed, combined with what follows, these scenes could be said to justify Ben Jago's resentment and support the offhand comment made by the prime minister at the film's end that the promotion of John Othello may have been a matter of "too much too soon." How, after all, are we to interpret what happens next as the officer who courageously settled a riot prompted by police violence disguises himself as a common criminal and utterly betrays his position by thuggishly assaulting Michael Cass in the dark confines of a parking garage?

Discernible to us by the whites of his eyes and by a trick of the camera that thickens his lips, John looks like a stalker waiting in ambush to attack his unsuspecting (stereotypically white) victim. He goes after Michael Cass with the same tenacious, robotic fixity with which he has just taken apart his and Dessie's apartment. Sax brings this shocking scene to an end by having the headlights of an approaching car prevent John from delivering a possibly fatal blow to Michael and by recording this picture of black-on-white violence in garishly lit slow motion. We may, if we like, attribute even this criminal act to the ministrations of Ben Jago. Yet it is hard to say which is worse at this point, to see John Othello as nothing more than the degraded product of Ben Jago's designs, or to see him acting on (and out of) his own inclinations and desires.

The stakes of casting John Othello as either the victim of Ben Jago or as an active agent in his own demise (and in the brutal killing of his wife) are raised by noting that these are the same choices the playtext of *Othello* always requires an audience to make. And this reception dynamic offers one of the most productive opportunities for adaptations willing to address the performative conditions of racial identity head on. There are important models for such an approach in the history of film *Othellos* and also in police procedural. The most powerful example of the former is probably *Che cosa sono le nuvole? (What Are Clouds?)*, a free, short adaptation of *Othello* conceived and directed in 1968 by Pier Paolo Pasolini. As Sonia Massai observes, Pasolini's film "anticipated in interesting ways the work of later critics, directors and adapters, by exposing the patriarchal and racist views associated with the play and its reception" (2005: 95). It foregrounds the extent to which Shakespeare's characters operate like puppets on a string by literally transforming them into "full-sized human puppets" (2005: 96). At the same time, the film liberates the audience from their role as complacent witnesses. Neither amused nor thrilled by the machinations of the Iago puppet, Pasolini's working-class "audience-within-the-film" saves the Desdemona puppet's life by attacking and "killing" the Iago and Othello puppets whose "bodies" are later dumped in a garbage pit. In an inspired twist, "Iago" and "Othello" respond to their demise by coming back to life, freed at last from the strings that bind them to the play and able for the first time to enjoy the "marvelous and heart-rending beauty of creation" ("straziante, meravigliosa bellezza del creato" (2005: 102, 169)).

Given their choice of genre, one would hardly expect Sax and Davies to construct an ending that runs against the grain of the gritty aesthetics of police procedural, dedicated to exposing prevailing power and social relations. That would give us an Othello *triumphans* as opposed to an Othello *agonistes*. Yet it is worth emphasizing here that their *Prime Suspect 2* avatar does find a third alternative, in the character of DS Oswalde (Colin Salmon), whose savvy suspicion of tokenism highlights a fundamental reflectiveness about racial scripting and misrecognition that the ITV *Othello* lacks. *Prime Suspect 2* opens on the scene of DCI Tennison, the series' central character (played by Helen Mirren), questioning a younger, black suspect: an apparent sexual predator who defends his actions in the most egregiously macho terms, implying that his victims sought out rough sex with black men. As the scene unfolds, it reverses into a classroom. We learn that the suspect is actually the gifted DS Oswalde, a colleague with whom Tennison is staging a training session and (it later turns out) with whom she is also having a secret affair. This opening and its reversals function as a sort of Othello test for the audience as well as for Oswalde: they deliberately invoke the racial misrecognitions Oswalde must be all too familiar with, in order to subject them to sustained interrogation.

By calling attention to the social clichés that prompt it, this prefatory scene rattles our complacency about maintaining a safe distance from the racially inflected misrecognitions that follow. And it has important consequences for character and plot. Oswalde is no more fully in control of racial misrecognition than anyone can be; but the role-playing does allow him space to distinguish himself from the parts (both negative and idealizing) socially scripted for him at the Met. He storms out of his affair with Tennison on suspicion that she sees him as a "black stud." When he finds himself assigned to her team, the token dark face on a racially charged case, his anxieties morph into competition with Tennison – the other target of tokenism and the other skilled performer who can use it and separate herself from it (as *Prime Suspect I* established). In short, this ambitious young, gifted, and black DS is as hyper-alert to the shoals and opportunities of racial misrecognition as Tennison is to gender misrecognition. By contrast, John Othello's credulity and helpless capitulation to obsessive anxiety seem conspicuously unexamined.

Public Speaking/Public Silence

We draw these extended comparisons because we want to call attention to the consequences of the mixed cultural and dramatic coding in this film. We also want to highlight important parallels between the Othello- and Desdemona-effects that are played out in the scene that most vividly foregrounds the social demands for racialized performance. The film does not sustain the pressure of a John Othello who calls ironic attention to his plantation heritage any more than it sustains the brief moment of ironic self-knowledge when Dessie tells Michael Cass how she met and fell in love with John. (This "posh" girl, we may recall, is also a freelance journalist, who meets her future husband in the process of writing precisely the kind of media spread about the "young, gifted, and black" male celebrity that is a staple of public relations tokenism.) Yet when John breaks down on a nationally televised public affairs show – as critical a transformation as his murderous violence – the film broaches the kind of self-reflection on permissible public scripts about race that we find in the scene from *Prime Suspect* or in Pasolini's adaptation.

Positioned to follow John's brutal assault on Michael Cass in the parking garage, this scene substitutes for Othello's lapse into a trance after uttering sexually charged epithets about "goats and monkeys" in Shakespeare's playtext. John's response to a white call-in viewer's question regarding what can we do about living in a racist society – "I say, enjoy the advantages it gives you" – is rejected less for its audacity than for being inconsistent with the expectations of his liberal-progressive auditors. When John answers the bewildered TV host's follow-up, "I think we were expecting a little more than that, John," with a silence that seems more like despair than a breakdown or trance, we may feel prompted to look at John with clearer eyes, noting just how much his emotional investment in Dessie has eroded his capacity to perform in public.

The film does not allow time for this impulse to develop. But it is important to take a moment to read against the forward drive of the plot – and against the grain of the on screen audience – to understand just how much may be at stake in John's public silence. This scene is the auditory corollary, in racial terms, of Dessie's muttering dream-speech, and we can understand it better by understanding how that dream-speech functions. We noted above the film's repeated inscriptions of John Othello's anxiety about the nature and extent of his emotional investment in Dessie, and about hers in him. This is the very first thing the film establishes in its opening images of John staring at the sleeping Dessie, and the film script repeatedly calls attention to his increasingly morbid fascination with what is running through her mind as she sleeps. This is a preoccupation that Ben Jago does not awaken so much as implicitly interpret for him. It is as if from the very start John cannot quite believe in his good luck, can't quite believe that he, the inner John, not just the great-looking John, has really "subdued" Dessie to his very "quality." We draw these words purposefully from the playtext because, as others have argued, Shakespeare's Othello seems in many ways *predisposed* to the idea of Desdemona's betrayal. The picture of sexual treachery that Iago paints is something Othello accepts so readily because he's already played out the possibility in his mind.

Yet crucially, in the ITV production, this predisposition derives as much from modern cinematic conventions as from Shakespearean ones. The desire to decode that secret language is something the film establishes as a mystery for the audience, enthralled by the spectacle of the almost knowable, desiring woman. We might, following Jago's voyeuristic lead, see this as a "luv" problem particular to film and video: specifically erotic film and video, in which the "truth" of female desire and pleasure is understood as *essentially* unrepresentable and therefore unknowable (Williams 1989: 30–2,115–19). Dessie's muttering, at-the-edge-of-hearing dream-speech is the audio corollary to this classic cinematic problem of visual proof of female pleasure.[9] The seductive power of those almost legible sounds and the fleeting expressions that accompany them has a great deal to do with the fact that these are involuntary expressions and therefore can be presumed not to be performed but to be authentic. Yet precisely because they are involuntary, unarticulated, they remain beyond the edge of legibility, as in the classic tradition of pornographic film. What obsesses John – indeed, what haunts him at the moment of his TV panel "trance" – is the speech he cannot quite hear.

Jago's earlier sex scene with Lulu elaborates the problem of male knowledge of female desire in more explicitly pornographic terms. At first, the scene appears to provide the authentic aural evidence that Dessie's muttering seems to withhold. "Good?" Jago asks. "You know it was," Lulu answers with satisfaction. Of course, Jago cannot know whether she is faking it any more than the audience can. But the camera seems to suggest – by positioning Lulu upside down, where it had moments before positioned us – that Jago's control of both Lulu and us is complete. His distinction as a function is as much to enforce speech or silence on others – including Dessie, whose testimony about her own sexual history he effectively overwrites – by deploying truths about the unreliability of social performance and the unknowability of inner lives. When he tosses off the aside "who knows what makes us do things?" we hear both the falseness and the truth of the rhetorical question. (No one but Ben is doing anything, but why precisely he does what he does remains a mystery.) Later he will seduce John by preying directly on his already established anxiety and uncertainty: "Who knows what's going on in their heads?" It is part of the Iago-function, in other words, to affirm the unspeakability and unknowability of female desire. Paired with this, the ITV production offers a critical Desdemona-effect: displacing the cause for this always already silencing of women by men, onto Othello and the modern dynamics of heterosexual coupling: "luv." Thus, the beginning of the breakdown of the marriage in this film involves a familiar cliché. He talks, she listens, and this imbalance is bad for the relationship. The marriage ends on the same theme: not the refrain "put out the lights," but with John Othello's repeated, urgent, "shh."

Returning to John's breakdown, we might fruitfully consider the scene of a public affairs show, on the topic of law enforcement and race, as the counterpart to the porn scenario: substituting a public performance of the "authentic, black" experience of racism for the performance of female pleasure. John Othello is introduced as part of a panel; he is the only person of color and the first question to the panel, about racism, of course goes to him (we can see the head of the panelist on the right turn towards him even before the questioner has finished speaking). John's initial response might be heard as a kind of structural resistance, like Iago's at the end of Shakespeare's play. In the TV moderator's follow-up, "I think we were expecting a little more than that, John," we might hear an echo of Iago's last lines, "What you know, you know/From this time forth I never will speak word" (5.2.303–4), and in John's refusal a surrogation of Iago's exit to torture.

Yet the "more" being sought on this TV show is pointedly fixed on the "truth" of racism. And John's resistance ought logically to be understood in that context, as resistance to the way in which he is being made to represent that "truth" in another public relations performance like the opening riot. In that earlier scene, he knew it was a performance ("Best if they just see me" he asserts, donning his hat for the cameras). But his passionate, inspiring promises suggest that he believes it was also authentic, fed by a fire within. By now, one might imagine, the moderator's question confirms that the tokenism he has feared all along is the only performable truth. Whatever answer he gives, the ultimate function of a panel such as this will be to help the establishment "enjoy the advantages" it gives them. So, like a female performer in a porn film, he is being asked here to testify to a truth that cannot be expressed inside the system of representation (white, objectifying, scopophilic) that is available. In this light, his initial refusal to answer is a perfectly consistent refusal of the position of black-male-as-feminized-object-of-desire that has haunted him in his relationship with Dessie and that inflects the Othello-effect in the culture at large.

The soundtrack explicitly invites this comparison when it dubs Dessie's dream-whispers over John's silence. But in part because of the intimacy of that over-dubbed memory, available only to the film auditors, John's silence cannot parse as anything but a breakdown to the audience in the scene. By a kind of reverse dramatic irony – in which what we know is colored by the understanding of the on-screen audience rather than vice versa – the possibility of perceiving silence as resistance disappears. And as the film races forward, John's state of mind is prejudged for us by the sight and sound of a hard-boiled egg Ben Jago cracks open the next morning and the front page of a tabloid that he considerately holds up to our eyes (figure 6.5). The headline,

6.5 "Police chief cracks up"

"Police Chief Cracks Up," definitively interprets the photo of John holding his head in his hands on TV the night before. This act of editorial suture compromises our understanding of John's mental state even as it seems to be posing the question: *has* he cracked up, or has he, instead, been cracked open? Avoiding this impasse, we might ask more pressingly, is John's cracking up or open to *our* advantage, or not? Who constitutes this film's interpretive community? Or better yet, how does *the film* constitute *us* as its viewing subjects?

One answer would be that the film constitutes us as subjects who will not be invited to ask questions about the textual effects of social scripts, including Shakespearean character functions as powerful as those enacted here. It constitutes "Shakespeare adaptation" as a peculiar realist sub-genre that involves the suspension of certain kinds of disbelief, including the fact that it will never occur to any of the highly educated, late-twentieth-century, British professionals who populate this story to remark on John's unusual surname. It seems almost nonsensical to ask why they do not. Yet were it possible to speak the name of Shakespeare's Othello within the fiction itself, it would also be possible for the fiction to reflect on the Othello effect, as constituted in the alchemy of racial history – and, further, to reflect on how and why we recycle it as a culturally privileged form of entertainment.

7 Surviving Shakespeare: Kristian Levring's *The King is Alive*

- documentary and experimental film
- voice-over
- cultural memory
- character function and effect
- subtitles
- substitution and translation

As we observed at the end of the last chapter, contemporary screen updatings of Shakespeare's plays typically avoid the problem of their long-term embeddedness in Western culture. It is not that these films shy away from naming the playwright in their titles, as Baz Luhrmann, Michael Radford, and others have done. Shakespeare's box-office appeal may be small by Hollywood standards but it has stood the test of time. Naming the playwright may also serve to finesse specific marketing challenges, alerting audiences that some degree of linguistic decoding may be required of them, as in a foreign-language film. Even films that use little or no Shakespearean language may engage in sly verbal or visual references of the kind that proliferate in Billy Morrissette's *Scotland, PA*, playing around with the rise and fall of intertextual awareness as it changes from moment to moment and from spectator to spectator. Such references establish a relationship with "knowing" audiences and keep high-school teachers and college professors interested in screening these films for their students.

Whatever their mode of adaptation, most film and video updatings demand that audiences suspend what knowledge of Shakespeare we do have in a very specific way. They ask us to accept the idea that characters that use the same names, speak the same lines, or act out the same plot as *Macbeth, Hamlet,* or *Romeo and Juliet* themselves have no acquaintance with these stories or their history. Despite being fundamentally absurd, this suspension of disbelief has become so normal that it seems odd even to raise the issue. Indeed, few screen updatings bring the question of what it means to retell a story that has been told numerous times before into the fiction represented on screen. Directors and films may be haunted by earlier films, as Branagh's *Hamlet* is haunted by the figure of Laurence Olivier. However, they rarely address this haunting directly. Michael Almereyda rather boldly cites the pre-existence and persistence of a play called *Hamlet* by showing a brief clip of *Hamlet* footage on "Hamlet's" monitor. Yet as we observe in chapter 2, Almereyda's film leaves out of the picture the problem of what Shakespeare's *Hamlet means* to his video-collaging main character.

The convention by which an audience agrees not to ask what Hamlet thinks about *Hamlet* – to suspend its disbelief in the ignorance of the characters – is, of course, the *premise* of these films. But it cannot be, and is not, the premise of audiences at the level of reception, whatever degree of familiarity we may have with the playtext. One reason that so many Shakespeare films since the 1990s are interesting is that they make visible the restored behaviors named by these different characters (Hamlet, Iago, Juliet).

In this chapter, we work through some of these concerns in relation to Kristian Levring's *The King is Alive* (2000), one of the few films that explicitly addresses the cultural, psychological, and social uses of a Shakespearean text and the constellation of characters and plot it furnishes. *The King is Alive* explores the fate of a group of Western tourists marooned in an abandoned mining town in the Namibian desert. Their struggles to survive include an intimate encounter with the text of *King Lear* – or rather, with as much of it as they can remember and use. The film works in a stripped-down cinematic style that places it well outside the mainstream of conventional film-production and "Shakespeare on film" alike. Its stark, elegant presentation, sometimes absurdist and sometimes brutal, connects it to the avant-garde *Lears* of Peter Brook, on the one hand, and to documentary traditions on the other. Indeed, the film seems at moments to be in conversation both with Brook and with Jorgen Leth, a pioneer of Danish documentary – as well as with the popular genre of survival film.

Graham Holderness has claimed that to reflect the break with "early twentieth-century models of narrative, character, action, imagery, and form" critically rehearsed in poststructuralist criticism and "postmodern readings," we had better look to experimental films that embody the changing notions of authorship, textuality, and reception we seek to bring to our teaching and writing (1993: 66, 74). Working within this experimental tradition, *The King is Alive* opens up questions conventionally suppressed when we suspend our disbelief in a cinematic world that specifically excludes the text being replayed. What does it mean to speak the words of a Shakespeare play, here and now? How do the specifics of different heres and nows change our answer to that question? How might the words, characters, actions, and story of a Shakespeare play be useful, not useful, and how do they use us? As the journalist Bernard Levin long ago pointed out, a good part of idiomatic English is effectively scripted by Shakespearean language, whether we know it or not. Although this is not the only – or even the primary – issue the film is interested in, it takes up the uncanny effects of this verbal inheritance in a sustained way. The turning point of the film is a moment in which, as a central character observes, those in the film find themselves playing "good old *Lear* again" and then, deliberately and with difficulty, begin to rehearse the play itself. Playing *Lear* in this film means two things. It means being inhabited by the character-functions and effects associated with Shakespeare's story of a king reduced (in great part by his own actions) to a "poor, bare, fork'd animal" (3.4.107–8). And it means adopting and adapting the subject-positions and speeches of various characters in *Lear*, as circumstances in the frame story require. Authentic experience and self-knowledge emerge, the film argues, through knowingly reusing Shakespeare's playtext for one's own purposes.

Unaccommodated Filmmaking

> Thou art the thing itself: unaccommodated man is no more but such a poor, bare, fork'd animal as thou art.
>
> *King Lear*

Image and ambient sound come before word in the first frames of *The King is Alive*, the fourth film certified by the Dogme95 "movement." In seemingly artless shots facing directly into sun and sky, light flares on the camera lens, and gusts of wind blow across a microphone. From these first paired sounds and images we are invited into a cinematic experiment with "unaccommodated" filmmaking. The Dogme95 movement's aims involve a Lear-like stripping down of the apparatus of Hollywood cinema, as a way of restoring a purer kind of cinematic experience that will get us back to human truth, "the thing itself." In keeping with these aims, these opening moments announce themselves as only what has been found at the moment of recording in a natural, unreconstructed space. Yet the quick flash of lens-flare also reminds us of the presence of the camera; nothing in this story will be unmediated. This stripped-down recording, which keeps us aware of the apparatus rather than hiding it, yields (the Dogme95 movement claims) a privileged access to the experience of mediation.[1]

The first words we hear in the film are similarly dislocated: spoken in voice-over by an unseen character in an African language, translated in English subtitles as in "foreign" films. The scene shifts under this gentle, bass voice as diffraction lines from two headlights on a road at night replace the hexagonal patterns of lens-flare. The rising hiss of approaching wheels replaces the sound of the wind. Moments later we find ourselves on a bus filled with white tourists being driven by a black man through a desert, our eyes the eye of a camera that moves among them and occasionally settles on one or two to provide us with characterizing signs and gestures, though little in the way of backstory. As in Gus Van Sant's *My Own Private Idaho*, there is no hint of Shakespearean intertext in these opening moments. That intertext (the tragedy of *King Lear*) will emerge later as both a means to and the object of radical cultural displacement. The journey down this road, the subtitles promise us, is a "long one."

Genre-watchers are apt to guess that "we" and these travelers are headed towards some kind of crisis or disaster as the anxiety levels of several of the passengers begin to rise, night turns into day, and the road on which the bus has been traveling devolves into little more than a desert-track. The crisis hits when the oldest and most assertive among them, Charles (David Calder), notices that the compass on which the driver, Moses (Vusi Kunene), has relied is broken. They have traveled hundreds of miles in the opposite direction from their destination, an unnamed airport from which they all plan to fly "home." Hope surfaces when they spy the outlines of an old mining settlement in the distance

7.1 Kanana's stage and throne

but dissolves when they find it all but abandoned and the bus out of gas. The lone inhabitant, we discover, is one Kanana (Peter Kubheka), the speaker of the film's first voice-over lines. He seldom budges from the shaded and elevated stage-like structure on which he sits for the duration of the film, and from which he supplies subtitled commentary on the "story" that is about to unfold before our eyes (figure 7.1). Given the retrospective nature of Kanana's commentary, all of it phrased in the past tense, we know that this story has ended by the time the film begins.

The three video cameras Levring deploys in both hand-held and fixed positions render the humans under inspection in a stark unadorned manner. The cameras often unflatteringly fasten on them, in pairs or in isolation, at moments of strain or tension. Their postures are configured in posed relation to the shifting curves and pyramids of sand or the lamp-lit spaces of empty rooms in abandoned houses that serve as the film's "found" setting. Levring takes the liberty of deploying overhead and panoramic shots of the ghost-town and surrounding desert, establishing the latter in particular as a space of astonishing beauty. He takes fewer liberties regarding sound. Apart from the periodic, editorial voice-overs of Kanana, the dialogue of the travelers, music blaring from a CD player, and voices occasionally played back from a mini-recorder, the only other sounds we hear are the "natural" ones of wind whistling through the desert and the crackling of flames from the bonfires the survivors set to attract would-be rescuers. Almost all of this is diegetic sound, originating in the story itself. Yet the way sounds get to us matters as much as where they come from. Even Kanana's voice-overs have a flat, thin quality that suggests they were made using the same hand-held tape-recorder that turns up later in the story. Most of the soundtrack seems to have been recorded on site, with the action. In accordance with Dogme95 principles, the production team has kept post-processing to a minimum, except in the final credits. Audio is usually scaled (in terms of distance and volume) to its apparent source. Cuts in sound and image tend to be tied together rather than staggered so as to smooth over the transitions, as they would typically be in mainstream Hollywood cinema.

All of these choices convey the same thing: we are getting the cinematic equivalent of "the thing itself" to which Dogme95 films are dedicated. However, like all certified Dogme95 films, *The King is Alive* is marked as much by how it doesn't conform, as by how much it does, to the austere strictures of the Dogme95 manifesto. That manifesto was published by the movement's "founders," Lars von Trier and Thomas Vinterberg, at the 1995 Cannes film festival and has since been used to "certify" some 35 films. Its central tenets comprise the Dogme95 "Vow of Chastity."

DOGME95 "Vow of Chastity"[2]

1 Shooting must be done on location. Props and sets must not be brought in (if a specific prop is necessary, a location must be chosen where prop is to be found).
2 The sound must never be produced apart from the images or vice versa. (Music must not be used unless it occurs where the scene is being shot.)
3 The camera must be hand-held. Shooting must take place where the film takes place. (No stationary camera, no cranes, helicopter shots, etc.)
4 The film must be in color. Special lighting is (for the most part) not acceptable.
5 Optical work and filters are forbidden.
6 The film must not contain superficial action. (Murders, weapons, etc. must not occur.)
7 Temporal and geographical alienation is forbidden. (The film must take place in the here and now.)
8 Genre movies are not acceptable.
9 The film format must be Academy 35 mm.
10 The director must not be credited. Furthermore I swear as a director to refrain from personal taste! I am no longer an artist. I swear to refrain from creating a "work," as I regard the instant as more important than the whole. My supreme goal is to force the truth out of my characters and settings. I swear to do so by all means available and at the cost of any good taste and any aesthetic considerations.

As we will have occasion to note, while Levring generally holds fast to at least four strictures of the manifesto (1, 2, 4, and 7), he takes considerable liberties with rules 3, 5, and 6, while crediting his writing and direction (10), filming in video (9), and working within several overlapping genres (8) at the same time. As we have already noted, the opening frames of the film directly mine generic conventions deployed in "survival-narrative" films and literature. From the days of *Robinson Crusoe* (1719) to those of *Lifeboat* (1944), *Lord of the Flies* (1963), *Flight of the Phoenix* (1965), *Walkabout* (1970), and beyond, this genre focuses on how presumably civilized people contend with surviving shipwreck,

airplane crashes, or natural disasters. Indeed, the first "action" that
occurs as Levring's characters begin to reckon with their situation is the
sudden emergence from their number of an otherwise undeveloped
character named Jack (Miles Anderson), who seems to have cut his
teeth on *King Solomon's Mines* and knows everything one needs to
know about surviving in the desert. That Jack will ultimately prove as
unequal as any of the other characters to this task, however, is but
one of many ways in which Levring sets out to subvert the very convention within which he seems to be working. And this is also one of the
ways Shakespeare, or more precisely, *King Lear* becomes embedded in
the film.

The "king," Levring suggests, is "alive" in that the pragmatism and
optimism that Jack brings to bear on their plight (and that in conventional survival-narrative films will be actualized on the level of plot)
prove entirely unfounded, and other ways of surviving (or at best, passing time) must be found. Jack's appearance proves to be nothing more
than a cameo. He gives orders, supplies directives, and marches off into
the desert never to be seen alive again. Indeed, it appears in the end that
he never gets more than a mile or so from the settlement before falling
victim to the desert sands and heat. Who or what takes Jack's place in
the film – and fulfills, in a decidedly different way, his function – is the
considerably more diffident Henry (David Bradley), a former stage-
actor in London, now professional Hollywood scriptreader. The
survival tool Henry offers his undistinguished cast of characters is *King
Lear*, or, more precisely, what he can memorially reconstruct of that
play, whose rolls/roles he painstakingly inscribes on the back of one of
the Hollywood screenplays (entitled *Space Killers)* he reads for a living.

How should we understand this mode of partial reconstruction?
There are several ways to approach it. In one of the few scholarly essays
written on this film, Amy Scott-Douglass contends that by inscribing
King Lear on the back of a movie script, Henry is performing a kind of
penitence in the desert for "selling out" his earlier career as a stage-
actor in London, and that Henry's action is part of a larger confronta-
tion between European artistic "purity" and American commercial
corruption that Levring is staging in the film. She concludes that
"Levring's film attempts to reclaim Shakespeare *for* Europe, *from*
Hollywood" (2003: 260). This interpretation both links Levring's effort
to, and distinguishes it from, what Al Pacino is trying to do in *Looking
for Richard*, reclaiming Shakespearean language for the American
street.[3] To be more precise, Levring's target here is less America than it
is the multinational monolith subsumed under the name "Hollywood,"
the production values associated with it, and the self-involved, know-
nothing philistinism of Euro-American bourgeois culture as represented by his cast of characters, who are as clumsy and unfamiliar with
the popular matter of their own culture (*Saturday Night Fever, Grease*)
as they are with the plot of a Shakespeare play.[4] In this respect, Levring's
film is consistent with Pacino's more theatrically oriented effort "to

communicate a Shakespeare that is about how we feel and think today," though both films may suffer (more than they would like to admit) from their own inevitable "glo-cali-zation" (Burt 2003: 14–36). Neither can escape the fact that their chosen medium is one of the dominant means of global transmission for Western (Hollywood-packaged) ways of seeing the world. Nor can they occlude the fundamental ties of those ways of seeing to the growth of Western capitalism. Indeed, Levring has deployed a largely Anglo-American cast of actors in his film (two of whom, Janet McTeer and Jennifer Jason Leigh, command international reputations). And he has also chosen the world's reigning lingua franca, English, as his film's primary linguistic medium while consigning the local Namibian setting to a stage-set for acting out and working through decidedly "first-world" preoccupations.

Henry's reconstruction of the play on the reverse side of a screenplay that is so overtly artificial may also be read in thematic terms. *The King is Alive* seems preoccupied with partial transmission: from the whip cuts that momentarily blur images, to misremembered tunes and plots, to the mismatch between dialogue and text in its subtitles. No cultural matter is recalled or conveyed perfectly here, by any character. But the fact that all human experiences are mediated – captured and transmitted only through artifice, incompletely – may be as enabling as it is limiting, because it opens space for making the old new. Moreover, according to the film, some modes of artifice are better than others, and those artificers that come clean about the limits of expression are more trustworthy than those that hide them.

The limits of expression (cinematic expression in particular) are of course the central concern of the Dogme95 project. The struggle with them explains an emphasis in Dogme95 films on "*auteur* thinking," "the director's creative process," that characterized the early and arguably most adventurous films of the French New Wave (Scott-Douglass 2003: 256–3). While such an emphasis would seem to contradict the most urgently expressed article of the Dogma manifesto (#10 in which the director swears "to refrain from personal taste" and, even, to disclaim his status as an artist), Levring confesses that "the most difficult thing for me was the aesthetic bit," finding it "difficult to look myself straight in the face and say: I am not creating a picture" (phone interview; Rundle 1999a). Levring is particularly insistent on the shaping role he played in making the kinds of aesthetic choices that are unavoidable in deciding to place his cameras here rather than there, and in having written the film script in the first place: "As soon as you direct an actor and you have written a script, you are not depicting reality."

Levring's candor on this count should remind us that for all the Dogmatic brethren, the articles of the manifesto function more in the way of a general template than as fixed, unbending rules. Even von Trier admits that, "many of the rules can't be kept and are as impossible to keep as the commandment 'Love your neighbor as yourself.'" They are better construed as "tool[s] to be used freely." In the same interview from which these remarks are drawn, von Trier likens the changes wrought in the preceding four years of Dogmatic practice to the conversion "from Catholicism to Protestantism," and concludes that "We are now by definition sinners due to the fact that the rules cannot be kept. Our position must be that the perfect Dogme-film has not been made and probably never will be" (interview; Rundle 1999b). This has not, however, discouraged von Trier and company from continuing to find cinematic virtue in technical constraint, or prevented them from finding in the very condition of constraint an unusually enabling form of creative freedom. As von Trier says of his effort to observe "rule number two, which states that the sound must never be produced separately from the images or vice versa: What makes it interesting is . . . that you have to make all the decisions on the spot. It is as if you were shooting the very first talk movies."

Some of the same kind of thinking seems to inform Scott-Douglass's observation that "*The King is Alive* is not just a film *by* a director following Dogme rules; it is a film *about* a director following Dogme rules . . . who attempts to put on a play having been stripped of all theatrical devices: props, costumes, technological tools, even the text itself," and that "To a certain extent, *The King is Alive* is a history of film in the twentieth century" (2003: 260). These are apt, but not perfect, analogies. Levring and his director-surrogate, Henry, seem more interested in process than product, and – not unlike Pacino and his own band of brothers – in "penetrating into what at every moment the [play] is about" (*Looking for Richard*). In giving his actors the freedom to improvise – to choose what they put in their baggage, to pick their own houses – and in filming the script chronologically such that "the time span of the story is roughly the same as the time it took to shoot the film" (Rundle 1999a), Levring pointedly allowed process, accident, and actors who "simply went out and burnt their heads to shreds" to make choices of their own – some fortunate, some not.

There is, of course, nothing accidental in Levring's decision to superimpose this particular Shakespearean script on the survival-narrative. Modern theatrical productions and films – most notably Akira Kurosawa's samurai epic, *Ran* (1985) – have interpreted the play as a story of regression to barbaric disorder, making it part of the prehistory of the survival genre. Yet Levring takes pains to make the connection with *Lear* seem to emerge spontaneously from Henry's mind as he sits beside Kanana on the latter's raised stage and takes stock of the human comedy before him. Henry is portrayed here as the polar opposite of the action-oriented Jack, whose estimated return date has all but passed, prompting the other remaining survivors to perform more drastic measures (like removing the bus tires and setting them alight) to attract the attention of rescuers. Henry views their "performance" with undisguised contempt in lines that only we and Kanana hear and that presumably only we can understand: "Assholes, fucking assholes. Repairing a roof out here in dead men's land. It won't be long before

7.2 "Some fantastic striptease act of basic human needs"

we're fighting over water, killing for a carrot. Some fantastic striptease act of basic human needs" (figure 7.2).

This surprisingly cynical outburst of vulgarity and eloquence combined signals a shift in the generic conventions the film is mining, as its center of gravity migrates from the pragmatic optimism of the swashbuckling Jack to the despairing pessimism of the witnessing Henry, and *King Lear* displaces works like *King Solomon's Mines* and *Robinson Crusoe* as the text of first resort.[5] The move to *Lear* is directly made by way of quotation and citation in a brief moment which, for the thoroughly informed cineaste, also "quotes" a seemingly impromptu dance movement drawn directly from the 1967 short, *The Perfect Human*, made by the Danish documentary filmmaker, Jorgen Leth (with whom the Dogmatics maintain a typically unresolved oedipal relation, as attested to in Leth's and von Trier's *The Five Obstructions* [2003]).

Henry sits, at this moment, with Kanana on the rusty structure that supports Kanana's throne-like chair and from which Kanana's cryptic, subtitled commentary issues. As Henry looks out on what he calls a "fantastic striptease act of basic human needs" (itself an implied citation of Lear's terrible epiphany of man as nothing more than a "poor, bare, fork'd animal" (3.4.107–8)), his gaze lingers briefly on the middle-aged American, Ashley (Brion James). Ashley has just entered the scene from a dark hut, as if into a performance space, squinting confusedly into the bright sun (figure 7.3). Soon to withdraw from his casting as Lear due to a pronounced case of DTs, Ashley enters performing an unprompted dance movement, reminiscent of the existential routines in Laurel and Hardy or Samuel Beckett. Henry observes: "Is man no more than this? It's good old *Lear* again . . . Hah . . . Perfect." Ashley's dance-step is the immediate prompt that brings *Lear* into Henry's mind. But its possible source in Leth's film draws *Lear* into the DNA of the Dogme95 movement and also brings that genealogy to bear on how *Lear* is remediated in Levring's film (figure 7.4).

7.3 "Is man no more than this?"

7.4 "Look at him now, look at him all the time"

The Perfect Human is a deliberately flattened, mechanically constrained but otherwise poignant 12-minute "documentary" representation of "basic human" gestures and actions, like getting dressed and brushing one's teeth. In the film, the narrator's voice-over directs our gaze on its subjects in a way that enhances our sense of their isolation: "The perfect human in a room with no boundaries, and with nothing, and a voice saying a few words, this voice, saying a few words. Look at him now, look at him all the time." These commentaries resemble Kanana's similarly detached refrains, "Together they said words. But they still didn't say them to each other," and Henry's rather Olympian assessment of characters he will later refer to as "these lost souls." However, Levring's barren landscape that starts everywhere and ends nowhere, which he often films in deep focus, and the sparsely furnished, but essentially featureless *mise en scène* against which he pins his subjects in isolation shots, is considerably more unforgiving than Leth's "room with no boundaries."

The set's status as a physical testament to the barren legacy of the European scramble for Africa also graphically underwrites the surprising cynicism of the usually soft-spoken Henry's initial casting of his fellows as "assholes" and the brutal eloquence of the seemingly more free-floating "Some fantastic striptease act of basic human needs." This last observation reads less like an observation and more like a design or plan. Levring will present Henry as the most considerate and patient of directors – thoughtfully lending his mini-recorder to Amanda (Lia Williams) so she can speak and replay her lines in private, and willing to allow Liz (Janet McTeer) to reprise an exchange between Goneril and Edmund three times, until it finally sends her despairing husband Ray (Bruce Davison) out into the desert. Yet there is, as Charles and Catherine (Romane Bohringer) sense, something perverse and degrading in the very idea of the project, something we also sense as we watch the over-matched actors struggle with their lines under the double pressure of the relentless desert sun and a diet of superannuated canned carrots.

As Scott-Douglass suggests, Henry's plan may well involve performing a kind of penitence in the desert. On this count, however, we would probably do better to identify the primary motive for his own eventual (clearly traumatizing) assumption of the role of Lear with his failure as a father and unresolved relationship with his daughter (which he describes and addresses in a voice-letter he composes on his mini-recorder). But if we ask why he decides to put the others through such hard paces under the desert sun, we may also need to ask questions like why did the Dogmatics take their "vow of chastity" in the first place and why in *The Five Obstructions* does von Trier have Jorgen Leth remake *The Perfect Human* under even more radically constrained and potentially disabling conditions?[6] All these questions directly link the strictures of unaccommodated film-making to Henry's unaccommodated re-staging of *King Lear*. We learn little more about Henry than we have already established – his personal and professional background, the combination of tenderness and contempt with which he treats and views his fellow survivors – but we do crucially witness something we also catch fleeting glimpses of in Leth's patient and profoundly humane responsiveness to von Trier's dictatorial edicts in *The Five Obstructions*: that is, Henry's growing attachment to people he had previously seen as nothing but "assholes," which is at least partly mediated by his own deepening immersion in what we would term the Lear-effect or *King Lear* phenomenon. As Henry evolves into a participant in the play-within-the film which he both co-authors and directs, he begins to purge himself of the assumption of superiority articulated in the clinical detachment of the director-*auteur*, exactly the detachment Levring confesses not to be able to achieve and Leth delicately sets aside.

Before turning to the film's unfolding of *Lear*, one more cinematic issue needs to be addressed and that is Kanana's choral commentary, delivered through a combination of voice-over, subtitle, and special camera-work. Kanana's commentary directs our gaze throughout the film and Henry's gaze in this particular sequence (DVD chapter 4, "Is Man No More Than This?"). Indeed, Henry awakens to the idea of *Lear* because, the camera-work suggests, he is beginning to see the group with some quality of the way Kanana sees. The sequence begins with Kanana's commentary ("Out here there is silence") over blurry isolation shots that signal we are looking through or "with" Kanana's uncorrected vision. The blurred images prepare us to see the varied activities of those awaiting rescue (playing with a coin, filling a lamp with fuel, repairing a roof) as dumb shows: abstract patterns of motion filling time and space. Kanana observes these scenes with what Slavoj Zizek terms the "penetrating power of the perplexed foreign gaze" which, by interpreting a scene awry and out of cultural context, facilitates a greater understanding for the audience (Zizek 2004: 292). The "audience" here is first Henry, who sees Kanana interpreting the scene, and then the film audience, who watch Henry re-interpret it through the clarifying but also foreign lens of *Lear*. When Henry wakes up and squints out on these existential dances, he has to put on his dark glasses. We start to look now *with* him, and the camera picks up speed as if in response to his quickening connections between the scene and *Lear*. This faster motion reproduces the signature quality of Kanana's point-of-view – the quality that made these scenes seem like performances in the first place – moving so quickly as it pans from person to person that it temporarily blurs. Most importantly, these "whip pans" reproduce that quality of seeing *for us*. As these juxtapositions proceed, we begin to see how transformative but also partial the process of watching someone looking may be. Henry's way of looking is not only more embittered and ungenerous than Kanana's (at this point) but also distinctly mediated: fostered by an understanding of *Lear* that is negotiated not only by his own cynicism and misanthropy but by the postwar status of *Lear* as an apocalyptic and absurdist dramatic document (Cartelli 2002).

That this witnessing has been limited and partial is an essential component of Levring's cinematic vision, which privileges such constrained perceptions as the only true ones. This privileging of constraint is particularly evident in the interaction between the voice-over and the subtitles. Kanana's remarks convey the usual authority associated with voice-over pronouncements: grave, masculine, analytically acute, particularly as the survivors begin hesitantly to rehearse ("Together they said words. They still didn't say them to each other"). Yet the subtitles qualify the usual effects of voice-over, situating Kanana's authority firmly beyond audience ken. These brief and sometimes stilted sentences are clearly incommensurate with what Kanana says (at least in the English-language version that we are working with). As with all subtitles, the text that makes it to the screen is constrained as much by the technical demands of audience reading time and visual space as by Kanana's meaning. Moreover, the fact that his observations fail to bridge a significant communication gap is something Kanana calls attention to, by prefacing many of his observations with "I don't know if," or "I think," and by declaring "I didn't understand a word they said. Nor did they."

Crucially, what the audience learns from Kanana is to be aware of that gap in communication, yet not to perceive it as exclusively a liability. Just as Kanana's blurry vision intensifies our sense that the castaways are engaged in timeless ritual, so too the strongest effect of the subtitles is their abstraction into what Leth calls "few words." The mismatch between the highly compressed medium of screened text and the more expansive medium of recorded speech reminds us that translation, always partial, is occurring. Catherine's mistranslation of her nasty story in French prepares us to be suspicious of how culturally biased as well as duplicitous translation can be.[7] Yet the spareness of Kanana's subtitles, like the spareness of Cordelia's expressions of love and Lear's language at the close of the play, reads differently. These few words seem stripped to essentials. Far from smoothing over the differences between Kanana's utterances and the target language, as if to make the foreign "ours" (as the idiomatic subtitles for Catherine's story do), these subtitles emphasize the labor involved in stripping language down so as to accommodate meanings that exceed the superficial. The wrestling involved in that accommodation is not with the "foreign" language but with the target language – the one normally transparent to its users. Thus, as Amresh Sinha describes the effect, "what is ours, our own language, is made foreign" in these subtitles (Sinha 2004: 189): made difficult, opaque, requiring effort, just as the text of *Lear* so clearly requires.

Lear Again

The Lear-effect, understood in these multiple contexts, involves the dislodging of a patriarchal figure from his established position of control or "effect" of authority, the haunting of that figure by feelings of loss and inadequacy, and the conviction of having made crucial, possibly unforgivable, mistakes that he nonetheless tries to redeem. The Lear-effect reaches out, in turn, to a Cordelia-effect that satisfies his need for forgiveness (indeed, forgives everything) and helps recuperate feminine qualities that have been degraded by what may be termed Goneril/Regan functions. A *function* does things, performs behaviors that are integral to the working out of a dramatic design; an *effect* suffers or embodies the consequences. Although the figure of Cordelia precipitates Lear's downfall by rejecting his overbearing demands in Shakespeare's play, she ultimately serves as little more than a passive redeemer of Lear's guilt and fellow-victim of her sisters' unrelenting rage. The Cordelia-effect thus operates as an attribute or aspect of the Lear-effect more than as a free-standing dramatistic unit in its own right.

The King is Alive begins to reconfigure these operations when Levring divides his two Cordelia surrogates into Catherine, who rejects, and Gina (Jennifer Jason Leigh), who accepts. In the process he delegates the functional (oppositional) aspect of the Cordelia-effect to Catherine, while limiting Gina's agency to her decision to sacrifice herself sexually to Charles. That sacrifice allows the play rehearsals to go forward and also eventuates in Gina's "adoption" by Henry. Henry's growing attachment to Gina, in turn, begins to erode his own directorial detachment (from which station he has, Lear-like, proclaimed his superiority) and bring him level with people he has previously denounced as "assholes." Thus, what starts out as "some fantastic striptease act" in which Henry's cast will be compelled to rehearse their already pronounced individual "crimes" of pride, vanity, arrogance, brutality, self-loathing, etc., evolves into something less clinical and more personally revealing as Henry is compelled to acknowledge the part he plays in "good old *Lear*."

That part is initially assigned to the middle-aged American alcoholic, Ashley, who falls off his chair during one of the first rehearsals, spends much of the rest of the film in a stupor, and is pointedly shown clawing the sand in his "house" in one of the film's many isolation shots. Henry's replacement of Ashley could be said to function as an enabling displacement of Henry's own less savory "effects:" his status as failed father, failed actor or director, and possibly recovering alcoholic in his own right. As noted above, Henry's decision to stage *Lear* has many possible motives, ranging from his personal and professional preoccupations, his apparent cynicism and misanthropy, to his channeling of peculiarly Dogmatic concerns about working within seemingly disabling constraints to get at the truth of human experience. However, it is also clear that Henry discerns in the emerging configurations he witnesses from his seat beside Kanana much that is already established in the *Lear* script. From this vantage point he sees a father (Charles) who treats his son (Paul) with contempt; a wife (Liz) who treats her husband (Ray) even more disdainfully; two young women competing in different ways for Henry's attention, one who presents herself as an arrogant intellectual (Catherine), and another who is more secure about the attractions of her body than her mind (Gina); a man marginalized and degraded by the "custom of nations" (the bus driver, Moses); and another young woman (Amanda), who will discover both a moral and creative force and function in taking on the role of the Fool. It seems like "good old *Lear* again" to Henry because he witnesses how close the "characters" already are to the roles he will have them assume in the play.

And yet, as the rehearsals begin, we note that, close though the connections between character and role may be, the actual speaking of the lines from Shakespeare's play appear to constitute an insuperable barrier that none of the "actors" seems able to clear. In these early rehearsals, Levring has most of his unusually gifted cast repeatedly stumble over lines and words that they cannot pronounce and, as Kanana contends, they do not understand. Levring's characters are not only compelled to act badly, but shown to have little to no acquaintance with the play or its plot or, for that matter, with anything that smacks of literature or high culture. Apart from Henry, the only character who shows any interest in reading is the self-styled French intellectual, Catherine, and even she has to ask Henry if she can borrow one of his books. To seal his point, Levring has Catherine, when prompted by Henry to read one of Cordelia's lines, get the play's title wrong, guessing, "C'est *Othello*?" Interestingly, it is Liz who, when asked by her husband

Ray to tell her what the play is about, offers an accurate synopsis. In her bland American accent, Liz says it's a story about a king who has two, maybe three daughters, "a couple of kids," in any event, and "he's old and wants to retire and divide his kingdom between his kids, so whoever says she loves him most gets to have the biggest share." To Ray's next question, "You get to play the evil daughter, right," Liz responds, "Sure, I get to play the real bitch," caustically adding "You don't have to worry, though, nobody has to fall in love and everybody gets to die in the end." Still mulling the subject, Ray later entertains an objection to the plot, which evokes the story about embedded cultural norms that Laura Bohannan recounts in her story of fieldwork with the West African Tiv tribe, "Shakespeare in the Bush" (1966).[8] "Maybe he's a king and maybe she's a princess," Ray observes, "but who ever heard of a daughter that loved her father and wouldn't tell him that she loved him. That doesn't make sense."

At first, the amateurism and ignorance of the characters, which Henry appears to have done little to alter by only supplying them with transcriptions of their own parts, situates Henry (in Jack's absence) not only as reigning authority-figure, but also as "author" of the "text" they are all about to act out or re-live, as Catherine indicates when she asks "Are you writing *King Lear* by hand?" and he answers "As much as I can remember of it, or what I think I can remember." Yet the casual authenticity, even accuracy, of Liz and Ray's first assessments complicates the picture. And while Henry's soft-spoken modesty is made to seem admirable, the gaps in his memory are confirmed by the several mistaken line readings he delivers, thereby making his assumed authority seem as flawed or limited as Lear's. Indeed, Henry's status as a bit of a fake in his own right is cued by another question Catherine asks when he hands her the part of Cordelia he's inscribed on the back of *Space Killers*, which she first reads wrong side up: "Did you write this, Henry?" to which he deprecatingly responds, "No, I'm paid to read that stuff." The exchange underscores these two characters' shared presumption of being more than they appear and – in Catherine's case in particular – their shared propensity to cruelly display their intellectual superiority to their fellow travelers. The extent to which Catherine interprets Henry's offer of the part to her as a sexual invitation also may unsettle our trust in Henry's authority, although Henry himself gives little indication of harboring this particular motive. For all these reasons, a reading of the film as an allegory of embattled European artistic purity, maintained against American commercial corruption, seems reductive. That reading founders especially on the film's characterization of Catherine, who not only rejects the part of Cordelia but assumes the competitive affect of Regan and the plot-function of Goneril as she proceeds to degrade and later poison Gina, the substitute Cordelia who claims the role in her place.

Catherine may be wrong about Henry's motives but she is surely right to suspect some degree of projection or surrogation in his offer. The

DVD's segmentation of the film into chapters allows us privileged access to how carefully Levring has structured Henry's Lear-effect as a matter that involves not only the competition for his regard of two daughter-surrogates, but also Henry's apparent failure to earn the trust and love of his own daughter. Chapter 8 of the film opens with a low-angle two-shot of Henry and Gina seated on a desert elevation over-looking the settlement and discussing the progress, or lack thereof, of the rehearsals. (This two-shot notably echoes the earlier two-shot of Henry and Kanana gazing out at the rest of the cast from the vantage point of Kanana's raised "stage.") The camera maintains this double-focus in successive framings of their ongoing conversation in a way that both establishes their growing intimacy and directly contrasts with the shot/reverse shot framing Levring deploys in Gina's ensuing negotiations with Charles. It cuts back after a few minutes to a daylight shot of Henry's workroom, where Catherine is unaccountably poking around among Henry's things before fastening on Henry's mini-recorder and playing back the voice-letter Henry is taping for his apparently estranged daughter. Hearing Henry's footsteps, Catherine puts the recorder down and backs away but is nonetheless caught in the act in a moment fraught with tension. Seeing the recorder set on his worktable equidistant between them, Henry pockets it and then engages in a fairly testy exchange with Catherine. Rather than explaining what she's doing there, she announces, "Your plan failed. You haven't even got a king," before unaccountably countering his response that he might take the role on himself with, "You would be a wonderful Cordelia. Better than what you have now."

Although we know that this second comment involves Catherine's one-sided competition with Gina (who appears never to notice, much less feel it), her attack seems motivated by the candid admission of the mistakes Henry has made as a father that Catherine has overheard. It's almost as if she's found what she was looking for in the recording (a sign of weakness?) and is using it to expedite her evolution from a chosen Cordelia who inexplicably rejects being chosen to a composite Goneril/Regan who can't get over having once been preferred and now replaced. When the next scene begins with Gina offering to serve as Charles's sex-slave in exchange for his assumption of the role of Gloucester so that Henry's play might go forward, we are surely meant to recognize the momentousness of what the chapter names Gina's "dignity in sacrifice," and how radically it contrasts with Catherine's repeated acts of treachery and betrayal. We may also notice here how radically Gina's commanding performance as a Cordelia-surrogate contrasts with the passivity of Cordelia's performance in *King Lear*. As one of our students, Rachel Harris, has observed, "Gina can be seen as an active version of the passive Cordelia, who sacrifices herself at the beginning of the play through near inertia." Gina not only "sacrifices herself for Henry and the play by agreeing to sleep with Charles," but "bluntly reeducates Charles at the end of the film" in a manner that "serves the same purpose as Gloucester's literal blinding – it makes Charles aware of reality and allows him, finally, to see himself closely in relation to others." Harris instructively concludes that this "altering of the Cordelia role serves not only to update the play, but to update Cordelia's purpose. Gina moves Cordelia from delicate ladylike subversion to unapologetic and uninhibited self-expression. This shifts – indeed, *elevates* – the Cordelia role from a character *effect*, waiting to be acted upon, to a character *function*, with purposeful action of her own."

The competition of the two daughters for Henry's regard/admiration, the emergence of Gina/Cordelia as a function, and Henry's consequent movement from aloof director to father-surrogate are several ways in which the film "overwrites" the Shakespearean plot while also keeping it available for inspection. This overlaid plot becomes one of several backstories that Levring complicates by embedding them in the *Lear*-plot as the rehearsals move forward. The already established conflicts of Ray and Liz, for example, continue to play themselves out as Liz opportunistically appropriates Goneril's infatuation with Edmund to arouse Ray's jealousy. Though initially cast as Kent, Ray effectively finds himself cast by Liz to double as Albany, or at least to endure the "effect" that Goneril's behavior has on Albany in the playtext.

Other ripple effects follow from the collision of filmic backstory with Shakespeare's plot. Initially cast as proud overbearing father to Paul's emotionally immature son (Paul and Amanda have been traveling with Charles to advance the younger man's plan to improve his relationship with his father), Charles has already been playing Gloucester outside the film's rehearsal space before he actually assumes the role within it. And when he does formally assume the role, the Gloucester he puts into play is not the kind old man who suffers horribly for trying to help Lear, but the Gloucester of the play's opening scene who degradingly refers to Edmund as his bastard son while proudly recounting the sexual "sport" that went into his making, and the Gloucester who later relentlessly pursues his legitimate son Edgar's life and hounds him into a kind of self-annihilation.

Whereas in conventional survival-narrative films and fictions, the body of the plot stages conflicts and nostalgic reveries that specifically point back to the lives the characters have left behind, *The King is Alive* operates almost entirely on the level of conflict and gives no one but Henry a specific career, place of origin, or life-trajectory (though enough hints are dropped about the two marriages to build a backstory on). The characters are, instead, "charactered" largely in terms of age, accent, temperament, and marital status: a fact which allows them to merge with, to overwrite, and to be overwritten by the *Lear*-plot, and effectively to be transposed into a series of functions and effects. At the same time, the film also disassembles any established sense we might have of the unitary wholeness of Shakespeare's cast of characters. The characters "acting" in Levring's film don't all play one Shakespearean role, nor do they ever play all of the role they variously quote, cite, or impersonate. At one point in the film, a character may speak the lines assigned to one role; at another point, the same character may fall into the "subject-position" of another role (e.g., Ray moving between Kent and Albany). Since the characters don't have "unitary" identities of their own in the first place, they can only bring their own fragmented subject-positions to bear on the different roles/scenes/speech acts they perform.

However, as the film moves forward, characters who, initially, are merely playing at/playing out assigned roles without understanding or conviction begin to move toward and "claim" lines or passages associated with their own emerging subject-positions in the film, so that the play begins to speak – haltingly, in bits and pieces – through them. As they begin to apprehend how the play speaks their positions more knowingly and efficiently than they can represent themselves to themselves, they either cede their grounding in their starting subject-position, or gain an enhanced purchase on it. Indeed, several of the characters begin to perform their assumed or assigned roles or effects more intently, and in so doing begin to assimilate themselves to the subject-positions prescribed for them. The first Cordelia-surrogate (Catherine) initially channels her nervous distress at being displaced by withdrawing into the physical likeness of Tom o'Bedlam – naked, wild-haired, keeping to the margins of the group. But as her resentment intensifies, Catherine performs the function of a secondary Goneril and surreptitiously poisons her successor, Gina. The callous and humanly insensitive Gloucester-function that Charles embodies becomes virtually all that "Gloucester" is in the film: the abuser of "Edgar" (Paul) and sexual master of "Cordelia" (Gina) who takes his own life after Gina has the temerity to degrade him, having first taken care to degrade her back and dress himself in the businessman's coat and tie that are his robes of authority. Alternatively, the character Amanda (Lia Williams), who is assigned the part of the Fool and takes close instruction from Henry whom she shadows throughout the rehearsals, seems to take from the role the moral clarity she needs to anatomize the disabling brutality of her husband, Paul (Chris Walker). This leads him, in turn, to mortify himself in the manner of Edgar.

Thus, while the "deep structures" of *Lear* appear to rise up like the return of the repressed to overtake the film's characters, the characters return the favor, changing roles and lines to suit their evolving subject-positions. In this way, they exceed what the plot makes available: coming to express drives and desires even they didn't know they had until they begin to perform them against the grain of the *Lear* script. This reassembling of roles and subject-positions works to particularly dramatic effect with respect to the film's re-staging of the frequently misogynistic, yet also anti-patriarchal, material that circulates throughout both competing editions of the *Lear* playtext. Each of the female leads, for example, has a dramatically privileged moment in which she lashes out at a husband (Ray, Paul), lover (Charles), or patriarchal figure (Henry), who uses her to construct a fantasy of himself as the center of her universe. The lone exception may be the occasions when Liz – the unregenerate Goneril-figure – abuses, berates, and degrades the seemingly unoffending Ray. Yet Liz may have reasons for what she does that range beyond what we know of her backstory and these – Ray's passive withdrawal and depression – emerge as she manages to strip away the defensive structures men build for themselves. Indeed, Liz's willingness to use the play self-exploratively, and her deep immersion in her part, suggest that even self-styled "bitches" may be motivated by a complex and reasoned drive for knowledge and self-possession. In this respect, even Catherine's early rejection of the part of Cordelia may constitute a performance of the very role she rejects, designed to qualify our otherwise unqualified trust in Henry's knowingness and authority.

The most conspicuous collision of playtext and film text with respect to this theme is Gina's bitterly detailed response to Charles's solicitousness as she begins to feel the effects of Catherine's poison. Gina has heretofore occupied a number of overlapping subject-positions as sexually charged "tart;" stupid American; naively trusting sister-friend; corrupted "daughter" seeking absolution from Henry; and "dignified" sacrificial lamb. She "performs" her sexuality for Charles to please Henry and out of her strong desire to claim the role of Cordelia, which amounts to the same thing. Although Henry appears not to notice, or to feign indifference to, the bargain she's struck, her death prompts his total immersion in the Lear-effect in the film's climactic fireside sequence in which the closing moments of the play take complete command of the film's *mise en scène*. Given the extent to which the film's Gloucester-function invades the Lear-centered plot, we may also "read" Gina's diatribe against Charles as a displacement of the Lear-effect itself, channeled through one of the several disaffected Cordelias the patriarchal Henry has either failed to protect or has let down. As Amy Mahn, another of our students, writes, "Gina wanted to play Cordelia so badly that she turned Charles into Lear in order to become her." In this exchange, Catherine effectively performs the "active" function of the resisting/rejecting Cordelia, while Gina displaces whatever hostility she may feel toward Henry to Charles, and thus remains "spiritually," though certainly not sexually, inviolate. This kind of doubling and displacement also informs the strikingly photographed tableau (figure 7.5) that soon follows when we discover that Charles has hanged himself and see Catherine kneeling, seemingly brought back to awareness of her fall into the Goneril-function. (Death is clearly differently distributed here than it is in *King Lear*.)

Gina's body is strikingly absent from this tableau, which resembles nothing so much as an incomplete Pietà, with mourning the precursor to rescue but not redemption. Indeed, the suspicion that Henry has let another daughter down inflects his otherwise impassioned embodiment of the Lear-effect, when he discovers the dead Gina/Cordelia, and

7.5 Pietà manqué

informs his subsequent channeling of Lear's last lines around the bonfire, where it is difficult to distinguish passion from performance. Is this Henry mourning over Gina, or Henry mourning over Cordelia in the guise of Lear? The two are clearly inseparable, suggesting that *Lear* is simultaneously being mapped onto feelings and drives that the characters already have and calling new ones forth.

The closing movement of the film is particularly notable for the way in which it remediates the distintegrative effects of the closing movement of *Lear*. This move toward closure begins in chapter 18 as the camera follows Ray out into the desert where he has effectively been sent by Liz's insistence on repeatedly rehearsing in his presence an exchange with Edmund (Moses) that centers on a kiss. Pushed out by his enforced positioning as Albany in this exchange, Ray resumes his role as Kent as he wanders aimlessly out into a desert photographed to suggest the voluptuous contours of the female body, and repeats fragments of Kent's closing lines, "My master calls me" (5.2.323), and of lines spoken at the start of the playtext's Storm scene: "Hard by here is a hovel," "Repose you there, while I to this hard house" (3.2.61, 63). This is the moment in the film when lines from *Lear* begin most fully to speak the subject-positions of the characters outside the bounds of the rehearsal space and within the confines of the presumably "real" drama they inhabit.

Yet while the force of these and later iterations of the *Lear* playtext need to be reckoned with, as the time-space of play rehearsals is left behind, the visual force of cinematic representation also begins to reassert itself. For example, after Ray despairingly howls at his discovery of Jack's mutilated body, Levring abruptly cuts to a series of starkly blocked and framed "still" shots of the grouped survivors, who seem at

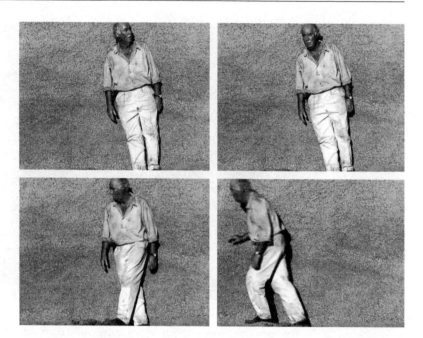

7.6 Exit Charles

once becalmed and defeated by their suffering and suffered to pose stiffly in configurations that embody their alienation from each other. Like the series of discretely framed and clinically detailed shots that announce the closing movement of Peter Brook's *King Lear*, the figures here are presented as entirely "unaccommodated" yet stylized at the same time. As Charles turns and walks out of the frame in an earlier moment of the film, the allusion to Brook's *Lear* is even more pronounced, bringing to mind as it does Lear's falling out of the frame to his death (figure 7.6).[9] By contrast, the return from stillness to speech, as Paul reprises Edgar's belated effort to reconcile himself with Gloucester in the last act of *Lear* in the form of the bathetic, "We need to talk," notably fails to satisfy the demand for dramatic truth that the film has already met on the level of visual realization.

In fact, the substitutions that Levring has his characters supply for the Shakespearean dialogue that mirrors their condition, consistently fall short of the intensity, force, and deep focus precision of the cinematography in the body of the film. Their lapse into colloquial speech seems expressly designed to highlight this disparity, revealing as it does the intellectual and emotional impoverishment of the characters, whose encounters and exchanges often operate at the level of the maudlin or soap operatic. By contrast, the characters' growing fluency in the delivery of dramatic verse in the film's last movement comes closer to approximating the expressive intensity of the cinematography. This growing fluency first emerges when Henry effectively claims the part of Lear, which is directly prompted by Liz's contention that she needs "to know who [Goneril] is and where she comes from" in order to better perform her part. Rather than answer her in the way a director might, Henry merely stands and speaks the speech beginning "Let it be so, thy truth then be thy dower" (drawn from 1.3.109–21 of the conflated edition), which is directed not at Goneril, but at Cordelia, in the playtext. Levring chooses to display more overtly than he needs to the honesty, power, and sheer dramatic truth of Henry's utterance by having the camera record a series of reaction shots of Liz, Gina, Ray, Amanda, and Charles. But what makes the speech riveting is the nuanced way in which Henry's pauses, elisions, and substitutions transform what in other hands might be a mere recitation into a carefully managed struggle to match words answerable to the part to the words that have been accurately remembered. However much we may suppose that Henry's private struggle with his failings as a father is being channeled into his performance, what's most striking is the command the words themselves have taken of his character's self-possession, which leaves Henry with nothing more to say as the rehearsing actors await further instruction, and Henry's surrogate-daughter, Gina, is trained away to resume her sexual sacrifice with Charles, who crudely asks, "Is that all?"

Henry's apparent inability here to break the spell his own acting the part of Lear has cast over him anticipates the moment when the entire cast becomes similarly spellbound after discovering the poisoned Gina and the hanged Charles in the film's final chapter, which propels the film into a complete immersion in *Lear* around the bonfire. In this last scene, the same impulse that took possession of Henry and moved *Lear* to speak through Ray outside the rehearsal-space – and, hence, to speak Shakespeare's lines more feelingly and articulately than ever before – takes hold of the rest of the cast. They take turns dropping their lines into the fire, which rages and flickers and blurs their images in an occasionally frantic montage of jump-cuts, flashbacks, and close-ups. And their turns are cued quite differently – not by prompts from other speakers but by the adequacy of specific lines to their own conditions at the moment. Liz belatedly tells Moses/Edmund that he has been "cozen'd and beguil'd" into answering "an unknown opposite" and absolves him of any guilt (5.3.153–4). Moses, who has been beaten by Paul for taking up, Edmund-like, with Goneril/Liz, counters that absolution, eloquently confessing Edmund's treasons to Paul who replies humbly with Edgar's line, "Let's exchange charity" (5.3.163–7). And Henry's climactic howls seem to well up out of this conflation of playtext and film, as if to mark the moment when the one overtakes, or is fully assimilated into, the other. Although the content of the lines, "A plague upon you, murderers, traitors all! / I might have sav'd her" (5.3.270–1), may seem to point a guilty finger at all the surviving characters for having allowed the play to subsume their hold on reality, the dignity, seriousness, and self-possession of the survivors appears to suggest otherwise.

The final words the film speaks are not, however, Shakespeare's. They are spoken by and through Kanana in his unidentified language which is interpreted to us in subtitles: "They are not here. Now they are gone." These words and those that precede them, "From the desert came peace; they didn't see everything, I saw it all," bring us as close as we get to understanding the film's last transaction as two truckloads of sympathetically rendered Africans (the soft expressive eyes of one of the younger men establishes compassion as the dominant mood of the rescuers) circle the fire. They share silent looks with the apprehensive survivors, who seem shocked into bewildered silence at the timing and suddenness of their discovery. They are clearly no longer waiting to be rescued, in fact well beyond it. After a cut sweeps this scene away, a last shot of Kanana establishes him sitting once again on his half-shaded platform, which suggests nothing so much as a patchwork stage: a stage that has not, crucially, been only a performance site but also a site of witnessing, storytelling and observation, inseparable functions in this film.

Although the stage may embed itself in our minds as an artifact of early theater history, it has effectively served as no more than a grandstand or staging-ground for the true genius of the place, the three video cameras that we never see working but which take the measure of Kanana himself, and reduce even him to the status of an actor reciting scripted lines, recorded and played back on screens that make his otherwise impossible presence in the desert worth noting. The slightly longer overhead shots that follow, of the now all-but-deserted ghost-town, fade to the sound of a vinyl record bumping off its track as the final credits roll. Possibly meant to suggest a heartbeat winding down, the sound certifies this latter-day embedding of *King Lear* as Dogme4, *The King is Alive*. While the title evokes everything from eternal recurrence to the old rendered new, this final beat records the mediations that make such recurrence possible.

Notes

Chapter 1 Beyond Branagh and the BBC

1 Peter Donaldson describes the powerful effect Olivier's "glorious film" had on Zeffirelli's decision to become a director in *Shakespearean Films/Shakespearean Directors* (1990: 145–88).

2 For a number of reasons box-office figures are an imprecise and crude measure of a film's success (see Acland 2003). However they can be useful for ballpark comparisons. Full-feature Shakespeare films of this period fall into three broad box-office groups. The vast majority grossed under ten million dollars (most under five million), regardless of style or industry category. A few films – including Blake Nelson's *O* and Branagh's *Much Ado About Nothing* – grossed between ten and 30 million. Lurhmann's film took in (by various estimates) around 160 million worldwide, the same order of magnitude as *The Matrix*.

3 Denise Albanese contends that Luhrmann's *Romeo + Juliet* has all the trappings of a "mall movie" (high production values blended with modish youth culture stylings and uniformly bad acting) (2001: 206–26).

4 We are using the term "mainstream," as Robert Stam does, as a shorthand for commercial film production practices specifically aimed at claiming the widest possible audience – what Stam calls practices of "aesthetic mainstreaming" (Stam 2005a: 43). Stam describes a specific set of production practices aimed at standardizing and homogenizing current commercial film products (see p. 35 of this volume). Yet it is important to remember that what is understood as "mainstream" regularly changes, often under pressure of what is understood as "avant-garde." And moreover that any so-called "mainstream" accommodates a wide variety of efforts at claiming an audience, from the most commercially driven action-adventure blockbusters and formulaic romantic comedies to moodily postmodern film-noir revampings such as David Lynch's *Mulholland Drive*. As the Italian film-critic, Adriano Apra, reminds us, even as daring a filmmaker as Antonioni made his seemingly avant-garde films within the "overground" of the "mainstream" as opposed to the "underground" of experimental cinema (Apra 2005).

5 On the heritage film in general, see Voigts-Virchow (2004). On "heritage Shakespeare," see Cartmell's contribution to that volume (2004: 77–86). Mark Burnett offers an extended counter-argument, making the case for Branagh's postcoloniality (2002: 83–105).

6 Our game-plan here is similar to the one Lisa Starks and Courtney Lehmann pursue in their estimable *The Reel Shakespeare: Alternative Cinema and Theory*, which "attempts to 'escape from Hollywood' and the restricted range of meanings it brings to the phenomenon of Shakespearean adaptation, examining instead the marginal, radical, and experimental uses to which Shakespeare has been put in twentieth-century film culture" (2002a: 14).

7 We use the term "realist" advisedly here, as it is often used in film studies: as a label for a network of narrative and cinematic conventions that help maintain coherent character and narrative continuity, long seen as a legacy of classic Hollywood cinema. A longer view reminds us that the underlying assumptions about and the representational conventions for verisimilitude change significantly from period to period and across cultures – just as what is perceived

as constituting "natural" acting has changed, although claims to transformative "naturalness" are recycled through theater generations (Roach 1993). Different genres and representational modes make different claims to realism. The vernacularity of documentary, for example, makes one kind of claim to be "true to life." Godard's close observance of the everyday – of narrative emerging out of the arbitrary, contradictory turns of unfolding life – makes another. The affective immediacy of action films make a third. We might well describe the roller-coaster camera rides in *Spider-Man* (2002, dir. Sam Raimi) as excitingly verisimilar (this is what it would feel like to dive off a building), while also recognizing them as completely implausible. In this longer view, as Christopher Williams explains, artistic realism is not a univocal style, but a historically conditioned "network of differing conventions" that make claims to reference – to "knowledge of how things really are," in "relation to different aspects of film and television works, and of emotional, cultural, and social life" (2000: 210–11).

8 For informed commentary on the BBC Shakespeare project, see Susan Willis's book-length study (1991), the essays and reviews assembled by James C. Bulman and H.R. Coursen (1988), and the chapters authored by Michele Willems and Neil Taylor in Anthony Davies and Stanley Wells (1994: 69–85, 86–98).

9 See Bruster (2000) on Mazursky; Holderness (1993) on Jarman; and Hapgood (1994) on Kurosawa.

10 Almereyda has contributed a brief essay on Kurosawa's deployment of *Hamlet* in *The Bad Sleep Well* (in which he also acknowledges his debt to Kaurismaki) in the booklet enclosed in the Criterion Collection's recent edition of the film.

11 With respect to Branagh's mining of "heritage film" conventions, Albanese notes that "Branagh's *Hamlet* approximates the period and style of Masterpiece Theater and Merchant-Ivory productions, aligns itself with them in interpelleting a US audience interested in, and comfortable with, British-inflected representations of texts from the distant – but not too distant – past. Given the attention to luxurious settings and interiors that characterizes these films, this time before might be called the upholstered past, made for ease and relaxation, a past that is domesticated, effortlessly knowable" (2001: 213–14).

12 On cinematic realism more generally, see note 7, above. At the start of his article Loehlin refers both to "the new wave [of Shakespeare movies] that followed Kenneth Branagh's *Henry V*" and to Jack Jorgens's typologies which we discuss above, making the same kinds of exceptional cases for Luhrmann's *Romeo + Juliet* and Loncraine's *Richard III* that we make (Loehlin [1997] 2003: 173). For Loehlin, "new wave" is less a term for formal and stylistic preoccupations than a chronological grouping.

13 Loehlin notes that "[Oliver] Parker's *Othello* was marketed in Columbia Pictures print ads as an 'erotic thriller' that was 'as accessible as *Fatal Attraction*' " (2003: 174), while Albanese contends that "Branagh's at times gratuitous casting reveals his investment in the nexus of value that is the Hollywood star system: witness the number of big-name American actors in minor parts, who are as likely there to secure funding as to represent the universality of the Shakespearean dispensation" (2001: 212).

14 Albanese asks if it is "enough that mall movie and art cinema have the apparition of Shakespeare in common for us to forget all the differences in direction, style, language, and cast – not to mention budget, production, and distribution – that would mark them as imperfectly distinct" (2001: 208). Like Albanese, we think it is not.

15 See Mallin (1999); Burt (1998); Deitchman (2002); Hodgdon 2003b.

Chapter 2   Adaptation as a Cultural Process

1 For accounts of this phenomenon see the essays collected in Cartmell and Whelehan (1999), Desmet and Sawyer (1999), Davies and Wells (1994), Burt and

Boose (2003), and Holland (2004). In this spirit, Robert Shaughnessy (2002) offers a cultural history of twentieth-century Shakespearean theater.

2 We can extend Grigely's metaphor to describe them as constantly expanding, infinite, and even divergent – but that may be to stretch the limits of the mathematical analogy too far. In applying McGann's ideas to Shakespeare adaptations we follow the lead of W. B. Worthen (1998), who follows the lead of Joseph Grigely (1995).

3 Thanks to Mark Burnett for this observation, offered at the Shakespeare Association of America seminar "Shakespearean Film Theory," Bermuda, 2005.

4 "Paratext" is Gérard Genette's term for "all the accessory messages and commentaries [that] at times become virtually indistinguishable from" the text they surround (Stam 2005a: 28; Genette 1982).

5 The convention was picked up by Adrian Noble as well, in his stage and film productions of *A Midsummer Night's Dream* (1996), and recycled back to the stage again with Mamilius, in Edward Hall's 2004 stage production of *The Winter's Tale*.

6 Of Radford, for example, we might conclude that his deep focus thematics – making everything and everyone seem equally significant in every scene – betray false pathos, the desire to please everyone and blame none. Certainly it has a peculiar discontinuity effect of changing our characterological readings from scene to scene: in making his pitch to Antonio and in the later banquet scene, Bassanio is a sleazeball; when he arrives in Belmont and makes his casket choice, he's wise and noble; a few moments later he's half undressed and sleazy again, etc. But one could also argue that Radford has here found a point-of-view equivalent for – and is calling attention to – the compelling but troubling dynamics of Shakespearean humanism: the play's characters have an equal ethical pull on us and generate equal repugnance (e.g. "hath not a Jew eyes" / "my ducats, my daughter").

7 Cf. Kenneth Burke's suggestive framing of dramatic character: "The essayist's terms serve to organize a set of interrelated emphases, quite as Othello, Iago, and Desdemona are interrelated emphases. There are 'hero' and 'villain' terms, with subsidiary terms distributed about these two poles like iron filings in a magnetic field, and tracing somewhat of a 'graded series' between them. Emphases cannot 'contradict' one another so far as the 'total plot' is concerned, any more than Iago's function in the play can be said to contradict Othello's" ([1937] 1984: 312).

8 See Lehmann (2002a) on the author function in film; see Worthen (1997) on the Shakespearean "authority of performance" in theater; see Lanier (2002b) on Shakespearean "purity" from things commercial; see Holderness (1988) on Bardolatry.

9 For accounts of these poststructuralist groundings see Grigely (1995) and Stam (2005a).

10 Stam elaborates: "aesthetic mainstreaming" involves an aversion to "all forms of experimentation and modernism," an adherence to the "dominant model of storytelling (whether in its classical Hollywood or its Sundance Hollywood-lite version)," and a "suburbanized Aristotelianism", calling for "three-act structures, principal conflicts, coherent (and often sympathetic) characters, an inexorable narrative 'arc' and final catharsis or happy end. . . . Aesthetic mainstreaming dovetails with economic censorship, since the changes demanded in an adaptation are made in the name of monies spent and box-office profits required" (2005a: 43).

11 Stanley Cavell (2004) traces the film's "witnessing" of "intellectual origins" including Shakespeare's play (p. 427) as a movement between skepticism and "something that resembles faith but that is also to be distinguished from what we may expect of faith" (p. 426).

12 For Cavell, these transformations raise "the issue of the competition of film with theater" (2004: 436) as well as their interdependency.

13 On Shakespeare as a field of transaction between the "high" and the "popular", see Lanier (2002b).

14 See Burt (2003) and Osborne (2002) for discussions of DVD mediations of Shakespeare film. Acland (2003) offers the most extensive account of the changing paratextual landscape in the global film industry.

15 Peter Donaldson develops the phrase "media allegory" over a number of essays (1990–2005) and uses it to describe Shakespeare films that use shifts of cinematic style to reflect on transitions between different media and the history of technological change. See also Douglas Bruster on these effects in Mazursky's *Tempest* (2000).

Chapter 3   *Hamlet* Rewound

1 The association between film and modernity in critical theory takes different forms and has passed through a number of phases, from early Russian and French film theory to the philosophies of a Cavell or a Deleuze.

2 See, for example, Marcel Gromaire's totalizing "A Painter's Ideas about the Cinema" ([1919] 1988) or Andre Bazin's exceptionalist "The Myth of Total Cinema" ([1946] 1967).

3 Robert Stam (2005b, chapter 6) discusses Godard's adaptations (including his *King Lear* (1987)) in the context of the larger "querelle de l'adaptation" that helped define the French New Wave as a cinematic movement.

4 For discussions of the classroom scene topos in American films since the 1990s see Semenza (2005), Deitchman (2002), and Burt (2002c).

5 "Presentism" is the tendency to interpret earlier works and events according to our own cultural standards, as if early modern culture were, in Margreta de Grazia's words, the "early now." In Shakespeare studies, de Grazia (1995a, 1995b, 1996) and Terence Hawkes (2002) have offered the most sustained analysis of this approach.

6 For Walter Benjamin, the newspaper and novel destroy the "chasteness" and embedded life of storytelling; for Fredric Jameson, photography challenges the fullness of novelistic representation (Frow 1997: 224). More recently television has played the role of the impoverished newcomer.

7 Unless otherwise indicated, all citations to Shakespeare's work reference *The Riverside Shakespeare*, ed. G. Blakemore Evans (Boston: Houghton Mifflin, 1974).

8 See Yates (1966), Carruthers (1990), Maguire (1996), Tribble (2005), and Sullivan (1999).

9 The still fresh insight that all new technologies lag behind our needs of them is Richard Lanham's (1993).

10 For a discussion of the history, art, and science of Pixelvision, see http://www.michaeloreilly.com/pixelpage.html. For a selection of Benning's work, see http://www.vdb.org/smackn.acgi$pkgdetail?SADIEBENNI. Almereyda has also experimented with this medium in earlier shorts and other films.

11 But see Hodgdon for an opposing view evocative of Nora's position: "overall the film marks not just the waning of affect but of rich verbal communication in present-day culture, substituting for the memory of that heritage the ephemera of media culture" (2003b: 202).

12 Hodgdon observes that the ghost's sudden physical presence is "made all the more startling because Hamlet and the spectator see the ghost simultaneously, one of the few times the film invites such specular identification" (2003b: 201).

13 Lanier explains: "Many of Hamlet's filmmaking efforts are directed toward using film to create a counter discourse, in effect turning the technological apparatus of media culture back on itself in an effort to expose its complicity with corporate corruption. This is, for example, how Hamlet confronts Claudius's opening news conference, training his independent lens on the 'official' media and creating his own unfiltered record of the event" (2002b: 174).

14 Lanier contends that this scene offers no "space of resistance" (2002b: 176).

15 On film pornography and fictions of presence, see Williams (1989).

16 The "snow" screens in Hamlet's videos recall the strips of blank film that punctuate Connor's shorts. Video "snow" is the textual record of a recorder turned off,
reminding us (Connor's signature gesture) that what we are looking at is a material and mechanical record. Moreover, Hamlet's credit line, "This is a film by
HAMLET," echoes a similar gesture in Conner's short, "A Movie," which prominently displays the tag "BY BRUCE CONNER" throughout. (Thanks to one of our
students, Andrew Hall, for noting the allusive play on authorship; 2006). The
credit line, an intertextual signature, is thus both an allusion and a pun. It simultaneously asserts the claim and the limits of authorship.

17 Although it helps: See Cynthia Fuchs, "Interview with Michael Almereyda,"
http://www.popmatters.com/film/interviews/almereyda-michael.html.

Chapter 4   Colliding Time and Space in Taymor's *Titus*

1 Taymor notes that her production designer, Dante Ferretti introduced her "to
E.U.R., Mussolini's government centre, whose principal building is referred to as
the 'square coliseum' because of its myriad arches. Built by Mussolini to re-create
the glory of the ancient Roman Empire, this surreal – almost futuristic – architecture was a setting that perfectly embodied the concept for the film" (2000: 178).

2 The first image to the left in figure 4.1 is drawn from Peter Greenaway's *The Belly
of an Architect*, the one below it from *Titus*. The taller image on the right is a
photograph made by Philip Greenspun to illustrate a webpage devoted to EUR
that is viewable at http://www.photo.net/italy/rom-eur.

3 Taymor may be mining a late twentieth-century genre, post-apocalyptic film,
exemplified by the *Mad Max* films (1979, 1981, 1985). Her adaptation evokes a
host of contemporary concerns, ranging from the recent ethnic cleansings in the
Balkans to the long-established threat of nuclear annihilation. As the first
sentence in Taymor's *Illustrated Screenplay* claims, "We could be in Brooklyn or
Sarajevo" (2000: 19).

4 In an interview that took place on February 25, 2000 at Columbia University
(*Titus* DVD 2), Taymor embraces her reputation as an accomplished stylist of
violence. Yet she also describes redesigning the role of young Lucius as a "counterpoint" to the unrelieved violence that makes Aaron and Titus "mirror images
of each other" in both play and film.

5 Richard Burt, for example, argues that Shakespeare's own cultivation of "aesthetic
excess" through "the media of theater and print narrative" effectively "destabilizes
precisely the kinds of oppositions Taymor wants to affirm and correlate: between
high art (film) and trash (blockbuster); Shakespeare and Shakesploitation; a
critique of violence and an embrace of violence; modesty versus sexual perversion; and sacred and profane" (2002a: 312–13).

6 Many reviews noted Taymor's debt to Fellini – which, it should be added, is as
much structural as conceptual. In addition to employing Cinécittà craftsmen,
Taymor enlisted a production designer, Ferretti, whose résumé includes five
Fellini films between 1980 and 1990. For extended discussions of the Fellini
connection see Stone (2000), Burt (2002a) and Donaldson (2006).

7 On Cumming's *Cabaret* haircut, linking homosexuality to perversion to Fascism,
see Burt (2002a: 315–16) and Anderegg (2004: 186). Anderegg observes, "the
danger of the kind of postmodern allusiveness Taymor practices is that the associations evoked will not be those the artist intends. Too many allusions to a diverse
mix of external signs can result in a work that has no ultimate center, no 'base'
from which the allusions can be launched and controlled" (2004: 186). We share
some of Anderegg's reservations about Taymor's free-floating postmodernity. Yet
if postmodernism is about anything, it involves the promiscuous relation of
signifier to signified. Searching for an example of Taymor's "fidelity" to anything
except the Shakespearean playtext (which Anderegg accounts "a virtue"), much

less a fixed "center" or "base," is apt to prove disappointing. Postmodern adaptations test the very notion of a clear boundary between what is "external" (in Anderegg's words) to a work and what "belongs" to it.

8 By "infrastructure" Grigely means the whole range of practices associated with the production, distribution, and formal reception of a given medium. As Donaldson has observed, *Titus* is poised at a moment of significant shift in all these aspects of cinema; advertising, celebrity lives of actors, director's cut editions on DVD, merchandise, toys, novels made from films, websites and the spectrum of fan reworkings are now part of the aesthetically and commercially dispersed experience of movies (2006: 257–8).

9 Taymor and Eileen Blumenthal survey Taymor's work in puppetry, mask making, theater, opera, and film in *Julie Taymor: Playing with Fire* (Blumenthal and Taymor 1995). See, in particular, the chapter on Taymor's 1994 stage production of *Titus Andronicus*.

10 Both the claim of cultural authority by comparison with Rome and the instability of such claims are central concerns of *Titus Andronicus*. Wayward allusions feature prominently in the stories of imperial expansion that Shakespeare adapts from classical epic.

11 If, as Grigely notes, "works are ontologized – that is to say, contextualized semantically – by the temporal history that surrounds their composition" (1995: 103), then Taymor's intervention gains added resonance from events like the widespread practice of arbitrary mutilation in the recently concluded civil war in Sierra Leone and from the efforts reportedly undertaken there by American prostheses suppliers to fit and sell legs and arms to its victims. This sequence also evokes the grave injuries caused by buried mines in Afghanistan. The topic is tragic-comically treated in a recent Iranian film, *Kandahar* (dir. Mohsen Makhmalbaf, 2001), set in a desert oasis in Afghanistan where people who have lost limbs due to the explosion of buried mines gather to be fitted for prosthetic arms and legs dropped from the sky by UN relief planes.

12 Starks (2002: 134) notes that Taymor may have borrowed the idea of channeling her film through young Lucius's point of view from Jane Howell's 1985 BBC *Titus Andronicus*. As Starks observes, "Taymor first incorporated it in the off-Broadway stage-production she directed in 1994" (2002: 140 n. 56).

13 In the Columbia interview, Taymor approvingly quotes Tamora's description of Titus's commitment to blood sacrifice, as "cruel, irreligious piety" (*Titus*, DVD 2).

14 Marvin Carlson describes "ghosting" as a theatrical effect of audience memory. "The recycled body of an actor, already a complex bearer of semiotic messages, will almost inevitably in a new role evoke the ghost or ghosts of previous roles if they have made any impression whatever on the audience, a phenomenon that often colors and indeed may dominate the reception process" (2001: 8). In cinema, ghosting is related to the familiar phenomenon of typecasting and also to the cult of the celebrity actor, whose personae in different films intersect with public behaviors off-screen.

15 Stone (2000) eloquently unfolds the audio and visual allusions to Fellini's *La Strada* (1954) in this scene.

16 All quotations from the text of *Titus Andronicus* are drawn from Jonathan Bate's Arden edition, 3rd series (London: Thomson Learning, 2000).

17 Shakespeare would likely have been familiar with Arthur Golding's 1567 translation, but for Taymor the text seems to be the translation by Sir Samuel Garth, John Dryden, et al. (1717) in which the key passage reads as follows:

> Scarce had she finish'd, when her feet she found
> Benumb'd with cold, and fasten'd to the ground:
> A filmy rind about her body grows;
> Her hair to leaves, her arms extend to boughs:
> The nymph is all into a lawrel gone;

The smoothness of her skin remains alone.
Yet Phoebus loves her still, and casting round
Her bole, his arms, some little warmth he found.
The tree still panted in th' unfinish'd part:
Not wholly vegetive, and heav'd her heart.

18 Thanks to Peter Donaldson for this observation (personal correspondence 2005).

19 It was also the "extraordinarily lifelike appearance" of the little dancer, "enhanced by the use of painted wax and actual clothing" that made her "so disturbing" to Degas's contemporaries. Degas's sculpture, however, was but "a figurine about two-thirds" of his model's actual size and, hence, more akin to "a puppet or doll" (Czestochowski and Pingeot 2002: 52).

20 Allusions regularly seem off-target in this way, an effect that is intrinsic to the act of comparison and that often stumps commentators. When Titus cites the example of Virginius, late in the play, the Riverside commentary puzzles that he has mis-remembered the story: "This Roman centurion killed his daughter to *prevent* her rape. Either the dramatist has got the story wrong or he is failing to convey the idea that Titus has a better case for killing Lavinia than Virginius had for killing his daughter" (Evans 1997: 1049 fn. 36). We would say rather that Titus has an interest not in getting his source "right" but in adapting it to his situation. In this context, it makes no more sense to hold Taymor to some standard of allusive decorum than it does Shakespeare.

21 Burt contends that "Resistance to fascism becomes in the film a kind of massive death-drive, and honor-killing in the play is transformed into psycho-killing in the film" (2002a: 309). He adds "Antifascism in *Titus* is not collective rational resistance to a tyrannical state, but is located in the subjectivity of a hero who is both sadistic and masochistic and whose acts of violence do not respect distinctions between people who are in or out of his family" (2002a: 310).

22 The notion that Taymor's ending is involved in trauma management is more favorably addressed by Lisa Starks (2002: 121–42).

Chapter 5   Vernacular Shakespeare

1 On Van Sant's appropriations of Shakespeare see Curtis Breight (1997: 295–325), Susan Wiseman (1997: 225–39), and Cartelli (1999: 27–9). For a broad discussion of *Idaho* and *Men of Respect*, see Robert F. Willson (1992: 34–7).

2 Foster Hirsch notes that a "central problem of the [Actors] Studio" approach has been "translating emotion into words, learning how to be as turned on by a playwright's words (especially if the playwright isn't a contemporary) as by recalling a powerful image from your life." He adds that "the chasm between feeling and words . . . seems like a continuing hurdle at the Studio" (1984: 198).

3 In an unpublished paper entitled "What country, friends, is this?" Gary Jay Williams remarks an "American ambivalence about Shakespeare" in Pacino's film: "In his film [Pacino] crosses his company's performance of the play dialectically with a performance of anxiety about the authenticity of Shakespeare for everyday Americans, the America from which Mr. Pacino, as a Hollywood film actor, wants and needs to derive his authenticity. Mr. Pacino is not prepared to give up either Shakespeare or America; his film gives us both unreconciled." (1997)

4 The full text of the panhandler's commentary reads: "If we think words are things and we have no feelings in our words, then we say things to each other that don't mean anything. But if we *felt* what we said, we'd say less and mean more." The speech is carefully edited to conclude with a spoken (self-authenticating) request, "Spare change?" directed at a pedestrian outside the frame of the shot and bridging to the next sequence.

5 As Hirsch notes of New York's Actors Studio, "many American actors, told for so long that they don't speak well enough to do justice to the language, have come to believe it" (1984: 200).

6 Barbara Hodgdon observes, "Pacino's strategy merges with that of Richard to generate a partial, incomplete kind of re-authored manuscript that, by showing his own body-in-process, affords an opportunity to examine how the actor's body functions as a lever to de-center, though not discard, the text-based core of Shakespeare studies" (1998: 209–10). About the Lady Anne scene, she adds " 'I'll have her, but I will not keep her long' becomes a mantra that not only propels the actor 'into' the character but which, when the scene continues, he uses to punctuate his own (double) performance" (1998: 211).

7 Oscar Kightley, a New Zealand playwright, director, hip-hop poet, screenwriter, sportscaster, and arts activist, is co-author (with Erolia Ifopo) of *Romeo and Tusi* (1996). Kightley claims never to have read a complete Shakespeare play. He made this comment during a plenary panel discussion entitled "Shakespeare in the Pacific" at the Sixth Biennial Conference of the Australia and New Zealand Shakespeare Association in Auckland, New Zealand on July 9, 2000.

8 Smith (2004) uses the term "sampling" to cover a broad range of postmodern Shakespearean citation, paraphrase, and allusion. We aim to mine the term's specifically musical reference.

9 Morrissette notes that he originally planned scenes with kidnapped children but was dissuaded by his production team (DVD commentary). Yet directorial intention seems less important here than consequence. Allusions (whether to a play or a TV show) always exceed intention by their very nature as a feedback loop between audience and text. Intertexts such as *Columbo* or *Macbeth* assert a gravitational pull on the experience of reception and on direction and composition as well. Could there be a Mrs McDuff on the scene in Scotland after *Columbo*? Probably not in this context.

10 For discussions of the Manson murders and Polanski's *Macbeth*, see Bryan Reynolds (2002) and Deanne Williams (2004).

11 Tellingly, what Morrissette elects to riff on – an action sequence – is one of the few formal conventions of 1970s television that John Caldwell describes as heralding a new, self-consciously "televisual" style in the 1980s (1995). The hallmark of that emerging style, for Caldwell, is an attempt to make the viewer see television as a special form, aesthetically distinct from other media.

12 These are Charles Siepmann's (1950) influential claims, extended in major studies by Lynn Spigel (1991) and Anna McCarthy (2001).

13 Morrissette notes that Sanko's theme sounds like Tom Waits (DVD commentary). What he responds to is the way Waits channels Weill, a master ironist Waits regularly pays homage to.

14 "Love the One You're With," by Stephen Stills, performed by Crosby, Stills, Nash, and Young, whose anthems were fading by the mid-1970s.

15 The first line is from "Danny's Song," Kenny Loggins's early 1970s tribute to the simple life.

16 Clear Channel, one of the largest US radio conglomerates, was founded in 1972 and made its first acquisition of a nation-wide frequency in 1975.

17 In fact radio and television were never wholly separate, sharing a complex history as the dominant broadcast media of the twentieth century, one that involved cross-pollination as well as competition. William Boddy notes important differences between the inception of radio – a widely debated, crowded, competitive, and open arena before the 1927 Radio Act – and television, with its planned and deliberately shepherded growth, which from the start saw regulatory barriers to competition and muting of public debates about its function (1990: 16–17).

Chapter 6   Channeling *Othello*

1 Other prominent modern instances are Orson Welles's performance in the role in his own film *The Tragedy of Othello* (1952) and later casting of a skin-darkened

Charlton Heston as a Mexican Othello-surrogate in *A Touch of Evil* (1958). See Nicholas Taylor on the former as "a complex meditation on the insidious temptations of racial essentialism" (2005: 11) and Scott Newstock (2005) for a convincing assessment of the latter as an *Othello* film. For a provocatively post-modern appraisal of the "Olivier *Othello*," see Timothy Murray (1993: 101–23).

2 Shakespeare's tragedy itself offers competing accounts of race, reflecting the emergence of modern notions of blackness and whiteness out of very different, earlier models of ethnicity. See Floyd-Wilson 2003 and Callaghan 1996.

3 Most of Daileader's examples are drawn from RSC stage-productions and demonstrate how stereotypes about black male sexuality migrate beyond the role of Othello to determine how black actors are deployed in other, non-traditional examples of "colour-blind" casting. Hodgdon (2003a) has elaborated many of these points regarding recent film-versions of *Othello*.

4 Stephen M. Buhler observes that under Parker's direction, Fishburne's Othello "speaks mostly with his body" while Branagh's Iago "has the most commanding voice in the film" (2002: 26–7).

5 In this respect and others, the work Eccleston does as Ben Jago bears an uncanny resemblance to the way Michael Kitchen channels class-based resentment and xenophobia in the role of Martin in the 1976 BBC production of Dennis Potter's controversial *Brimstone and Treacle* (dir. Barry Davis). The 1982 film version – featuring Sting in the role of Martin (dir. Richard Loncraine) – was considerably less successful in eliciting the politically incorrect pleasures of Potter's play.

6 Silverman adds: "On these occasions the discursive mode is direct rather than indirect. No distance separates teller from tale; instead, the voice-over is stripped of temporal protection and thrust into diegetic immediacy. Thus deprived of enunciatory pretense, it is no longer in a position to masquerade as the point of textual origin" (1988: 53). Whereas "the disembodied voice can be seen as 'exemplary' for male subjectivity" (1988: 164), embodied voice-over is "autobiographical and self-revealing," and therefore a precarious medium for establishing authority (1988: 52–3).

7 Sarah Neely offers an important corrective to Silverman's generalizations, analyzing vernacular voice-overs in contemporary Irish and Scottish film-adaptations. These films use the device ironically to expose the hierarchies of address in classical Hollywood cinema (2005). Jago's narration not only borrows the ironic intimacy of these counter-mainstream voice-overs but sidles up to the class-based grievances they address.

8 The histrionics of this scene bear obvious resemblances to the kind of "involuntary or constrained speech" that Silverman considers "a general characteristic of the embodied voice-over, as is vividly dramatized by that variant which seems most fully to turn the body 'inside out' – the internal monologue" (Silverman 1988: 53). But Ben's ability to recover his poise and to regain control of the film's momentum suggests that we are working here with a very special variant of the form: one rooted in the dramatic authority of the theatrical *aside* and rendered more intimate by its televisual mode of address, as we observe above.

9 See Linda Williams (1989: 122–6). The classic studies of visual pleasure are Laura Mulvey ([1975 and 1981] 1989).

Chapter 7   Surviving Shakespeare: Kristian Levring's *The King is Alive*

1 Some of the aims and effects of this subtle exposure of the filmic apparatus are explored by Lev Manovich (2001: 145–7), who differentiates them from the conventions of mainstream fiction cinema which are based upon "lying to the viewer" (146).

2 This manifesto may be found at the Dogme95 website, www.dogme95.dk/.

3 As Scott-Douglass writes, "the title 'Dogme95' suggests that the movement should be regarded, at least in part, as a reaction to GATT93, the final year of the

Uruguay round of General Agreement of Tariffs and Trade Talks, and GATT94, the international agreement that resulted from those talks." European representatives, particularly those from France, successfully "resisted the American initiative, arguing that films are works of art and, therefore, as François Mitterand put it, 'not mere merchandise . . . not simply commercial concerns' [quoted in Jeancolas 2000: 17]" (Scott-Douglass 2003: 253). Their success led to the exemption of films from the GATT94 agreement, an exception thus called *l'exception culturelle* or *l'exception française.*

4 In DVD chapter 3, "Turn On & the Married Man," Paul mistakes the opening chords of Errol Brown's "Every 1's A Winner" for the Bee Gee's "Staying Alive," an error compounded in the silly debate about John Travolta movies and dancing that follows. As Keith Harrison observes, this meta-critical moment humorously evokes "questions of performance, text, and scholarship" through a dispute over "low" culture (private communication, 2004). The dispute – and the arrogant and seductive posing that unfolds it – cues us to the film's general skepticism of arrogant experts (Jack, Henry, Catherine).

5 *Lear* has long served as an important intertext for critiques of the genre, at least since Peter Brook's work in the 1960s. Brook draws the connection both conceptually and artistically: his adaptation of William Golding's dystopic survival narrative, *Lord of the Flies* (1963), is in many ways a *King Lear* film and his own *Lears*, on both stage (1962/1964) and screen (1971), repay the debt.

6 The DVD edition of *The Five Obstructions* includes Leth's *The Perfect Human*, a pairing that makes the duel between filmmakers and films accessible to new viewers.

7 Bilingual viewers will find the English subtitles to Catherine's French "fairy tale" adequate to the main sense of the French. However, by making the English slightly less offensive than the French, and by varying idiomatic translations for *con* (literally "cunt," translated as "cow"), the subtitles fail to match the nastiness of the names Catherine calls Gina. What they convey clearly is that Catherine enjoys the unequal power of translator over listener. As one of our students, Lauren Everingham, notes, this disparity is ironically enriched by the fact that most of us "would not have understood Katherine's story without the subtitles, and yet we laugh at Gina's foolishness."

8 Like Bohannan, whose essay ironically turns on an American anthropologist being retaught the plot and meaning of *Hamlet* by a group of Tiv elders, *The King is Alive* is skeptical of claims to universal authority (and universalizing interpretations of Shakespeare). And as in Bohannan's essay, the figure who at once claims interpretive authority and embodies the limits of cross-cultural translation is a male African "elder." But in this instance, an American, Ray, inhabits the position delegated to an outspoken old man in Bohannan's account, who, while conceding that different cultures have different customs, nonetheless maintains that "people are the same everywhere; therefore, there are always witches and it is we, the elders, who know how witches work" (1966: 33). In this respect, Ray's normative Americanness and the elder's normative Tiv-ness speak the same language.

9 As Kenneth Rothwell observes, at the end of Brook's *King Lear* "a gravelly voiced Paul Scofield as the dying king literally falls out of the frame . . . to be replaced by white nothingness" (1994: 219).

References

Works Cited

Acland, Charles (2003) *Screen Traffic: Movies, Multiplexes, and Global Culture.* Durham, NC and London: Duke University Press.

Albanese, Denise (2001) "The Shakespeare Film and the Americanization of Culture." In Jean E. Howard and Scott Cutler Shershow (eds) *Marxist Shakespeares.* London & New York: Routledge, 206–26.

Altman, Rick, ed. (1992) *Sound Theory/Sound Practice.* New York: Routledge.

Anderegg, Michael (2004) *Cinematic Shakespeare.* Lanham, MD: Rowman & Littlefield.

Auslander, Philip (1999) *Liveness: Performance in a Mediatized Culture.* London: Routledge.

Bakhtin, Mikhail ([1965] 1984) *Rabelais and His World.* Trans. Helene Iswolsky. Bloomington: Indiana University Press.

Ball, Robert Hamilton (1968) *Shakespeare on Silent Film: A Strange Eventful History.* New York: Theater Arts Book.

Barbour, Reid (1998) *English Epicures and Stoics: Ancient Legacies in Early Stuart Culture.* Amherst: University of Massachusetts Press.

Barthes, Roland (1977) *Image–Music–Text.* London: Fontana.

Bate, Jonathan, ed. (2000) *Titus Andronicus.* The Arden Shakespeare. Third series. London: Thomson Learning.

Bazin, André ([1946] 1967) "The Myth of Total Cinema." Trans. Hugh Gray. In Bazin, *What is Cinema?* Berkeley: University of California Press, 17–22.

Belton, John (1994) *American Cinema/American Culture.* New York: McGraw-Hill.

Berger, Jr, Harry ([1980] 1997) "The Early Scenes of *Macbeth:* Preface to a New Interpretation." In *Making Trifles of Terrors: Redistributing Complicities in Shakespeare.* Stanford CA: Stanford: University Press, 70–97.

Black, Scott (2006) *Of Essays and Reading in Early Modern Britain.* New York: Palgrave MacMillan.

Blumenthal, Eileen and Julie Taymor (1995) *Julie Taymor: Playing with Fire.* New York: Abrams.

Boddy, William (1990) *Fifties Television: The Industry and its Critics.* Chicago: University of Illinois Press.

Bohannan, Laura (1966) "Shakespeare in the Bush." *Natural History* 75 (7): 28–33.

Bolter, J. David and Richard Grusin (2000) *Remediation: Understanding New Media.* Cambridge, MA: MIT Press.

Breight, Curtis (1991) "Branagh and the Prince, or a 'Royal Fellowship of Death.' " *Critical Quarterly* 33 (4): 95–111.

Breight, Curtis (1997) "Elizabethan World Pictures." In John J. Joughin (ed.) *Shakespeare and National Culture.* Manchester: Manchester University Press, 295–325.

Bruster, Douglas (2000) "The Postmodern Theatre of Paul Mazursky's *Tempest.*" In Mark Thornton Burnett and Ramona Wray (eds) *Shakespeare, Film, Fin de Siècle.* Houndsmill & London: Macmillan; New York: St Martin's, 26–39.

Buhler, Stephen M. (2000) "Camp *Richard III* and the Burdens of (Stage/Film) History." In Mark Thornton Burnett and Ramona Wray (eds) *Shakespeare, Film, Fin de Siècle.* Houndsmill & London: Macmillan; New York: St Martin's, 40–57.

Buhler, Stephen M. (2002) *Shakespeare in the Cinema: Ocular Proof.* Albany: State University of New York Press.

Bulman, James C. and H.R. Coursen, eds (1988) *Shakespeare on Television: An Anthology of Essays and Reviews.* Hanover, NH & London: University Press of New England.

Burke, Kenneth ([1937] 1984) *Attitudes Towards History.* Berkeley: University of California Press.

Burnett, Mark Thornton (2002) " 'We are the Makers of Manners': The Branagh Phenomenon." In Richard Burt (ed.) *Shakespeare after Mass Media.* New York & Houndmills: Palgrave, 83–106.

Burnett, Mark Thornton (2003) " 'To Hear and See the Matter:' Communicating Technology in Michael Almereyda's *Hamlet* (2000)." *Cinema Journal* 42 (3): 48–69.

Burnett, Mark Thornton and Ramona Wray, eds (2000) *Shakespeare, Film, Fin de Siècle.* Houndmills: Macmillan; New York: St Martin's.

Burt, Richard (1998) *Unspeakable ShaXXXspeares: Queer Theory and American Kiddie Culture.* New York: St Martin's; Houndmills, Macmillan.

Burt, Richard (2002a) "Shakespeare and the Holocaust: Julie Taymor's *Titus* is Beautiful, or Shakesploi Meets (the) Camp." In Richard Burt (ed.) *Shakespeare After Mass Media.* New York: Palgrave, 295–329.

Burt, Richard (2002b) "To e- or not to e-? Schlockspeare in the Age of Electronic Mass Media." In Richard Burt (ed.) *Shakespeare After Mass Media.* New York: Palgrave, 1–32.

Burt, Richard (2002c) "T(e)en Things I Hate about Girlene Shakesploitation Flicks in the Late 1990s." In Lisa S. Starks and Courtney Lehmann (eds) *Spectacular Shakespeare: Critical Theory and Popular Cinema.* Madison, NJ: Fairleigh Dickinson University Press; London & Cranbury, NJ: Associated University Presses, 205–32.

Burt, Richard (2003) "Shakespeare, 'Glo-cali-zation', Race, and the Small Screens of Post-Popular Culture." In Richard Burt and Lynda Boose (eds) *Shakespeare, the Movie II: Popularizing the Plays on Film, TV, Video and DVD.* London & New York: Routledge, 14–36.

Burt, Richard (2006) "Shakespeare, More or Less?" in *Shakespeare After Shakespeare: An Encyclopedia of Shakespeare in Mass Media and Popular Culture.* Westport, CT: Greenwood Press. In manifesto at www.clas.ufl.edu/~rburt/shakescentric.html.

Burt, Richard and Lynda Boose, eds (2003) "Introduction." In Richard Burt and Lynda Boose (eds) *Shakespeare, the Movie II: Popularizing the Plays on Film, TV, Video and DVD.* London & New York: Routledge, 1–13.

Caldwell, John (1995) *Televisuality: Style, Crisis, and Authority in American Television.* New Brunswick, NJ: Rutgers University Press.

Callaghan, Dympna (1996) " 'Othello was a White Man': Properties of Race on Shakespeare's Stage." In Terence Hawkes (ed.) *Alternative Shakespeares, vol. 2.* London & New York: Routledge, 192–215.

Carlson, Marvin (2001) *The Haunted Stage: Theater as Memory Machine.* Ann Arbor: Michigan University Press.

Carruthers, Mary (1990) *The Book of Memory: A Study of Memory in Medieval Culture.* Cambridge: Cambridge University Press.

Cartelli, Thomas (1998) "*Queer* Edward II: Postmodern Sexualities and the Early Modern Subject." In Paul W. White (ed.) *Marlowe, History, and Sexuality: New Critical Essays on Christopher Marlowe.* New York: AMS Press, 213–23. Reprinted in Avraham Oz (ed.) (2003) *Marlowe: Contemporary Critical Essays.* New York: Palgrave, 200–12.

Cartelli, Thomas (1999) *Repositioning Shakespeare: National Formations, Postcolonial Appropriations*. London: Routledge.

Cartelli, Thomas (2002) "Shakespeare in Pain: Edward Bond's *Lear* and the Ghosts of History." *Shakespeare Survey* 55: 159–69.

Cartelli, Thomas (2003) "Shakespeare and the Street: Pacino's *Looking for Richard*, Bedford's *The Street King*, and the Common Understanding." In Richard Burt and Lynda Boose (eds) *Shakespeare, the Movie, II: Popularizing the Plays on Film, TV, Video and DVD*. London & New York: Routledge, 186–99.

Cartmell, Deborah (2000) *Interpreting Shakespeare on Screen*. Houndmills: Macmillan.

Cartmell, Deborah (2004) "*Fin de Siècle* Film Adaptations of Shakespeare." In Eckart Voigts-Virchow (ed.) *Janespotting and Beyond: British Heritage RetroVisions Since the Mid-1990s*. Tübingen: Gunter Narr Verlag, 77–86.

Cartmell, Deborah and Imelda Whelehan, eds (1999) *Adaptations: From Text to Screen, Screen to Text*. London & New York: Routledge.

Castaldo, Annalisa (2002) "The Film's the Thing: Using Shakespearean Film in the Classroom." In Lisa Starks and Courtney, Lehmann (eds) *Spectacular Shakespeare: Critical Theory and Popular Cinema* Madison, NJ: Fairleigh Dickinson University Press; London & Cranbury, NJ: Associated University Presses, 187–204.

Cavell, Stanley (2004) "Shakespeare and Rohmer: Two Tales of Winter." In *Cities of Words: Pedagogical Letters on a Register of the Moral Life*. Cambridge: Harvard/Belknap Press, 421–43.

Chartier, Roger, J. Frank Mowery, Peter Stallybrass, and Heather Wolfe (2004) "Hamlet's Tables and the Technologies of Writing in Renaissance England." *Shakespeare Quarterly* 55 (4): 379–419.

Chion, Michel (1999) *The Voice in Cinema*. Trans. Claudia Gorbman. New York: Columbia University Press.

Cohen, Lisa (1998) "The Horizontal Walk: Marilyn Monroe, CinemaScope, and Sexuality." *The Yale Journal of Criticism* 11 (1) (Spring): 259–88.

Corrigan, Timothy (2004) *A Short Guide to Writing about Film* (5th edn) New York: Longman.

Crowl, Samuel S. (2003) *Shakespeare at the Cineplex: The Kenneth Branagh Era*. Athens: Ohio University Press.

Czestochowski, Joseph S. and Anne Pingeot (2002) *Degas Sculptures: Catalogue Raisonne of the Bronzes*. Memphis: International Arts and Torch Press.

Daileader, Celia (2000) "Casting Black Actors: Beyond Othellophilia." In Catherine M.S. Alexander and Stanley Wells (eds) *Shakespeare and Race*. Cambridge: Cambridge University Press, 177–202.

Davies, Anthony (1988) *Filming Shakespeare's Plays: The Adaptations of Laurence Olivier, Orson Welles, Peter Brook and Akira Kurosawa*. Cambridge: Cambridge University Press.

Davies, Anthony and Stanley Wells, eds (1994) *Shakespeare and the Moving Image: The Plays on Film and Television*. Cambridge & New York: Cambridge University Press.

Defoe, Daniel ([1719] 1994) *Robinson Crusoe*. Ed. Michael Shinagel. New York: Norton.

De Grazia, Margreta (1995a) "Fin de Siècle Renaissance England." In Elaine Scarry (ed.) *Fins de Siècles: English Poetry in 1590, 1690, 1790, 1890, 1990*. Baltimore & London: Johns Hopkins University Press.

De Grazia, Margreta (1995b) "Soliloquies and Wages in the Age of Emergent Consciousness." *Textual Practice* 9 (1): 67–92.

De Grazia, Margreta (1996) "The Ideology of Superfluous Things: *King Lear* as Period Piece." In Margreta de Grazia, Maureen Quilligan, and Peter Stallybrass (eds) *Subject and Object in Renaissance Culture*. Cambridge: Cambridge University Press.

Deitchman, Elizabeth (2002) "From the Cinema to the Classroom: Hollywood Teaches *Hamlet*." In Lisa Starks and Courtney Lehmann (eds) *Spectacular Shakespeare: Critical Theory and Popular Cinema*. Madison, NJ: Fairleigh Dickinson University Press; London & Cranbury, NJ: Associated University Presses, 149–71.

Derrida, Jacques (1981) "The Double Session." In Barbara Johnson (trans.) *Disseminations*. Chicago: University of Chicago Press.

Desmet, Christy and Robert Sawyer, eds (1999) *Shakespeare and Appropriation*. London & New York: Routledge.

Díaz-Fernández, José Ramón (1997a) "Shakespeare on Screen: A Bibliography of Critical Studies." *Postscript: Essays in Film and the Humanities* 17 (1) (Fall): 91–146.

Díaz-Fernández, José Ramón (1997b) "Shakespeare and Film-Derivatives: A Bibliography." *Postscript: Essays in Film and the Humanities* 17 (2) (Winter/ Spring): 109–20.

Díaz-Fernández, José Ramón (2000) "Shakespeare on Television: A Bibliography of Criticism." *Early Modern Literary Studies* 6 (1) (May): 4.

Donaldson, Peter (1990) *Shakespearean Films/Shakespearean Directors*. Boston: Unwin Hyman.

Donaldson, Peter (1991) "Taking on Shakespeare: Kenneth Branagh's Henry V." *Shakespeare Quarterly* 42 (1): 60–71.

Donaldson, Peter (1999) " 'All Which It Inherit': Shakespeare, Globes and Global Media." *Shakespeare Survey* 52: 183–200.

Donaldson, Peter (2002a) "Cinema and the Kingdom of Death: Loncraine's *Richard III*." *Shakespeare Quarterly* 53 (2) 241–59.

Donaldson, Peter (2002b) " 'In fair Verona': Media, Spectacle and Performance in *William Shakespeare's Romeo + Juliet*." In Richard Burt (ed.) *Shakespeare after Mass Media*. New York: Palgrave, 59–82.

Donaldson, Peter (2003) "Shakespeare in the Age of Post-Mechanical Reproduction: Sexual and Electronic Magic in *Prospero's Books*." In Richard Burt and Lynda Boose (eds) *Shakespeare: the Movie II*. London & New York: Routledge, 105–19.

Donaldson, Peter (2006) "Game Space/Tragic Space: Julie Taymor's *Titus*." In Barbara Hodgdon and W.B. Worthen (eds) *A Companion to Shakespeare and Performance*. Cambridge: Blackwell, 457–77.

Eliot, T.S. ([1919] 1932) "Tradition and the Individual Talent." *Selected Essays, 1917–1932*. New York: Harcourt, Brace and Company.

Emerson, Ralph Waldo (1968) "Shakespeare the Poet" in *Representative Men: Seven Essays*. In *The Complete Works of Ralph Waldo Emerson: Centenary Edition*, vol. 4. New York: AMS Press.

Enterline, Lynn (1977) " 'You Speak a Language that I Understand Not:' The Rhetoric of Animation in *The Winter's Tale*." *Shakespeare Quarterly* 48:1 17–44.

Evans, G. Blakemore, ed. ([1974] 1997) *The Riverside Shakespeare*. Boston: Houghton Mifflin.

Everingham, Lauren Constance (2005) "Foreign Languages in *The King is Alive*" (unpublished paper).

Floyd-Wilson, Mary (2003) *English Ethnicity and Race in Early Modern Drama*. Cambridge: Cambridge University Press.

Foucault, Michel (1977) "What is an Author?" Trans. Donald F. Bouchard and Sherry Simon. In Donald F. Bouchard (ed.) *Language, Counter-Memory, Practice*. Ithaca, NY: Cornell University Press, 124–27.

Frow, John (1997) "Toute la mémoire du monde." *Time and Commodity Culture: Essays in Cultural Theory and Postmodernity*. Oxford: Clarendon Press, 218–46.

Fuchs, Cynthia (1999–2001) "Interview with Michael Almereyda." http://www.popmatters.com/film/interviews/almereyda-michael.html.

Genette, Gérard (1982) *Palimpsestes*. Paris: Seuil.

Golding, William (1954) *Lord of the Flies: A Novel.* London: Faber and Faber.

Greenberg, Clement (1939) "Avant-garde and Kitsch." *Partisan Review* 7 (4): 34–49.

Green, Douglas E. (2002) "Shakespeare, Branagh, and the 'Queer Traitor:' Close Encounters in the Shakespearean Classroom." In Lisa Starks and Courtney Lehmann (eds) *The Reel Shakespeare: Alternative Cinema and Theory.* Madison, NJ: Fairleigh Dickinson University Press; London & Cranbury, NJ: Associated University Presses, 191–211.

Greene, Roland (1999) *Unrequited Conquests: Love and Empire in the Colonial Americas.* Chicago: University of Chicago Press.

Grigely, Joseph (1995) *Textualterity: Art, Theory, and Textual Criticism.* Ann Arbor: University of Michigan Press.

Gromaire, Marcel ([1919] 1988) "A Painter's Ideas about the Cinema." Trans. Stuart Leibman. Reprinted in Richard Abel (ed.) *French Film Theory and Criticism*, vol. 1. Princeton, NJ: Princeton University Press, 174–82.

Haggard, H. Rider ([1885] 1998) *King Solomon's Mines.* Ed. Dennis Butts. Oxford & New York: Oxford University Press.

Hall, Andrew (2006) "Hamlet and Bruce Conner: Filmic Reproduction and Authorship" (unpublished student essay).

Halpern, Richard (1997) *Shakespeare Among the Moderns.* Ithaca, NY: Cornell University Press.

Hapgood, Robert (1994) "Kurosawa's Shakespeare Films: *Throne of Blood, The Bad Sleep Well* and *Ran.*" In Anthony Davies and Stanley Wells (eds) *Shakespeare and the Moving Image.* Cambridge: Cambridge University Press, 234–49.

Harbord, Janet (2002) *Film Cultures.* London: SAGE Publications.

Harris, Rachel (2005) "Figurative Sight and the Wounding of Gloucester Characters in *King Lear* and *The King is Alive*" (unpublished paper).

Hatchuel, Sarah (2000) *A Companion to the Shakespearean Films of Kenneth Branagh.* Winnipeg and Niagara Falls: Blizzard Publishing.

Hayward, Susan (2000) *Cinema Studies: The Key Concepts* (2nd edn). London & New York: Routledge.

Hawkes, Terence (2002) *Shakespeare in the Present.* London & New York: Routledge.

Hedrick, Donald K. (1997) "War is Mud: Branagh's Dirty Harry V and the Types of Political Ambiguity." In Lynda Boose and Richard Burt (eds) *Shakespeare the Movie: Popularizing the Plays on Film, TV and Video.* London: Routledge, 45–66.

Hill, Erroll (1984) *Shakespeare in Sable: A History of Black Shakespearean Actors.* Amherst: University of Massachusetts Press.

Hirsch, Foster (1984) *A Method to Their Madness: The History of the Actor's Studio.* New York: Norton.

Hodgdon, Barbara (1998) "Replicating Richard: Body Doubles, Body Politics," *Theatre Journal* 50 (2): 207–25.

Hodgdon, Barbara (2001) Personal communication.

Hodgdon, Barbara (2003a) "Race-ing *Othello,* Re-engendering White-Out II." In Richard Burt and Lynda Boose (eds) *Shakespeare, the Movie II.* London & New York: Routledge, 89–104.

Hodgdon, Barbara (2003b) "Re-Incarnations." In Pascale Aebischer, Edward J. Esche, and Nigel Wheale (eds) *Remaking Shakespeare: Performance across Media, Genres and Cultures.* New York: Palgrave Macmillan, 190–209.

Holderness, Graham (1993) "Shakespeare Rewound." *Shakespeare Survey* 45: 63–74. Holderness, Reprinted in *Visual Shakespeare: Essays in Film and Television.* Hatfield: University of Hertfordshire Press, 2002.

Holderness, Graham, ed. (1988) *The Shakespeare Myth.* Manchester & New York: Manchester University Press.

James, Heather (1997) *Shakespeare's Troy: Drama, Politics, and the Translation of Empire*. Cambridge & New York: Cambridge University Press.

James, Heather (2003) "Ovid and the Question of Politics in Early Modern England." *ELH: a Journal of English Literary History* 70: 343–73.

Jameson, Fredric (1991) *Postmodernism, or The Cultural Logic of Late Capitalism*. Durham, NC: Duke University Press.

Jeancolas, Jean-Pierre (2002) "The Reconstruction of French Cinema." In Elizabeth Ezra and Sue Harris (eds) *France in Focus: Film and National Identity*. Oxford: Berg.

Jefferson, Margo (1996) "Welcoming Shakespeare into the Caliban Family," *New York Times*, November 12, 1996: C11, C16.

Jenkins, Bruce (1999) "Explosion in a Film Factory: The Cinema of Bruce Conner." *2000 BC: The Bruce Conner Story Part II*. Catalog of an exhibition held at the Walker Art Center, Minneapolis, MN, October, 9 1999–January 2, 2000.

Jones, Nicholas (2005) "A Bogus Hero: Welles's *Othello* and the Construction of Race." *Shakespeare Bulletin* 23 (1): 9–28.

Jorgens, Jack ([1977] 1991) *Shakespeare on Film*. Bloomington: Indiana University Press. Reprinted Lanham, MD and London: University Press of America.

Keen, Suzanne (2001) *Romances of the Archive in Contemporary British Fiction*. Toronto: University of Toronto Press.

Kightley, Oscar and Erolia Ifopo (1996) *Romeo and Tusi*. First performed in 1996 by the Pacific Underground Company, Christchurch, New Zealand. Details at www.smokefreearts.co.nz/romeo.html.

Kirschenbaum, Matthew G. (2001) "Media, Genealogy, History." *ebr 9, msn music-soundnoise*, Fall. www.altx.com/ebr/reviews/rev9/r9kir.htm.

Kliman, Bernice W. (1988) *Hamlet: Film, Television, and Audio Performance*. Rutherford, NJ: Fairleigh Dickinson University Press; London and Toronto: Associated University Presses.

Kushner, Tony (1993) *Angels in America: A Gay Fantasia on National Themes*, vols. 1–2. New York: Theatre Communications Group.

Lanham, Richard (1993) *The Electronic Word: Democracy, Technology, and the Arts*. Chicago: University of Chicago Press.

Lanier, Douglas (2002a) " 'Art thou base, common, and popular?': The Cultural Politics of Kenneth Branagh's *Hamlet*." In Lisa Starks and Courtney Lehmann (eds) *Spectacular Shakespeare: Critical Theory and Popular Cinema*. Madison, NJ: Fairleigh Dickinson University Press; London & Cranbury, NJ: Associated University Presses, 149–71.

Lanier, Douglas (2002b) "Shakescorp *Noir*." *Shakespeare Quarterly* 53 (2): 157–80.

Lawson, Chris (2000) "The Don Who Would Be King: *Looking for Richard* (USA, 1996), but Finding Al," *Shakespeare and the Classroom* 8 (1): 44–7.

Lehmann, Courtney (2002a) "Crouching Tiger, Hidden Agenda: How Shakespeare and the Renaissance Are Taking the Rage Out of Feminism." *Shakespeare Quarterly* 53 (2): 260–79.

Lehmann, Courtney (2002b) *Shakespeare Remains: Theater to Film, Early Modern to Postmodern*. Ithaca, NY: Cornell University Press.

Levin, Bernard (1984) "Quoting Shakespeare." *Enthusiasms*. New York: Crown Publishers.

Loehlin, James N. ([1997] 2003) " 'Top of the world, ma': *Richard III* and Cinematic Convention." In Richard S. Burt and Lynda Boose (eds) *Shakespeare, the Movie II: Popularizing the Plays on Film, TV, Video and DVD*. London & New York: Routledge, 173–85.

McCandless, David (2002) "A Tale of Two *Titus*es: Julie Taymor's Vision on Stage and Screen." *Shakespeare Quarterly* 53 (4): 487–511.

McCarthy, Anna (2001) *Ambient Television: Visual Culture and Public Space*. Durham, NC: Duke University Press.

McCullough, Malcolm (1996) *Abstracting Craft: The Practiced Digital Hand*. Cambridge, MA: MIT Press.

McGann, Jerome J. (1983) *A Critique of Modern Textual Criticism*. Charlottesville: University of Chicago Press.

McGann, Jerome J. (1991) *The Textual Condition*. Princeton, NJ: Princeton University Press.

McGann, Jerome J. (2001) *Radiant Textuality: Literature After the World Wide Web*. New York: Palgrave.

Maguire, Laurie E. (1996) *Shakespearean Suspect Texts: The 'Bad' Quartos and their Contexts*. Cambridge: Cambridge University Press.

Mahn, Amy (2005) "Functions and Effects in *The King is Alive*" (unpublished paper).

Mallin, Eric S. (1999) " 'You Kilt My Foddah': Or Arnold, Prince of Denmark." *Shakespeare Quarterly* 50 (2): 127–51.

Manovich, Lev (2001) *The Language of New Media*. Cambridge, MA: MIT Press.

Massai, Sonia (2005) "Subjection and Redemption in Pasolini's *Othello*." In *World-wide Shakespeares: Local Appropriations in Film and Performance*. London & New York: Routledge, 95–103.

Masten, Jeffrey (1997) *Textual Intercourse: Collaboration, Authorship, and Sexualities in Renaissance Drama*. Cambridge: Cambridge University Press.

Morse, Margaret (1990) "An Ontology of Everyday Distraction: The Freeway, The Mall, and Television." In Patricia Mellencamp (ed.) *Logics of Television: Essays in Cultural Criticism*. Bloomington: Indiana University Press.

Mulvey, Laura ([1975 and 1981] 1989) *Visual and Other Pleasures*. Bloomington: Indiana University Press.

Murray, Albert (1976) *Stomping the Blues*. New York: McGraw-Hill.

Murray, Timothy (1993) "Dirty Stills: Arcadian Retrospection, Cinematic Hieroglyphs, and Blackness Run Riot in Olivier's *Othello*." In *Like a Film: Ideological Fantasy on Screen, Camera, and Canvas*. London & New York: Routledge.

Neely, Sarah (2005) "Cultural Ventriloquism: The Voice-over in Film Adaptations of Contemporary Irish and Scottish Literature." In Kevin Rockett and John Hill (eds) *National Cinema and Beyond*. Dublin: Four Courts Press.

Neill, Michael (1989) "Unproper Beds: Race, Adultery, and the Hideous in *Othello*." *Shakespeare Quarterly* 40 (4): 383–412.

Nelson, Victoria (2001) *The Secret Life of Puppets*. Cambridge: Cambridge University Press.

Newstock, Scott L. (2005) "*Touch* of Shakespeare: Welles Unmoors *Othello*." *Shakespeare Bulletin* 23 (1): 29–86.

Nora, Pierre (1989) "Between Memory and History: *Les Lieux de Mémoire*." *Representations* 26 (Spring): 7–25.

Okri, Ben (1987) "Meditations on *Othello*." *West Africa*, March 23–30, 1987, 562–4, 618–19. Reprinted in Kwesi Owusu (ed.) *Storms of the Heart: An Anthology of Black Arts and Culture*. London: Camden Press, 1988.

Orgel, Stephen, ed. (1999) *King Lear: A Conflated Text*. New York: Penguin.

Osborne, Laurie E. (2002) "Clip Art: Theorizing the Shakespearean Film Clip." *Shakespeare Quarterly* 53 (2) (Summer): 227–40.

Ovid (1567) *Metamorphoses*. Trans. Arthur Golding. London.

Paster, Gail Kern (1993) *The Body Embarrassed: Drama and the Disciplines of Shame in Early Modern Europe*. Ithaca, NY: Cornell University Press.

Quarshie, Hugh (1999) "Second Thoughts About Othello." Chipping Camden: International Shakespeare Association Occasional Papers, no. 7.

Reynolds, Bryan (2002) "Untimely Ripped: Mediating Witchcraft in Polanski and Shakespeare." In Lisa S. Starks and Courtney Lehmann (eds) *The Reel Shakespeare: Alternative Cinema and Theory*. Madison, NJ: Fairleigh Dickinson University Press, London & Cranbury, NJ: Associated University Presses, 143–64.

Roach, Joseph (1993) *The Player's Passion: Studies in the Science of Acting*. Ann Arbor: University of Michigan Press.

Roach, Joseph (1996) *Cities of the Dead: Circum-Atlantic Performance*. New York: Columbia University Press.

Rosenbaum, Ron (2002) "Shakespeare in Rewrite." *The New Yorker*, May 13, 68–77.

Rothwell, Kenneth S. (1994) "Representing *King Lear* on Screen: From Metatheatre to 'Metacinema.'" In Anthony Davies and Stanley Wells (eds) *Shakespeare and the Moving Image: The Plays on Film and Television*. Cambridge & New York: Cambridge University Press, 211–33.

Rothwell, Kenneth S. (2004) *A History of Shakespeare on Screen: A Century of Film and Television*. 2nd edn. Cambridge: Cambridge University Press.

Rowe, Katherine (1999) *Dead Hands: Fictions of Agency, Renaissance to Modern*. Stanford, CA: Stanford University Press.

Rowe, Katherine (2003) " 'Remember Me': Technologies of Memory in Almereyda's *Hamlet*." In Richard Burt and Lynda Boose (eds) *Shakespeare, the Movie II: Popularizing the Plays on Film, TV, Video and DVD*. London & New York: Routledge, 37–55.

Rowe, Katherine (2004) "The Politics of Sleepwalking." *Shakespeare Survey* 57: 126–36.

Rundle, Peter (1999a) Phone interview with Kristian Levring, 10 November, http://www.dogme95.dk.news/interview/levring_interview.htm.

Rundle, Peter (1999b) Interview with Lars von Trier, 4 November, http://www.dogme95.dk/news/interview/trier_interview2.htm.

Schechner, Richard (1985) *Between Theater and Anthropology*. Philadelphia: University of Pennsylvania Press.

Schechner, Richard (1999) "Julie Taymor: from Jacques Lecoq to *The Lion King*, an Interview." *The Drama Review* 43 (3): 36–55. http://muse.jhu.edu/journals/the_drama_review_v043/43.3schechner.html.

Schlosser, Eric (2001) *Fast Food Nation: the Dark Side of the All-American Meal*. Boston, MA: Houghton Mifflin.

Schoenfeldt, Michael C. (1999) *Bodies and Selves in Early Modern England: Physiology and Inwardness in Spenser, Shakespeare, Herbert, and Milton*. Cambridge: Cambridge University Press.

Scott-Douglass, Amy (2003) "Dogme Shakespeare 95: European Cinema, Anti-Hollywood Sentiment, and the Bard." In Richard Burt and Lynda Boose (eds) *Shakespeare, the Movie II: Popularizing the Plays on Film, TV, Video and DVD*. London & New York: Routledge, 252–65.

Semenza, Gregory M. Colón (2005) "Shakespeare After Columbine: Teen Violence in Tim Blake Nelson's '*O*'". *College Literature* 32 (4) (Fall): 99–124.

Serres, Michel with Bruno Latour (1995) *Conversations on Science, Culture, and Time*. Trans. Roxanne Lapidus. Anne Arbor: University of Michigan Press, 43–62.

Shaughnessy, Robert (2002) *The Shakespeare Effect: A History of Twentieth-Century Performance*. Houndsmill & New York: Palgrave Macmillan.

Shohet, Lauren (2004) "The Banquet of *Scotland, PA*." *Shakespeare Survey* 57: 186–95.

Siepmann, Charles (1950) *Radio, Television and Society*. New York: Oxford University Press.

Silverman, Kaja (1988) *The Acoustic Mirror: The Female Voice in Psychoanalysis and Cinema*. Bloomington: Indiana University Press.

Sinha, Amresh (2004) "The Use and Abuse of Subtitles." In Atom Egoyan and Ian Balfour (eds) *Subtitles: On the Foreignness of Film*. Cambridge, MA & London: MIT Press, 172–90.

Sinyard, Neil (2000) "Shakespeare Meets *The Godfather*: The Postmodern Populism of Al Pacino's *Looking for Richard*," in Mark Thornton Burnett and Ramona Wray (eds) *Shakespeare, Film, Fin de Siècle*. New York: St Martin's, 58–72.

Smiley, Jane (1991) *A Thousand Acres*. New York: Knopf.

Smith, Kay H. (2004) " '*Hamlet*, Part Eight, The Revenge' or, Sampling Shakespeare in a Postmodern World." *College Literature* 31 (4) (Fall): 135–49.

Sontag, Susan ([1964] 1999) "Notes on 'Camp.' " Reprinted in Fabio Cleto (ed.) *Camp: Queer Aesthetics and the Performing Subject: A Reader*. Edinburgh: Edinburgh University Press, 53–65.

Spigel, Lynn (1992) *Make Room for TV: Television and the Family Ideal in Postwar America*. Chicago: University of Chicago Press.

Stam, Robert (2005a) "Introduction: The Theory and Practice of Adaptation." In Robert Stam and Allesandra Raengo (eds) *Literature and Film: A Guide to the Theory and Practice of Film Adaptation*. Oxford: Blackwell, pp. 1–52.

Stam, Robert (2005b) *Literature Through Film: Realism, Magic, and the Art of Adaptation*. Oxford: Blackwell.

Stam, Robert and Allesandra Raengo (2005) *Literature and Film: A Guide to the Theory and Practice of Film Adaptation*. Oxford: Blackwell.

Starks, Lisa (2002) "Cinema of Cruelty: Powers of Horror in Julie Taymor's *Titus*." In Lisa S. Starks and Courtney Lehmann (eds) *The Reel Shakespeare: Alternative Cinema and Theory*. Madison, NJ: Fairleigh Dickinson University Press; London & Cranbury, NJ: Associated University Presses, 121–42.

Starks, Lisa S. and Courtney Lehmann, eds (2002a) *The Reel Shakespeare: Alternative Cinema and Theory*. Madison, NJ: Fairleigh Dickinson University Press; London & Cranbury, NJ: Associated University Presses.

Starks, Lisa S. and Courtney Lehmann, eds (2002b) *Spectacular Shakespeare: Critical Theory and Popular Cinema*. Madison, NJ: Fairleigh Dickinson University Press; London & Cranbury, NJ: Associated University Presses, 149–71.

Stone, Alan (2000) "Shakespeare's Tarantino Play: Julie Taymor Resurrects the Despised *Titus Andronicus*." *The Boston Review*, April/May. bostonreview.net/BR25.2/stone.html.

Stone, Roseanne Allucquére (1995) *The War of Desire and Technology at the Close of the Mechanical Age*. Cambridge, MA: MIT Press.

Sullivan, Garrett (1999) " 'Be This Sweet Helen's Knell, And Now Forget Her:' Forgetting, Memory and Identity in *All's Well That Ends Well*." *Shakespeare Quarterly* 50 (1): 51–69.

Taub, Eric A. (2002) "Catch a Rising Star And Put It in Your Pocket." *The New York Times*, Thursday, January 10, Late Edition – Final. Section G; Page 3; Column 4; *Circuits*.

Taylor, Gary (2005) "Welcome to Bardworld." Wednesday, July 13, *The Guardian*. books.guardian.co.uk/departments/classics/story/0,6000,1527508,00.html. Consulted August 4, 2005.

Taylor, Neil (1994) "Two Types of Television Shakespeare." In Anthony Davies and Stanley Wells (eds) *Shakespeare and the Moving Image*. Cambridge: Cambridge University Press, 86–98.

Taymor, Julie (2000) *Titus: The Illustrated Screenplay, Adapted from the Play by William Shakespeare*. New York: Newmarket Press.

Tribble, Evelyn (2005) " 'The Chain of Memory': Distributed Cognition in Early Modern England." *SCAN: Journal of Media Arts Culture*, 2 (2) (September).

Turner, Bryan (1987) "A Note on Nostalgia." *Theory, Culture and Society*, 4 (1): 147–56.

Voigts-Virchow, Eckart, ed. (2004) *Janespotting and Beyond: British Heritage RetroVisions Since the Mid-1990s.* Tübingen: Gunter Narr Verlag,

Willems, Michele (1994) "Verbal-visual, Verbal-pictorial or Textual-televisual? Reflections on the BBC Shakespeare Series." In Anthony Davies and Stanley Wells (eds) *Shakespeare and the Moving Image.* Cambridge: Cambridge University Press, 69–85.

Williams, Christopher (2000) "After the Classic, the Classical and Ideology: The Differences of Realism." In Christine Gledhill and Linda Williams (eds) *Reinventing Film Studies,* London: Arnold, pp. 206–20.

Williams, Deanne (2004) "Mick Jagger Macbeth." *Shakespeare Survey* 57: 145–58.

Williams, Gary Jay (1997) "What country, friends, is this?" (unpublished essay presented at the Seminar on "Shakespeare and Popular Culture," Shakespeare Association of America convention, Cleveland, 1997).

Williams, Linda (1989) *Hard Core: Power, Pleasure and the Frenzy of the Visible.* Berkeley: University of California Press.

Willis, John (1621) *The Art of Memory.* London: W. Jones.

Willis, Susan (1991) *The BBC Shakespeare Plays: Making the Televised Canon.* Chapel Hill: University of North Carolina Press.

Willson, Robert F. (1992) "Recontextualizing Shakespeare on Film: *My Own Private Idaho, Men of Respect,* and *Prospero's Books," Shakespeare Bulletin,* 10 (3): 34–37.

Wiseman, Susan (1997) "The Family Tree Motel: Subliming Shakespeare in *My Own Private Idaho.*" In Lynda E. Boose and Richard Bart (eds) *Shakespeare, the Movie: Popularizing the Plays on Film, TV and Video.* London & New York: Routledge, 225–39.

Wither, George ([1635] 1975) *A Collection of Emblemes, Ancient and Moderne.* Columbia, SC: Newberry Library.

Woolf, Daniel (1991) "Memory and Historical Culture in Early Modern England." *Journal of the Canadian Historical Association,* New Series 3: 283–308.

Worthen, W.B. (1997) *Shakespeare and the Authority of Performance.* Cambridge: Cambridge University Press.

Worthen, W.B. (1998) "Drama, Performativity, and Performance." *PMLA,* 113 (5): 1093–107.

Yates, Frances (1966) *The Art of Memory.* Chicago: University of Chicago Press.

Zizek, Slavoj (2004) "The Foreign Gaze Which Sees Too Much." In Atom Egoyan and Ian Balfour (eds) *Subtitles: On the Foreignness of Film.* Cambridge, MA & London: MIT Press, 286–306.

Films, Videos, DVDs, Television Cited

24 (2001 to present) TV series created by Joel Surnow and Robert Cochran. USA. Twentieth Century Fox. Sound, col.

Aldrich, Robert, dir. (1965) The *Flight of the Phoenix.* USA. The Associates and Aldrich Company. Sound, col., 149 mins.

Almereyda, Michael, dir. (2000) *Hamlet.* USA. Miramax. Sound, col., 113 mins. DVD (2001): Miramax.

Animal Planet (1996 to present) USA. Discovery Channel. Film, TV production and distribution. Sound, col.

Antonioni, Michelangelo, dir. (1966) *Blow-Up.* Great Britain/Italy. Metro-Goldwyn-Mayer. Sound, col., 111 mins.

Apra, Adriano (2005) "Elements of Landscape." Video interview. Disc 2, Criterion Collection edition of Michelangelo Antonioni's *L'Eclisse.* USA. Col., 22 minutes.

Attenborough, Richard, dir. (1982) *Gandhi.* USA/India/Great Britain. Carolina Bank. Sound, col., 188 mins.

Badham, John, dir. (1977) *Saturday Night Fever*. USA. Paramount Pictures. Sound, col., 119 mins.

Baretta (1975–8) TV series created by Stephen J. Cannell. USA. Roy Huggins-Public Arts Productions/ABC. Sound, col.

Bedford, James Gavin, dir. (2002) *The Street King* (aka *King Rikki*). USA. Universal. Sound, col., 90 mins.

Benning, Sadie, dir. (1990) *If Every Girl Had a Diary*. USA. Sound, b/w, 6 mins. http://www.vdb.org/smackn.acgi$pkgdetail?SADIEBENNI.

Boyle, Danny, dir. (1996) *Trainspotting*. Great Britain. Channel Four Television. Sound, col., 89 mins.

Branagh, Kenneth, dir. (1989) *Henry V*. Great Britain. Renaissance Films. Sound, col., 137 mins.

Branagh, Kenneth, dir. (1993) *Much Ado About Nothing*. USA/Great Britain. Samuel Goldwyn. Sound, col., 110 mins.

Branagh, Kenneth, dir. (1996) *Hamlet*. USA/Great Britain. Castle Rock. Sound, col., 242 mins.

Branagh, Kenneth, dir. (1999) *Love's Labour's Lost*. Great Britain/France/USA. Kenneth Branagh/InterMedia. Sound, col., 93 mins.

Brook, Peter, dir. (1963) *Lord of the Flies*. Great Britain. Allen-Hodgdon Productions. Sound, b/w, 92 mins.

Brook, Peter, dir. (1970) *King Lear*. Great Britain/Denmark. Filmways Ltd. Sound, b/w, 137 mins.

Burge, Stuart, dir. (1965) *Othello*. Great Britain. BHE Productions. Sound, col., 166 mins.

Carpenter, John, dir. (1978) *Halloween*. USA. Falcon International Pictures. Sound, col., 91 mins.

Cimino, Michael, dir. (1978) *The Deer Hunter*. USA. EMI Films. Sound, col., 182 mins.

Columbo (1971–8) TV series created and produced by William Link and Russell Metty. USA. Universal TV. Sound, col.

Coppola, Francis Ford, dir. (1974) *The Conversation*. USA. Paramount Pictures. Sound, col., 113 mins.

Cox, Alex, dir. (2002) *Revengers Tragedy*. Great Britain. Revengers Ltd. Sound, col., 109 mins.

Davis, Barry, dir. (1976) *Brimstone and Treacle*. Great Britain. BBC. Sound, col., 87 mins.

Demme, Jonathan, dir. (1991) *Silence of the Lambs*. USA. Orion Pictures. Sound, col., 118 mins.

De Palma, Brian, dir. (1983) *Scarface*. USA. Universal. Sound, col., 170 mins.

Donner, Richard, dir. (1987) *Lethal Weapon*. USA. Silver Pictures/Warner Brothers. Sound, col., 109 mins.

Donner, Richard, dir. (1989) *Lethal Weapon 2*. USA. Warner Bros. Sound, col., 114 mins.

Duffell, Peter, dir. (1984) *The Far Pavilions*. TV mini-series USA. HBO Television. Sound, col.

Elliott, Stephan, dir. (1994) *The Adventures of Priscilla Queen of the Desert*. Australia/Great Britain. Latent Image Productions. Sound, col., 102 mins.

Eyre, Richard, dir. (1983) *The Ploughmans Lunch*. Great Britain. Greenpoint. Sound, col., 107 mins.

Fellini, Federico, dir. (1954) *La Strada*. Italy. Ponti de Laurentis. Sound, b/w, 104 mins.

Fellini, Federico, dir. (1969) *Satyricon*. Italy. Produzioni Europee Associati. Sound, col., 120 mins.

Fellini, Federico, dir. (1972) *Roma*. Italy/France. Ultra Film. Sound, col., 128 mins.

Fosse, Bob, dir. (1972) *Cabaret*. USA. ABC Pictures. Sound, col., 123 mins.

Franklin, Carl, dir. (1995) *Devil in a Blue Dress*. USA. Clinica Estetico. Sound, col., 102 mins.

Frears, Stephen, dir. (1985) *My Beautiful Laundrette*. Great Britain. Working Title Films. Sound, col., 97 mins.

Frears, Stephen, dir. (1987) *Sammy and Rosie Get Laid*. Great Britain. Sammy and Rosie Limited. Sound, col., 101 mins.

Friedkin, William, dir. (1973) *The Exorcist*. USA. Warner Brothers. Sound, col., 122 mins.

Gibson, Brian, dir. (1993) *What's Love Got to do With It*. USA. Touchstone Pictures. Sound, col., 118 mins.

Godard, Jean-Luc, dir. (1964) *Bande à part*. France. Anouchka. Sound, b/w, 95 mins.

Godard, Jean-Luc, dir. (1987) *King Lear*. USA. Cannon International. Sound, col., 90 mins.

Greenaway, Peter, dir. (1987) *The Belly of an Architect*. Great Britain/Italy. Mondial. Sound, col., 123 mins.

Greenaway, Peter, dir. (1989) *The Cook, the Thief, His Wife & Her Lover*. Netherlands/France. Allarts. Sound, col., 123 mins.

Greenaway, Peter, dir. (1991) *Prospero's Books*. Netherlands/France/Italy/Great Britain/Japan. Allarts. Sound, col., 125 mins.

Greengrass, Paul, dir. (1999) *The Murder of Stephen Lawrence*. Great Britain. ITV/BBC. Sound, col., 120 mins. Screened on PBS (Masterpiece Theatre) January 21, 2002.

Hare, David, dir. (1985) *Wetherby*. Great Britain. Greenpoint Films. Sound, col., 102 mins.

Heckerling, Amy, dir. (1995) *Clueless*. USA. Paramount. Sound, col., 97 mins.

Hitchcock, Alfred, dir. (1944) *Lifeboat*. USA. Twentieth Century Fox. Sound, b/w, 96 mins.

Hoffman, Michael, dir. (1999) *William Shakespeare's A Midsummer Night's Dream*. USA/Great Britain/Germany. Twentieth Century Fox. Sound, col., 116 mins.

Howell, Jane dir. (1985) *Titus Andronicus*. Great Britain. BBC/Time–Life Productions. Sound, col., 135 mins.

Hudson, Hugh, dir. (1981) *Chariots of Fire*. Great Britain. Enigma. Sound, col., 123 mins.

Hughes, Ken, dir. (1955) *Joe Macbeth*. Great Britain. Film Locations. Sound, b/w, 90 mins.

Ivory, James, dir. (1993) *The Remains of the Day*. Great Britain/USA. Columbia. Sound, col., 134 mins.

Jackson, Mick, dir. (1991) *L.A. Story*. USA. Carolco. Sound, col., 95 mins.

Jarman, Derek, dir. (1980) *William Shakespeare's The Tempest*. UK. World Northal. Sound, col., 90 mins.

Jarman, Derek, dir. (1991) *Edward II*. Great Britain/Japan. Working Title. Sound, col., 90 mins.

Jarmusch, Jim, dir. (1995) *Dead Man*. USA/Germany. 12-Gauge Productions. Sound, b/w, 121 mins.

Jewison, Norman, dir. (1999) *The Hurricane*. USA. Universal. Sound, b/w & col., 145 mins.

Jordan, Neil, dir. (1997) *The Butcher Boy*. Ireland/USA. Warner Brothers. Sound, col., 109 mins.

Junger, Gil, dir. (1999) *10 Things I Hate About You*. USA. Touchstone Pictures. Sound, col., 97 mins.

Kaurismaki, Aki, dir. (1987) *Hamlet Goes Business* (*Hamlet liikemaailmassa*). Finland. Villealfa Filmproduction Oy. Sound, b/w, 86 mins.

Kleiser, Randal, dir. (1978) *Grease*. USA. Paramount. Sound, col., 110 mins.

Kubrick, Stanley, dir. (1971) *A Clockwork Orange*. Great Britain. Warner Brothers. Sound, col., 136 mins.

Kurosawa, Akira, dir. (1961) *Throne of Blood (Kumonosu jô)*. Japan. Toho. Sound, b/w, 108 mins.

Kurosawa, Akira, dir. (1963) *The Bad Sleep Well*. Japan. Toho. Sound, b/w, 135 mins.

Kurosawa, Akira, dir. (1985) *Ran*. France/Japan. *Greenwich Film Production*. Sound, col., 160 mins.

Landis, John, dir. (1978) *National Lampoon's Animal House*. USA. Universal. Sound, col., 109 mins.

Lean, David, dir. (1965) *Doctor Zhivago*. USA. MGM. Sound, col., 197 mins.

Lean, David, dir. (1984) *A Passage To India*. Great Britain/USA. Thorn EMI Films. Sound, col., 163 mins.

Lee, Spike, dir. (1998) *He Got Game*. USA. Touchstone. Sound, col., 136 mins.

Leth, Jorgen and Lars von Trier, dirs (2003). *The Five Obstructions*. Denmark/Belgium/Switzerland. Zentropa. Sound, col., 91 mins. DVD (2004): Koch Lorber Films, includes Jorgen Leth, dir. (1967). *The Perfect Human*. Denmark. Laterna Film. Sound, b/w, 13 mins.

Levring, Kristian, dir. (2000) *The King is Alive*. Denmark/USA/Sweden/Norway/Finland. Zentropa Entertainments5 ApS. Sound, col., 110 mins. DVD (2002): MGM Video/DVD.

Loncraine, Richard, dir. (1982) *Brimstone and Treacle*. Great Britain. Namara Films. Sound, col., 87 mins.

Loncraine, Richard, dir. (1995) *Richard III*. Great Britain/USA. First Look Pictures. Sound, col., 104 mins.

Lynch, David, dir. (1986) *Blue Velvet*. USA. De Laurentiis Entertainment Group. Sound, col., 120 mins.

Lynch, David, dir. (2001) *Mulholland Drive*. France/USA. Les Films Alain Jarde. Sound, col., 147 mins.

Lyne, Adrian, dir. (1987) *Fatal Attraction*. USA. Paramount Pictures. Sound, col., 120 mins.

Luhrmann, Baz, dir. (1996) *William Shakespeare's Romeo + Juliet*. USA/Canada. Twentieth Century Fox. Sound, col., 120 mins. DVD special edition (2002): Twentieth Century Fox Home Entertainment.

McCloud (1970–7) TV series. USA. Universal TV/NBC. Sound, col.

McTiernan, John, dir. (1993) *Last Action Hero*. USA. Columbia. Sound, col., 131 mins.

Madden, John, dir. (1998) *Shakespeare in Love*. USA. Miramax. Sound, col., 122 mins.

Makhmalbaf, Mohsen, dir. (2001) *Kandahar* (*Safar e Ghandehar*). Iran/France. Makhmalbaf Productions. Sound, col., 85 mins.

Mankiewicz, Joseph, dir. (1953) *Julius Caesar*. USA. MGM. Sound, b/w, 121 mins.

Marshall, Penny, dir. (1994) *Renaissance Man*. USA. Cincergi. Sound, col., 129 mins.

Mazursky, Paul, dir. (1982) *Tempest*. USA. Columbia Pictures. Sound, col., 142 mins.

Miller, George, dir. (1979) *Mad Max*. Australia. Mad Max. Sound, col., 100 mins.

Miller, Jonathan, dir. (1981) *Othello*. Great Britain. BBC Shakespeare Plays. Sound, col., 210 mins.

Morahan, Christopher and Jim O'Brien, dirs (1984) *The Jewel in the Crown*. Great Britain/USA. Granada Television/WGBH. Sound, col. & b/w, 97 mins.

Morrissette, Billy, dir. (2001) *Scotland, PA*. USA. Abandon Pictures. Sound, col., 104 mins. DVD (2005): Sundance Channel Home Entertainment.

Nelson, Tim Blake, dir. (2001) *O*. USA. Miramax. Sound, col., 95 mins.

Noble, Adrian, dir. (1996) *A Midsummer Night's Dream*. Great Britain. Edenwood Productions. Sound, col., 103 mins.

Norrington, Stephen, dir. (1998) *Blade*. USA. New Line. Sound, col., 120 mins.

Nunn, Trevor, dir. (1996) *Twelfth Night or What You Will*. Great Britain/USA. Renaissance Films. Sound, col., 133 mins.

Olivier, Laurence, dir. (1944) *Henry V*. Great Britain. Two Cities Film Ltd. Sound, col., 137 mins.

Olivier, Laurence, dir. (1948) *Hamlet*. Great Britain. Two Cities Film Ltd. Sound, b/w, 155 mins. DVD (2000): The Criterion Collection, Carlton International Media Limited.

Olivier, Laurence, dir. (1955) *Richard III.* Great Britain. Big Ben Films. Sound, col., 158 mins.

Oz (1997–2003) TV series created by Tom Fontana. USA. Rysher Entertainment/HBO.

Pacino, Al, dir. (1996) *Looking for Richard.* USA. Twentieth Century Fox. Sound, col., 109 mins.

Parker, Oliver, dir. (1995) *Othello.* USA/Great Britain. Castle Rock. Sound, col., 123 mins.

Pasolini, Pier Paolo, dir. (1968) *Che cosa sono le nuvole?* Italy. Dino De Laurentiis. Sound, col., 20 mins. Released as one of six shorts by different directors, under the title *Capriccio All'Italiana.*

Polanski, Roman, dir. (1971) *Macbeth.* USA. Great Britain. Playboy. Sound, col., 140 mins.

Potter, Dennis (1987) *Brimstone and Treacle.* Great Britain. *Play for Today* TV Series (originally scheduled air date April 6, 1976; banned, then aired August 25, 1987). Sound, col., 87 mins.

Prime Suspect, 1 & 2 (1991–3) TV movies dir. by Christopher Menaul and John Strickland, created by Lynda La Plante. Great Britain/USA. Granada Television/WGBH Boston. Sound, col., 207 & 203 mins.

Radford, Michael, dir. (2004) *William Shakespeare's The Merchant of Venice.* Great Britain/Italy/Luxembourg/USA. Shylock Trading Limited. Sound, col., 131 mins.

Raimi, Sam, dir. (2002) *Spider-Man: The Movie.* USA. Columbia Pictures. Sound, col., 121 mins.

Reilly, William, dir. (1990) *Men of Respect.* USA. Central City. Sound, col., 113 mins.

Reinhardt, Max and Wilhelm Deiterle, dirs (1935) *A Midsummer Night's Dream.* USA. Warner Brothers. Sound, b/w, 132 mins.

Roeg, Nicholas, dir. (1970) *Walkabout.* Australia. Max L. Raab-Si Litvinoff Films. Sound, col., 100 mins.

Rohmer, Eric, dir. (1992) *Conte d'hiver* (*A Tale of Winter*). France. Films du Losange. Sound, col., 114 mins. Distributed in VHS in the USA by MK2 Diffusion (1995): New Yorker Films Video.

Sax, Geoffrey, dir. (2001) *Othello.* Great Britain/USA/Canada. LTW Productions. Sound, col., 99 mins. Screened on PBS (Masterpiece Theatre), January 28, 2002.

Scorsese, Martin, dir. (1990) *Goodfellas.* USA. Warner Brothers. Sound, col., 145 mins.

Seed, Paul, dir. (1990) *House of Cards.* TV series written by Andrew Davies from the novel by Michael Dobbs. Great Britain. BBC. Sound, col.

Sharman, Jim, dir. (1975) *The Rocky Horror Picture Show.* Great Britain. Houtsnede Maatschappij NV. Sound, col., 101 mins.

Spielberg, Steven, dir. (1982) *E.T. The Extra-Terrestrial.* USA. Universal Pictures. Sound, col., 115 mins.

Stone, Oliver, dir. (1987) *Wall Street.* USA. Twentieth Century Fox. Sound, col., 126 mins.

Sturges, John, dir. (1960) *The Magnificent Seven.* USA. Mirisch. Sound, col., 128 mins.

Suzman, Janet, dir. (1988) *Othello.* Great Britain/South Africa. Focus. Sound, col., 199 mins.

Taymor, Julie, dir. (1999) *Titus.* USA/Great Britain. Clear Blue Sky Productions. Sound, col., 162 mins. DVD special edition (2000): Twentieth Century Fox Home Entertainment. 2 discs.

Tykwer, Tom, dir. (1998) *Run, Lola, Run* (*Lola rennt*). Germany. X-Filme Creative Pool. Sound, b/w & col., 81 mins.

Van Sant, Gus, dir. (1991) *My Own Private Idaho.* USA. New Line. Sound, col., 104 mins. DVD special edition (2005): Criterion. 2 discs.

Von Trier, Lars, dir. (1996) *Breaking the Waves.* Denmark/France/Sweden/Italy/ Netherlands. Zentropa Entertainments. Sound, col., 148 mins.

Wachowski, Andy and Larry Wachowski, dirs. (1999) *The Matrix*. USA/Australia. Warner Brothers. Sound, col., 136 mins.

Welles, Orson, dir. (1948) *Macbeth*. USA. Literary Classics Productions. Sound, b/w, 86 mins.

Welles, Orson, dir. (1952) *The Tragedy of Othello: The Moor of Venice*. Morocco. Mercury Productions. Sound, b/w, 90 mins.

Welles, Orson, dir. (1958) *Touch of Evil*. USA. Universal. Sound, b/w, 108 mins.

Welles, Orson, dir. (1966) *Chimes at Midnight* (Swiss/USA title *Falstaff*). Spain/ Switzerland. Internacional Films Española. Sound, b/w, 119 mins.

Wenders, Wim, dir. (1977) *The American Friend (Der Amerikanische Freund)*. Germany/France. Road Movies Filmproduktion. Sound, col., 125 mins.

Wilcox, Fred McLeod, dir. (1956) *Forbidden Planet*. USA. Loews Inc. Sound, col., 98 mins.

Wilder, Billy, dir. (1955) *The Seven Year Itch*. USA. Twentieth Century Fox. Sound, col., 105 mins.

Wise, Robert and Jerome Robbins (1961) *West Side Story*. USA. Beta Productions. Sound, col., 152 mins.

Zeffirelli, Franco, dir. (1967) *The Taming of the Shrew*. USA/Italy. Royal Films International. Sound, col., 122 mins.

Zeffirelli, Franco, dir. (1968) *Romeo and Juliet*. Great Britain/Italy. BHE Productions. Sound, col., 152 mins.

Zeffirelli, Franco, dir. (1990) *Hamlet*. USA/France. Marquis Productions. Sound, col., 134 mins.

Resources

Working with film and new media: basic terms, strategies, tutorials

Hamlet on the Ramparts (http://shea.mit.edu/ramparts/welcome.htm). Public website collaboration of MIT Shakespeare Project and Folger Shakespeare Library. *Collection of teaching and other resources* focused on the ghost scenes from *Hamlet*, including a *comprehensive film lexicon.*

Folger Shakespeare Library "Teach and Learn" (www.folger.edu). *Lesson plans* archive for working with film and interactive media.

Writing with Audio-Visual Texts. www.brynmawr.edu/filmstudies/writing/index.html. Bryn Mawr College Film Studies site with *student tutorials and handouts*: close reading film, capturing clips, taking screening notes, copyright links, etc.

A Short Guide to Writing about Film, Fifth Edition. Timothy Corrigan. New York: Harper Collins College Publishers, 2004. *Basic questions for student writers* on a variety of film-analysis topics.

Sound Theory, Sound Practice. Ed. Rick Altman. New York: Routledge, 1992. Introduction serves as a sophisticated but accessible *primer on film audio.*

Film Art: an Introduction. David Bordwell and Kristin Thompson. Boston: McGraw-Hill, 2004. A standard *textbook.*

Literature and Film: A Guide to the Theory and Practice of Film Adaptation. Ed. Robert Stam and Alessandra Raengo. Oxford: Blackwell, 2005. Introduction serves as a sophisticated but accessible *primer on film adaptation.*

Shakespeare on screen: bibliography, history, production information, reviews

Shakespeare on Screen: An International Filmography and Videography. Ed. Kenneth S. Rothwell and Annabelle Henkin Melzer. London: Mansell; New York: NealSchuman, 1990. Searchable online at the Internet Shakespeare Editions, ise.uvic.ca/Theater/sip/about.html.

A History of Shakespeare on Screen: A Century of Film and Television. Ed. Kenneth S. Rothwell. Cambridge: Cambridge University Press, 2001.

The Cambridge Companion to Shakespeare on Film. Ed. Russell Jackson. Cambridge: Cambridge University Press, 2000.

Annotated bibliographies of criticism by José Ramón Díaz-Fernández (full citations in Works Cited). "Shakespeare on Television" (http://purl.oclc.org/emls/06-1/diazbibl.htm), "Shakespeare on," and "Shakespeare and Film-Derivatives."

The British Film Institute and American Film Institute catalogues. (Note that The Internet Movie Database is not authoritative.) *The Movie Review Query Engine* (www.mrqe.com/lookup).

Journals focused on Shakespeare adaptation

Borrowers and Lenders: The Journal of Shakespearean Appropriation. Online, peer-reviewed. (www.borrowers&lenders).

Shakespeare Bulletin.

Early Modern Literary Studies (online, peer-reviewed; www.emls.net). *Literature/ Film Quarterly, Shakespeare Survey, Shakespeare Quarterly, Postscript, Cineaste.* Occasional essays on special issues.

Purchasing and rentals

The Poor Yorick Shakespeare Catalogue (www.bardcentral.com): Shakespeare-related videos, DVDs.

Best Video (www.bestvideo.com). Hard-to-find and out-of-print titles.

Index